MW01062038

THE HEMINGWAY SHORT STORY

THE HEMINGWAY SHORT STORY

A STUDY in CRAFT for WRITERS and READERS

ROBERT PAUL LAMB

Louisiana State University Press

Baton Rouge

Published by Louisiana State University Press

Manufactured in the United States of America
First printing

Designer: Laura Roubique Gleason
Typeface: Minion Pro
Printer: McNaughton & Gunn
Binder: Dekker Bookbinding

LIBRARY OF CONGRESS CATALOGING-IN-PUBLICATION DATA

Lamb, Robert Paul, 1951–
The Hemingway short story : a study in craft for writers and readers / Robert Paul Lamb.
p. cm.
Includes bibliographical references and index.
ISBN 978-0-8071-4742-9 (cloth : alk. paper) — ISBN 978-0-8071-4743-6 (pdf) — ISBN 978-0-8071-4744-3 (epub) — ISBN 978-0-8071-4745-0 (mobi)
1. Hemingway, Ernest, 1899–1961—Technique. 2. Short story. I. Title.
PS3515.E37Z6886 2013
813'.52—dc23

2012007901

The paper in this book meets the guidelines for permanence and durability of the Committee on Production Guidelines for Book Longevity of the Council on Library Resources. ♾

For Kip Robisch

A beloved, multi-award-winning educator who has taught
generations of students to examine everything they take for granted
and to think for themselves

An unswervingly ethical man who always stands up for what is right,
devotes himself to helping others, and never ditches his principles
out of inconvenience or fear

An advocate for those who cannot speak for themselves—animals
in the wild—dedicated to protecting them and the earth's ecosystems
from a culture of death bent on senseless extermination
for "fun" and profit

A brilliant scholar whose masterpiece, *Wolves and the Wolf Myth
in American Literature,* is the absolute gold standard
of contemporary, scientifically based ecocriticism

An author of original ecocritical fiction

and

A true friend whose wisdom, kindness, and decency
I will forever cherish

This one's for you, #54

But giants of his sort are truly modest; there is much more behind Hemingway's form than people know.

—James Joyce

Of his own writing Ernest said, "Nobody really knows or understands and nobody has ever said the secret. The secret is that it is poetry written into prose and it is the hardest of all things to do."

—Mary Welsh Hemingway

Contents

Preface xi

I. *Full Encounters of the Close Kind*

1. Really Reading a Hemingway Story: The Example of "Indian Camp" 3

   Prologue: The Contexts of "Indian Camp" 3

   Failure: The Original Opening 14

   Triumph: The Achievement of "Indian Camp" 26

   Coda: Coming Full Circle in "Fathers and Sons" 84

II. *How Craft Readings Contribute to Understanding Stories*

2. Dueling Wounds in "Soldier's Home": The Relation of Textual Form, Narrative Argument, and Cultural Critique 89

3. The "Pointless" Story: What Is "A Canary for One"? 112

III. *Metacritical and Metafictional Hemingway*

4. Hemingway on (Mis)Reading Stories: "God Rest You Merry, Gentlemen" as Metacriticism 153

5. Hemingway on (Mis)Writing Stories: "Big Two-Hearted River" as Metafiction 167

Acknowledgments 193

Notes 197

Works Cited 215

Index 225

Preface

This book is a sequel to *Art Matters: Hemingway, Craft, and the Creation of the Modern Short Story* (2010). In *Art Matters,* my goal was to provide the definitive study of Hemingway's short story aesthetics, exploring what he learned from previous artists—such as Poe, Cézanne, Maupassant, Henry James, Chekhov, Crane, Stein, Joyce, Eliot, and Pound—and how he developed this inheritance to create the unique style and innovative techniques that would revolutionize the craft of both fiction and the short story over the past century. The book was framed by a polemical preface, introduction, and coda arguing for Hemingway's central place in the canon through his unsurpassed influence on his contemporaries and later authors, an influence that has cut across the artificial boundaries which culture and politics create: nationality, race, gender, class, ethnicity, sexual orientation, and religion. These authors, among them fourteen Nobel Prize Laureates, include writers as diverse as Raymond Chandler, Isaac Babel, John Dos Passos, F. Scott Fitzgerald, William Faulkner, Sean O'Faolain, Nathalie Sarraute, John Steinbeck, Halldór Laxness, Evelyn Waugh, Graham Greene, Jean-Paul Sartre, Simone de Beauvoir, Elio Vittorini, Eudora Welty, Albert Camus, Bernard Malamud, Ralph Ellison, Saul Bellow, William Burroughs, Camilo José Cela, Heinrich Böll, J. D. Salinger, Jack Kerouac, Norman Mailer, Nadine Gordimer, Flannery O'Connor, Elmore Leonard, Gabriel García Márquez, John Munonye, Edna O'Brien, Derek Walcott, John Updike, Joan Didion, Cormac McCarthy, Kenzaburo Oe, Ellen Gilchrist, Mario Vargas Llosa, Raymond Carver, Russell Banks, Jean-Marie Gustav Le Clézio, Robert Olen Butler, Ann Beattie, Terry Tempest Williams, and Junot Díaz. The bulk of the book examined through close readings the major elements of Hemingway's art and explained exactly how each functions: dispassionate presentation, authorial judgment, suggestiveness, concision, omission, impressionism, focalization, repetition, juxtaposition, story openings and endings, the illustrative stamp, constructive dialogue, story characterization, and setting. In addition, it introduced and developed a new set of terms and concepts for analyzing the short story as a distinct literary genre while also redefining older literary terms, such as *impressionism* and *expressionism*, which had become hopelessly misunderstood by critics.

I did not have the necessary space in *Art Matters* to explore any individual story fully. Instead, in order to analyze the many technical aspects of Hemingway's art, I drew upon exemplary passages from most of the fifty-three stories and eighteen vignettes he wrote between 1922 and 1939. Early in the book, I observed:

> Such a dissection has its obvious value; it gets beneath the surface to show how texts actually work. But it also tends to make stories into clinical specimens, treating parts of them rather than looking at each story as a whole. Hemingway, I should hasten to note, would probably have detested what I am doing here. As penance, in a future book I intend to examine a number of stories thoroughly as autonomous texts, putting back together what here I so callously take apart. The short story is a living thing; even in its final form it continues to grow, change, and reveal hidden aspects of itself to new generations of readers. But, as with human bodies, a certain knowledge of basic anatomy illuminates.[1]

Encouraged by, and grateful for, the response of critics and creative writers to *Art Matters,* I wish to make good on that penance I promised and present readings that do justice to a number of individual Hemingway stories. Although *The Hemingway Short Story* is best read after *Art Matters,* I have shaped it so that it can be read on its own. Therefore, whenever I use a term coined in the previous book, I explain it in a shorthand fashion so that the reader will get its gist. I also use endnotes to *Art Matters* for those interested in reading fuller definitions of the terms along with detailed analyses of examples drawn from Hemingway's stories. In this manner, I hope, the craft readings in this book can be enjoyed with profit on their own while not being constantly interrupted by forays into the critical terminology developed in my earlier volume.

The same three premises articulated in the preface and introduction to *Art Matters* also inform *The Hemingway Short Story,* although—once we are done with this preface—I will try to refrain from repeating my polemics and occasionally combative tone. I have no desire to beat a dead horse and, to be candid, I'm done trying to justify a study of the aesthetic principles and techniques of the most influential fiction writer of the past hundred years. It's not that I've ceased to care, but the importance to all literary critics of understanding craft *should* be self-evident. Eavesdrop on any group of professionals—musicians, surgeons, athletes, jurists, fly fishermen, psychologists, pilots, political strategists, actors, firefighters, poets, journalists, skilled artisans, engineers, teachers, comedians, soldiers, or *fiction writers*—and you will discover that, whatever else they may discuss, when they get serious they talk about their craft. If it's deemed essential by actual fiction writers, then it should matter to anyone claiming authority about fiction. A literary critic indifferent to craft is like a football analyst uninterested in the mechanics of pass blocking. It's manifestly ridiculous but, unlike the football analyst (or the offensive tackle practicing his craft), such literary critics will not lose their jobs as a result of their ignorance. Nevertheless, I'm a realist, and all putative critics of fiction who dismiss literary art are welcome to cast a cold eye on this book and go their merry way. I wish them well. But for anyone who believes that art does, and will always, matter, and that cultural studies, however important (and they certainly are), do not possess a monopoly on literary criticism, the following three assumptions underlie both books.

My first premise is that a writer is not merely a social construction, a site upon which cultural forces contend, but a complex human being, a professional in his or her craft, and capable of agency in consciously making decisions that create a literary text from blank pages of paper. In 1968, when Roland Barthes famously declared the "death of the author," he did so for three related, necessary, and beneficial purposes. First, he wanted to open up the study of literature, which he rightly felt was "tyrannically centered on the author, his person, his history, his tastes, his passions. . . . [*E*]*xplanation* of the work is still sought in the person of its producer, as if, through the more or less transparent allegory of fiction, it was always, ultimately, the voice of one and the same person, the *author,* which was transmitting his 'confidences.'" Second, he wanted critics to view texts (to use Mikhail Bakhtin's term) as "unfinalizable," to see a literary work as "a fabric of quotations, resulting from a thousand sources of culture" with everything "to be *disentangled,* but nothing to be *deciphered*[.]" By divorcing the text from our obsession with the "Author-God," we could view it "in all its reprises, all its stages," and thus there would be "no end to it, no bottom; the space of writing is to be traversed, not pierced." Third, he wanted to liberate not only the text, but also to emphasize the vital role of the reader in the consumption of a work of literature: "a text consists of multiple writings, proceeding from several cultures and entering into dialogue, into parody, into contestation; but there is a site where this multiplicity is collected, and this site is . . . the reader[.]”[2]

Barthes’s landmark essay on the death of the author made perfect sense, but over time many in the academy began to literalize what he had clearly intended as a metaphor. Scholarship that focused on actual writers of fiction consciously practicing their craft became, in the minds of many academics, a “fetishization” of the author and tantamount to heresy. If the purpose of Barthes’s essay was to open up criticism to a multiplicity of methodological approaches—*none* of them dominant—unfortunately and ironically it was undermined by the religious right of cultural studies, which stigmatized any scholarship on the formal elements of fiction as a return to the dreaded “New Criticism.” Like branding someone a “Communist” in the 1950s or a “Liberal” today, invoking the label “New Critic” effectively dismissed any further discussion. All too typical of academia, which boasts of its love of diversity but often betrays little appreciation for what diversity really means, and which shows scant tolerance toward anything different from what’s currently fashionable, a new hegemony simply replaced an older one. Or, as one perplexed junior colleague condescendingly asked me about *Art Matters,* “What cultural labor does your project perform?” To which I replied in my best native Bronx accent, “yuh mean my book?—well, uh, none, I guess.” For critics, who suffer from what I think of as “an anxiety of significance,” the death of the author served another, unconscious purpose. It made the critic paramount and the author secondary, putting the cart before the horse. But let’s be painfully honest here, shall we? I know of no critic who wouldn’t kill to have written *Ulysses,* but I seriously doubt that Joyce would have preferred to have been a Joyce critic. Again, some plain speech: without literary critics, we would still have literature, but without writers, literary critics would either have to retrain themselves as historians or else get a real job.

A second premise of both volumes is that the bifurcation between art, craft, technique, and form, now the province of creative writing programs, and cultural critique, the current territory of literary studies, is spurious. Nowhere is this divide more striking than in the approaches to the texts of Hemingway, who is arguably the single most studied fiction writer in creative writing craft courses while, in literary criticism, he has become mainly the subject of gender, sexuality, ideological, historicist, and biographical studies.[3] Such a division is nonsensical, because an understanding of art informs, complicates, and deepens cultural studies, and vice-versa; they are far from incompatible. For example, modernist fiction is well known for such formal techniques as breaking up linear chronology, returning to the same scenes through the eyes of different focalizers, abdicating the (author)ity of the writer, withholding exposition, and leaving texts open ended. The authors of these works did not engage in such practices to be clever or to make reading their books difficult; opacity, for them, was never the goal. Instead, there is an important relationship between their form and their content. In modernism, emerging in a period in which cultural absolutes were crumbling, we see a focus on epistemology—not what we know but *how* we know what we know. This is as true of an explicitly epistemological novel such as William Faulkner's *Absalom, Absalom!* as it is of Hemingway's impressionism or Willa Cather's expressionism, which foreground the immediacy of experience over retrospective understanding and force readers to fill in interstices in the texts with their own experiential knowledge. Modernism's concern with epistemology is linked to the modernist belief that "reality" is multiple and intangible; it is produced by the individual perceiver. For this reason, modernism focuses on the consciousness and the unconscious, where reality resides. The many formal techniques of modernism, then, serve to question the false order that previous historical genres like realism and naturalism imposed upon life. This weakening of traditional narrative structures, which compels the reader to become more active in producing meaning from the text, creates a homology between the fragmented world as seen by the writer and the fragmented text as presented to the reader. Far from an empty formalism, then, studies of such modernist techniques are essential to any understanding of what modernism was and how it created its cultural representations and critiques. To sum up—and I cannot state it too strongly—*what* a text means and *how* it means are interconnected. Form and content are two sides of the same coin.

The third premise of both books is that a short story is not merely fiction that takes up less room. Rather, the short story is a distinct literary genre, complete with its own conventions that have developed over time, and different from such longer forms of fiction as the novella and the novel. In many ways, as I demonstrated in *Art Matters*, the story is closer to lyrical poetry than to the novel—a point made by authors as different as Frank O'Connor, Wallace Stevens, and Hemingway himself.[4] The language of the short story is more complex because it has more to do in a smaller amount of space, and therefore relies on multiple meanings, compression, omission, suggestiveness, implication, and nuance. As a result, it demands, and rewards, the sorts of full close readings usually reserved for poems rather than readings of selected passages that are, for practical purposes, necessarily typical of criticism on the novel.

These are the sorts of close readings that comprise this book: readings in which we observe the author consciously practicing his craft, how that craft is inextricably entwined with the story's cultural representations, and the many ways in which close examinations of stories reward us. The lengthy first chapter is a full craft reading devoted to "Indian Camp" that presents the biographical contexts of the story's creation and speculates on how these found their way into the narrative, analyzes the shortcomings of its deleted opening, presents a complete reading of the final text, and concludes with a coda on "Fathers and Sons." I chose "Indian Camp" for several reasons. It is Hemingway's initial story masterpiece and, by first analyzing the amateurish opening, which he simply chopped off, and then proceeding to the final story, we can see the exact moment in which Hemingway became Hemingway, the story in which he originally brought into play many of the technical innovations of his craft. It is also the story in which he introduced his most memorable and autobiographically based character, Nick Adams;[5] combined with the coda on "Fathers and Sons," we view Nick at the first and final chronological points in his saga, and there are surprising connections. Following the exhaustive reading of "Indian Camp," the second chapter, on "Soldier's Home," examines a story that has been the subject of an ongoing critical debate in Hemingway studies and demonstrates how a focus on form, technique, and narrative argument can help us to resolve that debate and deepen our understanding of the story's terrain of cultural meaning. The third chapter is on "A Canary for One," which exemplifies a number of Hemingway stories where nothing appears to happen. Or, to put it more precisely, it is a story that seems to elude all methodological approaches (except for biographical ones) and, as a result, has been admired but neglected by scholars. The chapter shows how such a story must be read in terms of craft to be fully appreciated. In the final two chapters, I let Hemingway have his own say on the nature of reading and writing. The fourth chapter explores "God Rest You Merry, Gentlemen" as a metacritical story about the act of interpreting and misinterpreting texts themselves. This story, also admired but neglected by scholars, shows Hemingway fully aware of what would later be termed "reader-response" or "reader-oriented" criticism: how the different intertexts, conceptual frames, and experiences that readers bring to a text determine the ways in which they interpret that text. The fifth chapter, on the much analyzed "Big Two-Hearted River," employs its deleted ending to view both the original and final versions of the story as metafictional, that is, a story about the nature of writing stories, including the writing of itself. Throughout these chapters, my methodology is best defined as *craft analysis,* the sort of approach that Flannery O'Connor proclaimed essential if one wishes "to understand a story" because it gives us the "tools that operate inside the work and not outside it": tools that "are concerned with how this story is made and with what makes it work as a story."[6]

In *Art Matters,* I appropriated Henry James's famous metaphor from his preface to *The Portrait of Lady,* about the "house of fiction" and its many windows, in order to posit that the house of criticism, too, should have many windows. Inclusiveness, in both criticism and life, is always more rewarding than exclusiveness. Diversity and multiplicity help us to see the world, and the literature that represents it, more complexly and accurately. For James and Hemingway, and I suspect for most writers and readers, a greater awareness is always the ultimate goal of reading. Northrop Frye's statement, made over half a century ago, seems a particularly apt admonition to critics today: "that every increase of appreciation has been right, and every decrease wrong: that criticism has no business to react against things, but should show a steady advance toward undiscriminating catholicity."[7]

For those readers, then, who appreciated the vista afforded by *Art Matters,* I hope that the view presented in this new volume proves equally illuminating and enjoyable.

I

Full Encounters of the Close Kind

As the contract only mentions excisions it is understood of course that no alterations of words shall be made without my approval. This protects you as much as it does me as the stories are written so tight and so hard that the alteration of a word can throw an entire story out of key.

—HEMINGWAY TO HORACE LIVERIGHT (1925),
Ernest Hemingway: Selected Letters

I write one page of masterpiece to ninety one pages of shit. I try to put the shit in the wastebasket.

—HEMINGWAY TO F. SCOTT FITZGERALD (1934),
Ernest Hemingway: Selected Letters

1

Really Reading a Hemingway Story

THE EXAMPLE OF "INDIAN CAMP"

> I'm trying to do it so it will make it without you knowing it, and so the more you read it, the more there will be.
>
> —Ernest Hemingway (on his work in the mid-1920s), *A Moveable Feast*

Prologue: The Contexts of "Indian Camp"

From mid-February through April 1924, the start of an extraordinary period of creativity that would last five years, Hemingway completed eight of the stories that would comprise the bulk of *In Our Time.*[1] The first of these stories, "Indian Camp," marked the introduction of Nick Adams, who had briefly appeared in an earlier *in our time* vignette and would become Hemingway's most memorable and autobiographical character.[2] "Indian Camp" was both the first Nick Adams story and, as it would turn out, the earliest story in Nick's chronology. It was also something else. Of his three previously published stories, "Up in Michigan" and "My Old Man" had been derivative, heavily influenced by Gertrude Stein and Sherwood Anderson, respectively, and "Out of Season" was merely competent. "Indian Camp" was therefore another "first"; it was Hemingway's initial masterpiece in the genre.

The original version of the story begins with Nick undressing inside a tent. As he watches the shadows of his father and Uncle George projected by the campfire on the wall of the tent he feels ashamed of something that happened the night before. In a flashback to that night, the two men head off in a rowboat to troll for fish. Before they leave, Nick's father tells him that in the event of an emergency the boy should fire three rifle shots and they will return immediately. Nick walks back to the tent and tries to sleep, but the dark and silent woods frighten him, and his vague anxiety turns into a fear of death. In a flashback within this flashback, Nick recalls sitting in church a few weeks earlier singing a hymn and realizing, for the first time, that he will someday die. He remembers spending that night in the hall reading a book to keep his mind off of dying. The story then returns to the original flashback as Nick's fear overwhelms him, he fires the three shots, feels relieved, and goes to sleep. On the lake the two men hear the shots, with Uncle George angry about having his fishing ruined and making a number of nasty comments while Nick's father feebly defends his son. The men enter the tent, Uncle George awakens Nick by shining his flashlight on him, and the boy tells a lie about having heard something that sounded like a cross between a wolf and a fox prowling about the tent. The story then flashes forward to the morning of the night on which it opened, as Nick's father finds two trees leaning against each other in the wind and asks Nick if that was what he heard. The boy is evasive, but his father calms him by giving advice on how to protect himself in a thunderstorm. The story returns to the present as Nick, still undressing, hears a boat pull up on the beach; the shadows of the two men disappear, and his father yells for him to get dressed and put on his coat.

On the beach two Indians and a second rowboat await. The Indians row them across the lake as Nick's father explains to Nick that there is an Indian lady at the Indian camp who is sick. After docking, the five characters walk up the beach, through a meadow, along a trail in the woods, and up a logging road into the hills. When they get to the camp, they enter a shanty in which a pregnant Indian woman lies in a bunk while her husband, who had hurt his foot with an ax, is in the bunk above her. Nick's father explains to his son that she is having a difficult childbirth, and Nick is unnerved by her screams. Nick watches his father prepare to operate, and then assists in a brutal, makeshift Caesarean performed with fishing equipment and no anesthetic. A boy is born, but Nick, despite his father's explanations, is too upset to watch. His father's post-operative exhilaration is cut short when he checks on the Indian father in the upper bunk and discovers that sometime during the operation the man cut his own throat from ear to ear with a razor. Nick also sees the gruesome sight. As he and his father leave the camp at dawn, Nick asks a series of questions about death, questions to which his father can offer no satisfactory answers. The story ends with two paragraphs of description of Nick and his father on the lake, concluding with the phrase that Nick "felt quite sure that he would never die."[3]

In an interview near the end of his life, Hemingway was asked, "How complete in your own mind is the conception of a short story? Does the theme, or the plot, or a character change as you go along?" The author replied with a disarmingly frank statement about how stories get written:

> Sometimes you know the story. Sometimes you make it up as you go along and have no idea how it will come out. Everything changes as it moves. That is what makes the movement which makes the story. Sometimes the movement is so slow it does not seem to be moving. But there is always change and always movement.[4]

What were the background and biographical contexts of this story? What materials did the author draw upon in writing it? What, in short, did Hemingway "know" when he sat down to write it in mid-February 1924 upon his return to Paris?

In the ten months between writing "Out of Season" in April 1923 and "Indian Camp," Hemingway's life had been hectic, leaving him little time for his fiction. In May, he worked on the vignettes that would be published in 1924 as *in our time.* In June, accompanied by friends, he left Paris for his first visit to Spain, where he would fall in love with the country, begin a lifelong *afición* for the bullfights, and take copious notes that would reemerge in his writings over the years. The next month, he returned to Spain with his wife Hadley, who was six months pregnant, for the feast of San Fermin at Pamplona and, of course, the bullfights. He spent the rest of July and August 1923 caring for Hadley, who was ill, finishing the vignettes, including writing five of the six bullfighting sketches, and going over the proofs of his first book, *Three Stories & Ten Poems.*[5]

At the end of August, Ernest and a very pregnant Hadley left Paris to take up residence in Toronto so that their first child could be born in North America. Intending to stay for a year, Hemingway took a position on the *Daily Star,* the newspaper for which he had served as a foreign correspondent since February 1920. But there he was immediately targeted by the sadistic new assistant managing editor, Harry Hindmarsh, the son-in-law of the *Star*'s owner, who tried to establish his authority by humiliating the handsome, charismatic, star journalist with menial cub reporting jobs and "junk assignments," denying him his proper share of by-lines, deliberately working him long hours, sending him off on out-of-town assignments, and even misspelling his name. In October, while returning from one such grueling assignment—in New York City to cover British Prime Minister Lloyd George's arrival and train trip to Canada—Ernest received a telegram stating that Hadley had delivered her baby prematurely the night before. He reached the hospital overcome by "fatigue and strain" and was subsequently castigated by Hindmarsh because, upon arriving in Toronto, he had gone directly to the hospital to see his wife and baby before personally filing his story. This confrontation, which concluded with Ernest offering to knock Hindmarsh down if he opened his "trap" again, finalized the rift between the ace reporter and the truculent editor who had tried to break him. Remarkably, given Hemingway's disposition toward bullies and petty bureaucrats, it did not also finalize the assistant managing editor.[6]

Hadley worried that the job would "kill or scar" Ernest if he did not quit soon. To Ezra Pound he wrote that his stomach was "shot from nervous fatigue" and that he suffered from insomnia. He wanted badly to write a story for Ford Madox Ford's *transatlantic review,* but felt "so full of hate and so damned, bitchingly, sickeningly tired that anything I do will be of little value." To Gertrude Stein and Alice B. Toklas he admitted his feelings of guilt about having been absent during the childbirth, and he complained that the "whole thing here is a sort of nightmare. I work anywhere from 12 to 19 hours a day and am so tired at night that [I] can't sleep." He also recalled from his time in New York, or possibly made up, an incident in which a man who was drawing pictures in chalk in front of the Stock Exchange shouted repeatedly: "He sent his only begotten son to do this. He sent his only begotten son to die on a tree. He sent his only begotten son to hang there and die."[7]

Ernest and Hadley decided to return to Paris in January, where they could live more cheaply and he would have time to write fiction. Although he had begun "Indian Camp" in November, the pressing need to earn and save money for the relocation to Paris prevented him from working on it. In a letter to Edward J. O'Brien, he described his frustration:

> Have felt pretty low and discouraged here. Working so that you're too tired at night to think let alone write and then in the morning a story starts in your head on the street car and have to choke it off because it was coming so perfectly and easily and clear and right and you know that if you let it go on it will be finished and gone and you'd never be able to write it. I'm all constipated up with stuff to write, that I've got to write before it goes bad in me. And am working 14 to 18 hrs [hours] a day to keep the show going until the 1st of the year.[8]

The depth of his frustration can be gauged by the way he mixes metaphors of birth and excretion to describe the stories inside of him that will miscarry if he lets them out too soon or holds them inside too long. This metaphor would later emerge in his fiction. In *A Farewell to Arms,* Catherine and Frederic's baby dies in her womb before he can be born. The baby in "Indian Camp," like the story itself, is extracted before it can "go bad."

Hemingway also had to attend to other family relationships. Before leaving for France he was obliged to pay a call on his parents in their Chicago suburb of Oak Park. His father had sent him a check to help out with Hadley's hospital expenses and had mentioned that Ernest's Uncle George, whom Hemingway disliked, had recently been on a hunting trip. Hemingway thanked his father for the check and complained that he himself had not the time to go hunting. On the day before Christmas, he paid a brief visit home, by himself, and gave his sister Marcelline a copy of his first book, *Three Stories & Ten Poems,* knowing that she would be repulsed by the rape in "Up in Michigan." He told her not to read it until after she left Oak Park because he did not want his parents to know about the offensive story. But when he got back to Toronto he arranged to have his publisher send his parents an order form for his second book, the recently published *in our time,* realizing full well that they would be equally disgusted by the "vulgarity" and violence of these vignettes. Indeed they were, most especially his father. Having ordered six copies of the book, they read with horror the contents (including the story of an American soldier who contracts gonorrhea from a Chicago salesgirl in the back of a taxicab), and promptly returned the copies to the publisher. The incident had, for Ernest, the desired effect; he now had an excuse to avoid writing to his parents for a while.[9]

When Ernest and Hadley returned to Paris with their baby John in January 1924, he was ready to write the stories that would launch his career. Although some of this writing was done at the dining room table in their new flat, during the day he worked at a nearby café, the Closerie des Lilas, driven out of the apartment by his four-month-old's crying and by the noise of a saw mill next door that operated constantly from seven in the morning until five in the evening. As he sat writing in a small, blue notebook, he observed among the Lilas patrons many French war veterans who had been mutilated in battle: men with missing limbs, artificial eyes, and reconstructed faces. In the evening he returned to the flat and his new paternal duties. Hadley was ill and had been suffering from insomnia ever since their return, and the baby wailed incessantly. Hemingway, who had also fallen ill and been laid up in bed, was determined to "write something" for Ford's *transatlantic review* but, he confessed to Ezra Pound, although he had "about 7 stories" inside him, he did not know "when or where" he would be able to write them. The stories would eventually get written "in cafes and one place and another."[10]

Often, they would return in a body bag. A quarter of a century later, Hemingway still remembered the experience:

> I had finally shucked off the journalism I had been complaining about and I was finally doing all the good writing I had promised myself. But every day the rejected manuscripts would come back through the slot in the door in that bare room where I lived over the Montmartre sawmill. They'd fall through the slot onto the wood floor, and clipped to them was that most savage of all reprimands—the printed rejection slip. . . . I'd sit at that old wooden table and read one of those cold slips that had been attached to a story I had loved and worked on very hard and believed in, and I couldn't help crying.[11]

This, then, is the biographical background to the writing of "Indian Camp." It is all we "know" about what Hemingway "knew" when he began to write the first of the eight stories that had preoccupied him for the previous four months. But from this tableau of emotions, events, and relationships we can see how details, incidents, and characters accrued to the story as it developed in his mind and in his notebook.

All fiction, Raymond Carver observes, is "in some way, autobiographical." But the relationship between life and art is complex, subtle, and elusive. It is, as Eudora Welty states, "by its nature . . . not very open to generalization or discoverable by the ordinary scrutinies of analysis." In the deleted original ending of "Big Two-Hearted River," Hemingway would admonish his readers: "Nick in the stories was never himself [i.e., neither Nick nor Hemingway]. He made him up. Of course he'd never seen an Indian woman having a baby. That was what made it good. Nobody knew that. He'd seen a woman have a baby on the road to Karagatch and tried to help her. That was the way it was." But if Nick was never Hemingway, he was nonetheless the autobiographically based, fictive creation of a particular man, the product of experience, memory, emotion, and imagination. We can therefore offer a number of necessarily inconclusive speculations that may prove illuminating, but with the twin caveats offered by Carver—that the "circumstances surrounding the writing are something else, something extraliterary"—and by Welty—that these are "of merely personal importance."[12] To add my own qualifier, I should note that I am attempting to address the question of how material from Hemingway's life was transmuted into his fiction, not trying to use the fiction to shed light on the life (always a very risky enterprise).

The theme of "Indian Camp" is death; more specifically, the story is about the fear of death, what I shall term *ontological shock*—the numbing, existential recognition of one's own finitude. The action of the story revolves around a Caesarean operation performed under primitive conditions. And the central relationship concerns a father and his young son. From these statements on theme, action, and character we can see how "extraliterary" events may have worked their way into the story. Clearly, childbirth and fatherhood were very much on Hemingway's mind, forming the emotional matrix from which this story emerged. During John's delivery in Toronto, he had been absent while others attended to his wife and child. The strain, guilt, and helplessness he felt seem in some way embodied in the figure of the Indian father who lies incapacitated in the upper bunk, powerless and emotionally isolated, while others hold down his wife and bring forth his baby son. This sense of helplessness—both the Indian father's and the Indian mother's—might also have as their analogue Hadley's frequent illnesses over the past four months (in the story, Dr. Adams first explains the journey to his son with the words, "There is an Indian lady very sick"). The times Ernest and Hadley both lay ill in bed while the baby cried have their fictional counterpart in the scene of the Indian father and mother lying in their bunks, the shanty filled with her screams caused by the unborn child, screams that seem to affect the Indian father. Like the other male Indians of the story, who had moved up the road "out of the range of the noise" in the shanty, Hemingway had been driven from the apartment by his baby's crying, in order to write this very story. Furthermore, the Indian father's ax injury resonates with the mutilated French war veterans of the Lilas whom Hemingway observed as he wrote, just as the Caesarean operation is reminiscent of the desperate conditions under which he may have tried to assist in the baby's delivery on the road to Karagatch during the horrific evacuation of Greek refugees from eastern Thrace in October 1922.

Hemingway's impending fatherhood surely must have caused him to reflect upon his relationship with his own father, especially during the one-day visit to Oak Park. Dr. Clarence Hemingway was someone toward whom his son felt ambivalence. He admired his father's excellence as a physician and an outdoorsman, but resented his paternal inadequacies. Dr. Adams is a similarly flawed character. He is competent but immodest;

he is loving toward his son but self-absorbed when most needed by him. Just as Dr. Adams is proud of successfully performing a Caesarean without proper equipment, so too was Dr. Hemingway proud of having invented a laminectomy forceps praised by the Rush Medical School faculty.[13] Both fathers in the story, Dr. Adams and the Indian husband, fail their sons. The words of the deranged artist Hemingway recalled from the streets of New York when he was missing his son's birth echo eerily in the story: "He sent his only begotten son to do this. He sent his only begotten son to die on a tree. He sent his only begotten son to hang there and die."

"Indian Camp" is set in the northern Michigan woods, the locale of Hemingway's fondest memories of childhood and adolescence. The daily noise of the Parisian sawmill would have reminded him of that region's semi-abandoned lumber towns, like Hortons Bay and Seney, the settings of other stories he would write during the months after "Indian Camp." The news of Uncle George's hunting trip must have evoked memories of similar northern Michigan hunting and fishing excursions from his youth. Linda Lizut Helstern points out that the term "Indian camp" is described in Ernest Thompson Seton's *The Woodcraft Manual for Boys* as a synonym for the "all-male primitive camping where activities were carried out with the bare minimum of protective gear." Hemingway owned the 1917 edition of this book, and Seton was one of his favorite authors.[14] Remembering the many such camps of his youth, in which Indian skills and values played an integral part in the construction of his own sense of Anglo-American masculinity, he must have yearned—as he found himself a husband, father, former journalist, and aspiring writer sitting in a Parisian café—for the simpler times of those Indian camps and his immersion in the empowering ethos of "primitivism" they provided. As for his lifelong dislike of his uncle, this also found a place in the story; he neither concealed his feelings nor even bothered to change the character's name.

All of these elements from Hemingway's life came together in "Indian Camp": childbirth, father-son relationships, hunting/fishing, northern Michigan, physical mutilation, competence, and powerlessness. They came together in the mind of a writer whose great and pervasive theme was man's efforts to control his fate, efforts marked by small successes and ultimate failure. The emotions evoked by such thematic concerns—exhilaration, hope, fear, anxiety, and despair—colored the terrain of his imagination. These emotions can be found at the start in this, his first great story.

"Indian Camp" originally appeared in the April 1924 issue of Ford's *transatlantic review.* It was published without a title and grouped under the heading "Works in Progress" along with selections from Tristan Tzara, the founder of Dadaism, and from James Joyce's as yet untitled *Finnegans Wake.* Also omitted, almost certainly by Hemingway himself, was the first third of the original story, so that "Indian Camp" now began with the two Indians waiting by the rowboats for the doctor. The deleted opening was posthumously published in 1972 by Philip Young in his collection of Nick Adams stories and given the title "Three Shots."

Speculating on Hemingway's motives for removing the original beginning of the story, biographer Carlos Baker states that they "remain obscure":

> He may have shortened it to fit the available space in Ford's review. He may have been trying out his new critical theory that something omitted can still affect the reader as if it were there. He may have decided that the comic aspects of the small-boy story softened unduly the hammerblows of violence in the main story's double climax of birth and death. Finally, he may have made the deletion because it clearly indicated the presence of cowardice in Nick Adams, whom he was planning to develop as a hero of tougher fiber.[15]

But it is difficult to believe that an author of Hemingway's own tough fiber, a writer who waged a thirteen-year campaign to get Scribner's to include "Up in Michigan" in a collection of his stories, would have cut a story so radically in the interests of "available space," or that, had he been forced to shorten the story, he would have merely lopped off the beginning, or that, had he done so, he would have chosen not to restore it at a later date when he was free to publish whatever he saw fit. Nor did his theory of omission at any time include simply severing the opening of a narrative. Last, there is nothing especially comical about a small boy's fear of death, nor does such a fear indicate, in one so young, the presence of cowardice, even taking into account this particular author's hypersensitivity to such a charge.

The reason why Hemingway deleted the opening is obvious. As he went along making up the story, to paraphrase his own statement on story-writing, it "changed" as it moved. From that movement, the real story that emerged, the one he wanted to tell, was the second part, in contrast to which the first part was a muddle. If "Indian Camp" is, in Kenneth S. Lynn's words, a "miracle of compression,"[16] then "Three Shots" is unfocused, mistake-ridden, and verbose. It is also, as the story turned out, gratuitous, and as such detracts from the narrative. On this point we may turn to Anton Chekhov, the master storyteller. In one of his many exasperated letters to mediocre would-be storywriters, he spoke of "the compactness that makes short things alive. . . . To make a face from marble means to remove from the slab everything that is not the face. Do I make myself clear?"[17] To Hemingway, clearly, he had.

Although we may muse, as I have, on how elements from Hemingway's life were transmuted into fiction as he wrote "Indian Camp," what he actually "knew"—how much of the story and plot were complete in his mind when he began—can never be known. In the absence of such information, though, we could do worse than to observe that the theme of the original story, as well as of its two component parts, concerns a small boy's first encounter with what I have labeled ontological shock—the gripping existential realization of one's own mortality, the overwhelming comprehension that someday one will cease to be. This was more than just an interesting topic to Hemingway; it was a lifelong obsession. "When asked what he is afraid of," wrote Ernest's mother of her five-year-old son, "he shouts out *fraid a nothing* with great gusto."[18] Yet to be afraid of nothing, of "no thing," can mean to live in a state of undefined fear, that is, in a state of anxiety. This sort of naked anxiety, where fears are unspecific and attached to no things in particular, is emotionally unbearable. The fear of nothingness, the experience of one's own finitude, overwhelms comprehension and produces ontological shock. The twentieth century's greatest theologian, Paul Tillich, observes:

> Finitude in awareness is anxiety. Like finitude, anxiety is an ontological quality. . . . As an ontological quality, anxiety is as omnipresent as is finitude. Anxiety is independent of any special object which might produce it; it is dependent only on the threat of nonbeing—which is identical with finitude. In this sense it has been said rightly that the object of anxiety is "nothingness"—and nothingness is not an "object." Objects are feared. A danger, a pain, an enemy, may be feared, but fear can be conquered by action. Anxiety cannot, for no finite being can conquer its finitude. Anxiety is always present, although often it is latent. Therefore, it can become manifest at any and every moment, even in situations where nothing is to be feared.[19]

I might add, parenthetically, that Hemingway's attempts to conquer what some have mistakenly termed his "fears" were doomed to failure; it was his anxiety about non-being that drove him to his futile acts of "courage." Hemingway's sensitivity to non-being was a dominant presence in his life and writing, most powerfully addressed in the story "A Clean, Well-Lighted Place" with its arresting "nada-ization" of "The Lord's Prayer." He spent a lifetime trying to conquer the anxiety of non-being by demonstrating control through his mastery of craft: fiction—achieving immortality through art—fishing and hunting—killing "game" animals and fish to become, in effect, the very thing he dreaded: death. In the end, he aggressively surrendered to ontological shock by attacking the repository of his finitude—himself.

From whatever seeds "Indian Camp" grew, and however much of the story was complete when Hemingway started to write it, lurking beneath the creative impulse and its subsequent stages of composition was the original question—the matter of ontological shock. "The artist," says Chekhov, "observes, chooses, guesses, compounds—these actions in themselves already presuppose a question at the origin; if the artist did not pose a question to himself at the beginning then there was nothing to guess or to choose." The writer, he concludes, does not create "unintentionally," nor is art the result of a "temporary aberration." Although not all authors are so fully conscious as Chekhov of the "question at the origin," nevertheless he is quite right when he says that the writer must "approach his work consciously" in "*the correct formulation of a problem.*" This, he flatly states, is the main requirement for an author.[20] Chekhov refers here to the *treatment of theme*, that which distinguishes the storywriter from the philosopher, the theologian, the sociologist, the person on the street—or the literary critic. It is in the "correct formulation of a problem," the treatment of theme, that storywriters practice their craft.

What is especially fascinating about the original version of "Indian Camp," then, is that not only did the story change as it moved along, but that the two parts of the story are nearly autonomous, constituting two separate treatments of the same theme. For our purposes, they are strikingly respective examples of an unsuccessful and a successful treatment of that theme, and, as such, wonderfully illustrate many of the basic principles of Hemingway's craft at the very moment when he was developing them. Of course, to make such a comparison is grossly unfair to Hemingway, for he wisely discarded "Three Shots" and never intended for it to come to light. Nor did he ever conceive of it as a separate story; at most, it was the original opening of "Indian Camp." But because such a comparison is instructive, and since it is a tribute to Hemingway that he could master so quickly the techniques of storywriting, I should like to examine these two texts, the deleted opening and the published story, as though they were two separate stories. Technique in any craft is often easier to demonstrate by analyzing bad examples; what makes bad art bad is easier to take hold of than what makes great art great. As Hemingway himself stated about the art of bullfighting in *Death in the Afternoon,* "It should be a good thing for him [a new spectator] to see a novillada first . . . if he wants to learn about technique, since the employment of knowledge that we call by that bastard name is always most visible in its imperfection."[21]

Failure: The Original Opening

> Beginners have often to do this—fold in two and tear up the first half [of the story]. . . . the first half is superfluous. One must write so that the reader should understand, without the author's explanations . . . what it is all about.
>
> —Anton Chekhov (quoted in O'Faolain, *The Short Story,* 150)

The original opening of "Indian Camp" is to the final version of the story as a *novillada* (a type of amateur bullfight) is to a *corrida de toros* (a formal bullfight); it stumbles out of the gate in the first paragraph:

> [1] Nick was undressing in the tent. [2] He saw the shadows of his father and Uncle George cast by the fire on the canvas wall. [3] He felt very uncomfortable and ashamed and undressed as fast as he could, piling his clothes neatly. [4] He was ashamed because undressing reminded him of the night before. [5] He had kept it out of his mind all day.

It's a bad idea to begin a short story, as Hemingway does here, with the past progressive tense. Not coincidentally, he refrained from doing so in any of the stories written for his first three major collections.[22] The storywriter does not have the novelist's luxury of opening in a leisurely manner. Readers, who since the days of Maupassant and Chekhov have been trained to bring to a story a higher degree of alertness than to a novel, are "eager to process"—to digest, sort out, and make sense of the details, images, relationships, and other elements of the story that will enable them quickly to get their bearings in, to use Eudora Welty's apt phrase, the "little world" they have entered.[23] The storywriter must accordingly play to the reader's eagerness by trying to keep pace with it, not by putting on the brakes, for in a story "[i]f the first stroke be vivid and telling," as Edith Wharton observes, "the reader's attention will be instantly won."[24] The past progressive is a vague tense, expanding a past action by continuing it into an undefined point of time also in the past. As John Gardner notes, "verbs with auxiliaries . . . are never as sharp in focus as verbs without auxiliaries, since the former indicate indefinite time, whereas the latter . . . suggest a given instant."[25] Moreover, auxiliaries are abstract words serving merely as time markers and nothing more. The past progressive is therefore precisely not the way to start a story unless there is some effect toward which the writer is working. In this story, it only slows down the narrative at its inception.

To make matters worse, Hemingway further hinders the reader by employing, in a five-sentence paragraph, the past progressive tense, the simple past, and the past perfect. By the end of the paragraph, the reader has been slowed down considerably just trying to figure out the sequence of the actions indicated by the verb tenses. There is also no particular logic to Hemingway's usage. If he is concerned with accuracy, then the third sentence should read: "He *was feeling* very uncomfortable and ashamed and *undressing* as fast as he could, piling his clothes neatly." These are ongoing past actions just like those of the first sentence. The past progressive is a seductive verb tense; once writers start using it they usually continue to do so until "ing" words cover the page and they realize they have been snared. Then they go back and change to the simple past tense.

Why, then, did the young author get so caught up in these different verb tenses? Why was he unable simply to rewrite the paragraph, and other paragraphs, so that the reader would not be slowed down sorting out the actions? The answer to these questions points to a more fundamental problem with the paragraph (and the whole aborted opening). He got trapped into using the grammatically correct verb tense at the expense of storycrafting because from the start he was busy telling and explaining rather than showing and implying. As Nick undresses, he sees the shadows of the two adults. So far, so good, except that it would have been more effective to pique the reader's curiosity by saying that he saw "the shadows of the two men" rather than identifying them as Nick's father and uncle (this would also have made his sense of shame more palpable because it would have appeared, perhaps, archetypal). But then the author *tells* us that Nick feels uncomfortable and ashamed, so now he feels compelled to explain *why.* This not only explicitly links undressing to his feelings of shame instead of allowing the image to resonate, it also jerks the reader's attention out of the present to an event that occurred "the night before." The story, already wounded, starts to bleed. In the brief space of the last two sentences of the first paragraph and the opening sentence of the next paragraph, the reader goes from the night of the story to the night before, back across the day to the night of the story, and then back to the night before. One can almost hear the frustrated Chekhov's advice to his brother Alexander—"avoid depicting the hero's state of mind; you ought to . . . make it clear from the hero's actions"—and to young Maxim Gorky: "The brain can't grasp all that at once, and art must be grasped at once, instantaneously."[26]

Hemingway's desire to explain finds him, like Frank O'Connor's hypothetical bad playwright, telling the reader more than is necessary. Far from leaving the author "everywhere felt but never seen," as Gustave Flaubert advised, his expository prose is, to return to Chekhov, a "terrible thing" that "reveals the author's hands and feet."[27] Hemingway is so concerned that the reader see everything just as he himself sees it, and understand it exactly as he understands it, that he will not let the reader participate in the story. Only in the single phrase, "piling his clothes neatly" does he write like an artist and not a child psychologist. The phrase suggests a deliberate action by a character trying to ward off unpleasant emotions—in this case a sense of shame associated with deeper feelings of anxiety. Yet the author does not trust the reader enough to allow the image to remain suggestive (as he subsequently would with an extended series of similarly functioning actions in "Big Two-Hearted River"). Instead, he explains it in the last sentence and thus kills its potential resonance.

In the second paragraph, Hemingway flashes back to "the night before":

> [1] His father and uncle had gone off across the lake after supper to fish with a jack light. [2] Before they shoved the boat out his father told him that if any emergency came up while they were gone he was to fire three shots with the rifle and they would come right back. [3] Nick went back from the edge of the lake through the woods to the camp. [4] He could hear the oars of the boat in the dark. [5] His father was rowing and his uncle was sitting in the stern trolling. [6] He had taken his seat with his rod ready when his father shoved the boat out. [7] Nick listened to them on the lake until he could no longer hear the oars.

In the opening paragraph, the action sequence was difficult to grasp; here it is out of order. The first sentence is written in the past perfect tense, indicating a past action completed before another past time; the two men went across the lake (the completed past action) before the next night (the past time in which the story begins). The rest of the flashback could then be written in the simple past, for convention allows the writer to revert to the simple past after first establishing through the past perfect that the past action being described was completed. This convention is necessary since otherwise all flashbacks would have to be narrated in the past perfect, a tense encumbered with auxiliaries that cannot sustain a lengthy section of narrative.

But Hemingway again begins a paragraph with a mistake. He sends the two men across the lake with the irrevocable finality of the past perfect tense before bothering to explain the actions preceding their journey. Therefore, in the very next sentence, he must yank them off the lake and put them back on the shore so that he can summarize what Nick's father told his son. He has no other choice; there is no "past past perfect" tense in English. With the two men back on shore, he gives up the struggle and puts the first two verbs of sentence 2 in the simple past tense ("shoved" and "told") even though "had told" is indicated. The whole second sentence also creates an unnecessary minor flashback immediately following a major flashback; it continues the verb tense problem that has plagued the story from the beginning; and it is another example of inartistic "telling" in a story that is already suffocating in explanations.

In the third sentence, the beleaguered author sends Nick from the shore through the woods to the camp. But sentences 4 through 6 are hopelessly confusing. Either the two men set out before Nick left the shore, in which case Hemingway has repeated the mistake he made in the first sentence, or else Nick was already gone when they left, in which case the story's point-of-view has been compromised. In either case, there is simply no way to tell where Nick, our camera eye, was when the men left. If Nick was by the lake when they set out, then the story is still being told from his point-of-view in a third-person fixed internal focalization with Nick as the central consciousness, and Nick saw the actions of sentences 5 and 6. But if that is what happened, then these actions should have taken place before Nick returned to camp, and sentence 3 is out of sequence (just as sentence 1 was). The only other possibility, presuming that Nick was by the lake, is that he saw his father shove the boat out; he returned through the woods to the camp; during the time it took for him to return to the camp the two men did not go very far (even though they will shortly end up on "the other side of the lake"); and when he hears the oars it reminds him of the actions he observed in sentences 5 and 6. This is all pretty unlikely, but even if that is what happened, then sentences 5 and 6 are yet another flashback within a flashback, indicating a paragraph that is rather carelessly arranged. I might add that no matter which of these versions is true, in relation to each other the two sentences in question (5 and 6) are still out of sequence, unless his father was rowing and his uncle trolling while the boat was still on land.

On the other hand, if Nick was back at camp when his father pushed the boat out, then sentences 5 and 6 are no longer being narrated from Nick's point-of-view. Since Hemingway will shortly abandon his adherence to Nick as the fixed internal focalizer, to the story's detriment, when he reports the dialogue of the men out on the lake, this assumption is plausible. But such a strategy is dangerous; to shift the point-of-view so soon, suddenly, and briefly in such a short story is a bad mistake. My own belief is that Nick probably watches the two men depart. Three uses of the pronoun "his" with Nick as the antecedent make it seem as though Nick is present, even though the antecedent to the final possessive pronoun in sentence 6—"He had taken his seat with his rod ready when his father shoved the boat out"—is grammatically vague and potentially ludicrous. (The first three pronouns refer to Uncle George, but the fourth, one can only hope, refers to Nick.) Although the paragraph is a mess, such a brief shift in point-of-view for no good reason would be incredibly amateurish. Much more likely is that Hemingway sent Nick back to camp too soon, just as he had sent the two men across the lake prematurely. That the very next paragraph begins with Nick once more walking back from the lake to the camp lends weight to this conclusion.

By the end of the first two paragraphs, a narrative pattern has emerged that will continue until Hemingway works his way out of it toward the close of the original opening. He writes a sentence depicting an action, then feels the need to explain the action, and ends up explaining not only the action but other peripheral actions and the original explanation as well. This leads him to retreat backwards from each action in a series of explanatory flashbacks. Some are formal flashbacks (e.g., the entire second paragraph and, perhaps, the actions described in sentences 5 and 6 of that paragraph). Others are implied flashbacks, made necessary by the author's need to explain what led up to each action (e.g., sentences 2 and 6 of the second paragraph). The constant flashbacks and explanations hinder the reader's progress while the plot confuses the sequence of the actions. This confusion is exacerbated by a faulty and inconsistent choice of verb tenses. Moreover, the explanations—sentences of mere information lacking vivid detail—enervate the few suggestive images (e.g., "piling his clothes neatly"; hearing the oars in the dark; his uncle taking his seat with "his rod ready") and prevent the reader from entering the story imaginatively. All of these problems stem from one source: the author's need to explain, which prevents the commencement of what John Gardner terms the "fictional dream."[28]

The story reaches its nadir in the third paragraph, which opens with Nick's "second" return to camp: "Walking back through the woods Nick began to be frightened." Again, the author directly explains his character's state of mind, and in the next sentence adds that Nick "was always a little frightened of the woods at night." After these unnecessary sentences, the third sentence reads: "He opened the flap of the tent and undressed and lay very quietly between the blankets in the dark." This suggestive image of Nick could then have been developed in later sentences so that readers could sense, on their own, Nick's unease. But by directly stating Nick's fear, Hemingway again prevents the image from being effective. Also, since what Nick feels is anxiety and not fear, the preemptive explanations of the first two sentences are misleading. The images suggest anxiety, but the explanations state that it is fear, and because the explanations are so insistent and the images so few and undeveloped, the reader is trapped between them.

Despite this, the story briefly attempts to assert itself as fiction. After the third sentence, which should have opened the paragraph, there are four consecutive sentences that might have worked had they not been undermined by the actual opening of the paragraph: "The fire was burned down to a bed of coals outside. Nick lay still and tried to go to sleep. There was no noise anywhere. Nick felt if he could only hear a fox bark or an owl or anything it would be all right." These specific images imply Nick's growing anxiety, which reaches its climax when he fires the shots. Even the last sentence, which tells us what Nick "feels," works because Hemingway does not address his anxiety directly. Instead, the sentence tells us something about which Nick is conceivably conscious—his desire to hear a noise—rather than discussing a psychological state that Nick would neither be aware of nor able to articulate. Which is to say that these sentences are narrated from Nick's point-of-view. But the passage is rendered ineffective by the sentences that precede it, and it is obliterated by the sentences that follow: "He was not afraid of anything definite as yet. But he was getting very afraid. Then suddenly he was afraid of dying." There is no need for the first of these sentences; the preceding passage already makes it clear that Nick's fears are unfocused. The anticipatory "as yet" is a cheap attempt to create momentary suspense and an unwelcome omniscient focalization that provides information Nick would not know. His sharply increasing anxiety is never portrayed; the author merely informs us of it in six uninspired words. As for the last sentence of explanatory information, how else can feelings of anxiety turn into ontological shock except suddenly? Moreover, what Nick feels is not fear, which is always attached to a specific object, but anxiety, which never is. Even the fear of death that Nick "suddenly" feels is not fear, but naked anxiety, the most intense form of anxiety. It's bad enough that the author feels obliged to explain his character's every feeling; he should at least know what he is trying to explain.

But things can get worse, and do. Because he directly stated Nick's fear of dying, Hemingway now feels compelled to sketch the history of that fear by way of yet another explanation. This leads him into the biggest foul-up in a story full of blunders. In the middle of what is already a major formal flashback, indeed in the middle of only the third paragraph, he gives us an even greater formal flashback, hurling the bewildered reader back a few weeks to the day in church when Nick first felt ontological shock. *Suddenly,* unity of time (which was on the verge of collapse) and unity of place (which, remarkably, had been holding its own) are gone; the bottom falls out of the story. "Just a few weeks before at home, in church, they had sung a hymn, 'Some day the silver cord will break.'" During the hymn, "Nick had realized that some day he must die. It made him feel quite sick. It was the first time he had ever realized that he himself would have to die sometime." The "at home, in church" phrase is yet more evidence of how the author's unwillingness to trust the reader leads to silly prose. Does it make any difference to the story where the church was? As Sean O'Faolain notes, "detail for its own sake is . . . pointless."[29] With the adjective "quite," the author once more intrudes; in keeping to Nick's point-of-view "very" would be more appropriate. "Quite," like the use of the verb "to commence" instead of "to begin," is one of Hemingway's peculiar verbal tics that, when they do not work, come across as affectations. "Quite" works best for him when he uses it in first-person narratives for purposes of understatement, or in dialogue for characterization. The final sentence of the paragraph is needlessly awkward and verbose.

In the next paragraph the flashback stumbles forward: "That night he sat out in the hall under the night light trying to read *Robinson Crusoe* to keep his mind off the fact that some day the silver cord must break." The nurse discovers him and makes him go back to bed by threatening to tell his father. When she returns to her room, he comes back into the hallway and reads until morning. The sentence quoted is again awkward, wordy, and repetitive. The image of Nick under the night light trying to read speaks for itself; there is no need to explain why he is doing it. In addition, a child would never picture his anxiety in terms of "the silver cord" breaking, even if he first had the revelation of his mortality while the hymn was being sung. Ontological shock grips the entire being viscerally; it is not experienced metaphorically. The scene with the nurse is completely gratuitous and introduces a character who serves no conceivable purpose. The story then jumps back to the night of the original flashback as Hemingway explains to the readers, just in case they are complete idiots, that the fear Nick now experiences is the same as the fear he'd had in church: "Last night in the tent he had had the same fear." He adds: "He never had it except at night." This information is both useless and makes no sense; how many times could Nick have had such an extreme experience in a few weeks? Because the narrative flow of the story, such as it is, has been disturbed, the author now recapitulates the last three sentences before the flashback, the ones in which Nick was suddenly afraid of dying: "It was more a realization than a fear at first. But it was always on the edge of fear and became fear very quickly when it started." Quite! What these sentences, like the previous passage, mean to say is that whenever Nick experienced anxiety over his mortality, it quickly turned acute. Neither Hemingway's attempts to describe Nick's feelings nor my own rephrasing of those descriptions is particularly effective, but at least my version is comprehensible.

After this passage, Hemingway mercifully quits explaining and the dying story briefly stirs. Nick grabs the rifle, points it out the tent flap, fires the three shots, and feels better. He lies down and falls asleep almost immediately, before the two men on the other side of the lake start back. These sentences don't do a great deal of work, but they do establish, for the first time in the story, a chronological sequence of actions in clear, precise prose with consistent verb tenses and no authorial explanations. When the author depicts actions, instead of explaining them, all aspects of the story improve. Until this last passage, the story has been told almost entirely through digressive explanatory exposition. There have been scenic elements, but these are undeveloped and hidden in summary treatment. Not coincidentally, dialogue has been absent. But although the story, as written, is by now beyond all hope of repair, the author has finally purged himself of the need to explain. The next three passages are scenes mostly in dialogue. The action of "Three Shots" proper, considered as a separate story, really ends with the third of these passages, but even the fourth passage, which serves as a bridge to "Indian Camp," is skillfully done. Through scene and dialogue Hemingway will leave behind the muddled, ineffective prose he has been writing and ascend into the realm of art.

He ascends; he does not leap. Although dialogue will lift him from the quagmire, at first it serves only to tear apart the story more completely. Each scene with dialogue improves upon the previous one until the final passage that, along with the bridge passage, is but a tiny step from the mastery of "Indian Camp." The first passage treats the reaction of the two men upon hearing the shots:

> "Damn that kid," Uncle George said as they rowed back. "What did you tell him to call us in for? He's probably got the heebie-jeebies about something."
>
> Uncle George was an enthusiastic fisherman and his father's younger brother.
>
> "Oh, well. He's pretty small," his father said.
>
> "That's no reason to bring him into the woods with us."
>
> "I know he's an awful coward," his father said, "but we're all yellow at that age."
>
> "I can't stand him," Uncle George said. "He's such an awful liar."
>
> "Oh, well, forget it. You'll get plenty of fishing anyway."

What purpose does this scene serve? In what ways, as Elizabeth Bowen would ask, is the dialogue relevant?[30] Unlike the earlier scene on shore, where the fixed internal focalization was possibly compromised, here it is wholly discarded. Nick is present only as the absent antecedent of the possessive pronoun in the inadvertently ridiculous sentence: "Uncle George was an enthusiastic fisherman and his father's younger brother." The scene does nothing to advance the plot; if it were simply removed, the story would actually improve. Nor does it further our understanding of the characters. We learn from the scene that Uncle George is an avid fisherman, Dr. Adams's younger brother, and an insensitive person. But the earlier image of George having "taken his seat with his rod ready" much more effectively conveys to the reader this character's love of fishing. In addition, it is irrelevant to the story (though perhaps not to the writer who transferred intact to that story the uncle he so hated) that Dr. Adams is the older brother. Furthermore, Uncle George is not an important enough character to waste so much space depicting as insensitive. In "Indian Camp," Hemingway will accomplish this characterization through the scrupulous use of a few details that do not get in the way of the plot (e.g., when George passes out cigars, curses at the Indian woman, and mocks Nick's father after the operation). These details, which work *within* the story, are the signifiers that bring Uncle George to life in a way that this stilted dialogue does not.

Nor does the passage illuminate the character of either Nick or his father. What we already know about Nick makes trite the men's characterizations of him as an "awful coward" and an "awful liar." Dr. Adams's dialogue is also at odds with the character we will meet later on. Here he is almost as insensitive as his brother, to whom he abjectly apologizes for his son's perfectly understandable behavior. The Dr. Adams of a few pages later would have either ignored his brother's insults or else told him to shut up. The Dr. Adams in this passage, however, with his tepid "Oh, well" excuses, is pretty much unbelievable. He has left his young child all alone in the woods and is separated from him by an entire lake when he hears the warning shots, and it does not even cross his mind that there might possibly be genuine cause for concern. For all he knows, Nick is presently being devoured by feral dogs!

The dialogue is not just repetitious; it is stagnant. Both Uncle George and Dr. Adams talk to each other in awkward sentences that in no way resemble the shorthand manner by which people who know each other well converse. Not only does the dialogue fail to conform to the characters' personalities, but both speak in the same way, a cardinal error in writing dialogue. The next scene, however, is a vast improvement:

> They came into the tent and Uncle George shone his flashlight into Nick's eyes.
>
> "What was it, Nickie?" said his father. Nick sat up in bed.
>
> "It sounded like a cross between a fox and a wolf and it was fooling

> around the tent," Nick said. He had learned the phrase "cross between" that same day from his uncle.
>
> "He probably heard a screech owl," Uncle George said.

The compressed action of the first sentence efficiently locates the scene. The sentence is highly suggestive and the word choice is impeccable. With the phrase "came into the tent" instead of, say, "went into the tent," and the phrase "into Nick's eyes" instead of "on Nick's face," Hemingway subtly returns to fixed internal focalization with Nick as the central consciousness. This is precisely how Nick, and only Nick, would have experienced the action. The sentence even carries a hint of George's insensitivity. Each character has one speech, each of which reveals the speaker's unique personality; they do not sound alike. Dr. Adams's use of the diminutive "Nickie" expresses his tenderness and concern for his child. George's humiliating comment about the screech owl shows his contempt for Nick. Nick's speech suggests his embarrassment as he tries to make the danger seem serious, especially when he ups the ante by saying that it was "more like a wolf." The sentence informing us that he had learned the phrase earlier from his uncle is a nice psychological touch that shows how a small child unconsciously tries to placate a bully by aping him. The dialogue reveals not only involuntary self-revelation, but conscious calculation as well—the father wants to know what it was; Nick wants to persuade them it was serious; and George wants to get at Nick for ruining his fishing.

The following scene, which could have served as the ending to a much better story, is technically almost flawless:

> In the morning his father found two big basswood trees that leaned across each other so that they rubbed together in the wind.
>
> "Do you think that was what it was, Nick?" his father asked.
>
> "Maybe," Nick said. He didn't want to think about it.
>
> "You don't want to ever be frightened in the woods, Nick. There is nothing that can hurt you."
>
> "Not even lightning?" Nick asked.
>
> "No, not even lightning. If there is a thunder storm get out into the open. Or get under a beech tree. They're never struck."
>
> "Never?" Nick asked.
>
> "I never heard of one," said his father.
>
> "Gee, I'm glad to know that about beech trees," Nick said.

Again, Hemingway effectively locates the scene with a precise, concrete sentence. The use of the word "found" (instead of "saw") is suggestive; Dr. Adams has deliberately sought out a forest noise for his son, either to console him by offering a palpable reason for Nick's fear on the previous night, or, equally revealing, because he believes in his son despite the evidence and George's opinions. The author does not waste words directly telling us that Dr. Adams purposely took Nick with him on this little expedition; he allows a good reader to infer it and a careless one to miss it. The ensuing dialogue perfectly accords with the speakers' personalities. Dr. Adams both respects and wishes to encourage his child's autonomy. He *asks* Nick if he thinks it was the trees he heard. The child, still ashamed of his earlier behavior, is warily noncommittal. The author then adds the comment that Nick did not want to think about it, which is unnecessary because the reader already senses it. Dr. Adams also senses his son's reticence, and tactfully directs the conversation away from the particular embarrassing incident onto the general topic of how nothing in the woods "can hurt you." The "you" here refers to Nick, of course, but it also implies the more general sense of "one." The tactic succeeds. Because his father has addressed Nick's fears indirectly, the boy no longer feels ashamed and his curiosity causes him to engage in conversation. The subsequent dialogue about lightning and beech trees allows the two characters to settle into the security of a father-as-teacher/son-as-learner pattern of behavior. It produces a sort of catharsis, with Nick's final speech coming across almost as a sigh of relief.

As I've said, this would be a wonderful ending to a good story, but it is much too good for this story. Although the deleted opening is only three pages long, this passage is at odds with its beginning, which chronologically takes place later that night and in which Nick is again feeling "uncomfortable and ashamed." But this lonely passage without a story has served an enabling function. The author, after a brief return to the murky opening scene, is now ready to write "Indian Camp." In the final lines of "Three Shots," Nick is "undressing again in the tent" as Hemingway forgets that he has never stopped undressing in the past progressive throughout this extended flashback. This time he is "conscious of the two shadows on the wall" but is not watching them, and his father shouts for him to get his clothes on, comes into the tent to search for some surgical equipment, and tells Nick to get his coat on as well. A sentence later, we have thankfully left

"Three Shots" and entered "Indian Camp." There is no longer any cause for embarrassment. Dr. Adams is off to demonstrate his competence as a surgeon, and Hemingway is ready to demonstrate his own as a storywriter.

Triumph: The Achievement of "Indian Camp"

> [I]f you can get to see [the world] clear and as a whole . . . [t]hen any part you make will represent the whole if it's made truly. The thing to do is work and learn how to make it.
>
> —Ernest Hemingway (*Death in the Afternoon,* 278)

"Indian Camp" is a remarkably compressed story that eschews authorial explanations and makes its appeal to the reader's senses in an efficient, suggestive prose. Superfluities are negligible, and words are carefully chosen that resonate with implications on many levels. Hardly anything is explained; the characters are evoked with economy; the theme pervades the narration but lies beneath the surface of the action; and elements of the story (e.g., exposition, dialogue, action, settings) often perform multiple functions. A complex and carefully crafted unity holds the narrative together: the duration is roughly twelve hours; the main events take place in a shanty and are framed by a trip to and from that setting; and the plot is chronological, with each part contingent upon what precedes it and necessitating that which comes after it. The text's various elements are completely integrated. Not just the dialogue, but the entire story mimics the randomness of real experience, yet everything is thoroughly relevant and pointed, held together not only by the unities but by the author's subtle foreshadowing techniques. These techniques maintain an artful symmetry far from the clumsy flashbacks that Hemingway used to impose a false envelope of unity upon the earlier story. In short, "Indian Camp" is everything that its original opening was not: it is a masterpiece, the author's first.

Nick is the central consciousness, and Hemingway goes to great lengths to maintain a strict adherence to fixed internal focalization. Instead of making Nick the center of the story by making him the center of the action (and by "explaining" him), the author moves him to the periphery of the action and reflects that action through the child's consciousness. By making Nick an observer, as the reader, too, is an observer, Hemingway feels free to focus on the concrete events as they filter through Nick's consciousness, and this enables him to set aside the abstract language he had hitherto used to describe Nick's thoughts and feelings. Nick experiences ontological shock not by metaphorically pondering his own death, but in the wake of witnessing a real death. The reader also witnesses this death, witnesses, in fact, Nick's witnessing of this death, and thus is drawn into Nick's consciousness in a compelling manner. In "Indian Camp," the narrator remains dispassionate. In the discarded opening, the reader's knowledge was the same as the narrator's knowledge, which, oddly enough, was not much greater than Nick's knowledge. But here the narrator is effectively invisible and the reader, left alone with Nick, feels closer to him and to the story, yet is more aware than is Nick of the meaning of what the boy experiences. Thus the third-person fixed internal focalization is used to its fullest advantage; we are connected to the story by Nick's consciousness and yet not limited to the narrow comprehension of that consciousness.

"Indian Camp" begins with no preambles, explanations, or exposition. Our contact with the story is, in Sean O'Faolain's words, "immediate" and "intimate";[31] we are forced from the start to concentrate:

> [P1] At the lake shore there was another rowboat drawn up. The two Indians stood waiting.
>
> [P2] Nick and his father got in the stern of the boat and the Indians shoved it off and one of them got in to row. Uncle George sat in the stern of the camp rowboat. The young Indian shoved the camp boat off and got in to row Uncle George.

This opening casts us into an unfamiliar world, forcing us to be alert. It also strikes the keynote of suspense that carries the story and the reader up to the point where we discover the purpose of the journey, and it does so in a suggestively subtle fashion. The suspense is implicit in the phrases "another rowboat" and "two Indians" (preceded by the definite article). The reader immediately wonders what "other" rowboat and what two Indians, and proceeds to the next paragraph to find out the answers to these questions. Readers half a century earlier, by the way, would have assumed that the first page was missing from their copy of the story.

The very structure of the first sentence also produces suspense; it invites the reader into the text by mimicking the process by which a reader takes up a story. The construction of the sentence is inert, just like a story, which lies passively on the physical page waiting to engage a potential reader. But the rowboat, like the story, is "drawn up," ready to spring into action and carry us into the narrative once we start reading. The two Indians stand "waiting" for Nick and his father to get into the boat, but they are also waiting for the reader. The boat therefore functions on three levels simultaneously: it carries the doctor to his patient; it carries the central consciousness to the event that will be narrated from his point-of-view; and it carries the reader into the story. It does all of this in a mere two sentences of scenic description of 15 words totaling 21 syllables that are narrated from Nick's perspective without any authorial intrusion or explanation.

The second paragraph presents a precise sequence of actions *exactly* as Nick would have experienced them that focuses the reader's attention on these actions. Before we know it, we find ourselves in Nick's boat, about to cross the lake. In narrating these sentences, Hemingway immediately establishes Nick as the focalizer. There are two parallel sequences of action occurring here: Nick and his father getting into the Indians' boat, that boat being shoved off, and an Indian getting in to row; and Uncle George getting into the camp boat, that boat being shoved off, and the young Indian getting in to row. Because Nick is engaged in the first of these sequences, it is narrated in one sentence so that the continuity of Nick's felt experience is mimetically expressed in an unbroken manner: three consecutive actions linked by the non-subordinating conjunction "and." A sequence of action contained in one sentence reads more quickly than a similar sequence broken into two or more sentences. Once Nick is in the boat, he sees that Uncle George is already in the other boat. The second sequence of action began before the first was completed, so that Nick did not actually see Uncle George get into the other boat. Once he has completed his own sequence of action, Nick can now sit back and observe—his experience of the passage of time slows down—which effect is conveyed by breaking the second sequence of action, the one in which Nick does not participate, into two sentences. Nick now has time to see that one of the Indians is younger than the other. That he could notice this fact means that the age difference must be obvious. That he did not notice it right away shows how absorbed he was in the first sequence of action.

There are other indications that this will be Nick's story. The two men are identified as "his father" and "Uncle George," which shows them only in their relation to Nick. There will be no silly sentences like the one from "Three Shots" ("Uncle George was an enthusiastic fisherman and his father's younger brother"), or sentences that convey unnecessary information about the characters. Uncle George is referred to as "Uncle George" throughout the text (11 times) except when directly addressed by his brother. And Dr. Adams is always identified as "Nick's father" or "his father" (17 times) except when pronouns are substituted, and also in four consecutive references to him as "the doctor" in the aftermath of the operation during which his professional role displaces his parental function. Nowhere is his last name "Adams" used, which would be superfluous from Nick's point-of-view. (I use it merely as a convenience.)

Third-person fixed internal focalization achieves access to the central consciousness in two ways. First, the narrator can delve into the mind of the focalizer objectively, something that would not be possible with the hopelessly subjective nature of first-person narration. Second, the narrator sights events through the focalizer, making the central consciousness the story's "camera eye." The narrator, writing in the third-person, gives over to the central consciousness the role of perceiver traditionally associated with first-person narrators. In "Three Shots," Hemingway broke no rule of third-person fixed internal focalization when he told us that Nick felt "uncomfortable and ashamed." The sentence simply lacked specificity. In "Indian Camp," although the author makes a few unnecessary statements about Nick's state of mind, not until the very end does he take advantage of his unlimited access to Nick's consciousness. In other words, he proceeds mainly through external focalization (refraining from accessing Nick's feelings and thoughts), which would become a *sine qua non* of Hemingway's art. What he does do throughout the story, however, and with enormous success, is employ Nick as his camera eye.[32] The subtlety with which he does this is apparent in the second paragraph during the narration of the two sequences of action.

It is equally apparent in the third paragraph as the journey across the lake begins:

> [P3] [1] The two boats started off in the dark. [2] Nick heard the oarlocks of the other boat quite a way ahead of them in the mist. [3] The Indians rowed with quick choppy strokes. [4] Nick lay back with his father's arm aroun.d him. [5] It was cold on the water. [6] The Indian who was rowing them was working very hard, but the other boat moved further ahead in the mist all the time.

This paragraph immerses us in the physicality of the story. The first sentence engages our senses of touch and sight; we feel the boats start forward and, since this will turn out to be a moonlit night and the young Indian in the other boat has a lantern, perhaps, on rereading, we see them as well. In the second sentence we hear a specific sound, the noise of the oarlocks, while we feel the mist against our faces. In the third sentence we see the Indians rowing with "quick choppy strokes"—an image of men engaged in strenuous activity; we hear the sound of the oar blades cutting into the water; and we feel the boat progress across the lake in the steadily lurching fashion implied by the strokes. The fourth sentence appeals purely to touch; Nick feels the security of his father's arm that enables him to lean back without fear. He also implicitly feels his father's warmth, both literally and figuratively. This is juxtaposed to the "cold on the water" that he feels in the next sentence. In the final sentence, the older Indian is "working very hard"—we see and hear him straining against the oars—but we dimly see the other boat steadily moving farther ahead in the cold mist.

The sequence of action that began in the previous paragraph continues its forward progress in sentences 1, 3, and 6, in which the narrator reports that the boats are moving or the Indians are rowing. The three mentions of the noun "boat" provide a thread (an object associated with an action sequence) that runs from the first sentence of the story up through the paragraph where the boats reach the other shore (a thread that is then suspended until the return home). The main function of the paragraph, though, is not to fix our attention on the progress across the lake, but to expand the moods of strangeness and foreboding that pervade the story. The reader and Nick start off "in the dark," this phrase working on the literal level for the story's setting and on the symbolic and figurative levels for both the readers and for Nick. It gives way, in sentences 2 and 6, to the phrase "in the mist," a phrase that maintains the metaphor of obscured vision (in terms of both sight and knowledge), yet one in which there is increased light.

But what Hemingway does here is even subtler. The paragraph is pointed and relevant; it serves the story by continuing the action, by building up an air of suspense, and by providing a scene that will serve as the foundation for a crucial echo scene at the end of the story (when Nick and his father return). Yet the passage also establishes verisimilitude by mimicking the randomness and disconnectedness of Nick's sensory impressions. Because he does not know where he is going or why, Nick has nothing around which to structure these impressions. They are unprocessed because thus far his journey is unfocused. Therefore they are reported as he consciously experiences them, randomly, and the sentences of the paragraph seem correspondingly disconnected and unstructured. His confusion is particularly evident in the final sentence when he observes what seems, to him, an incongruity. The reader feels Nick's confusion even though he or she can easily explain why the other boat is moving quicker than Nick's boat (the young Indian in the other boat is stronger and perhaps the boat carries less weight). Such a passage, which so effectively establishes the dominant mood of the story, would not have been possible had Dr. Adams been the central consciousness.

Nick's experience of disconnected impressions is further mimicked by the way Hemingway breaks up the paragraph into short declarative sentences. The author even describes the nature of this prose in a concrete phrase that primarily works on the literal level ("quick choppy strokes"). This phrase especially draws attention to itself because Hemingway's quick choppy sentences scan mainly as anapestic ("Ĭt wăs cóld ŏn thĕ wát[er]") or iambic ("wăs wórkĭng véry hárd"), but in "quíck chóppy strókes" we get consecutive stresses. Such a marriage of sound and sense pervades this paragraph, in which the final three anapests, following the three consecutive stresses of "bóat móved fúr[ther]" seem to float the other boat off into the distance. Together, the spondee followed by the three anapests ("móved fúrthĕr ăhéad ĭnthĕ míst ăll thĕ tíme") imitate the actual movement of rowing—the stroke of the oar and the subsequent glide along the water. In fact, the only flaw in the paragraph is Hemingway's pet word "quite" in the second sentence; "quite a way" should have been replaced by "far."

After this intensification of suspense comes the first brief passage of dialogue, which appears unremarkable on the surface but is actually richly suggestive:

> [P4] "Where are we going, Dad?" Nick asked.
> "Over to the Indian camp. There is an Indian lady very sick."
> "Oh," said Nick.
> [I refer to this dialogue as paragraph 4 for clarity's sake.]

Nick's question is precisely what the reader would like to ask at this point. Due to the matter-of-fact way that Nick asks it and his waiting this long to ask it, we can assume one or more of the following: events have moved so quickly that he has not had time to ask; his trust in his father is so great that he did not think to ask; he sensed his father was preoccupied so he refrained from asking; and he has been so caught up in the action that he forgot, for a time, to ask. His father's answer is equally suggestive. Either he gives his child all that Nick needs to know for now, or else he is too preoccupied with what lies ahead to explain it more fully, or both. Nick's reply is intriguing. A doctor's son who has possibly gone on house calls with his father before, he may require no further answer. Or else, he may still be curious, but he senses his father's concern and/or the seriousness of the occasion from his father's laconic reply, and is therefore just a touch apprehensive about pursuing the matter further either because he does not wish to upset his father or because he is hesitant to find out more. Among these possibilities, a feature that stands out is Dr. Adams's preoccupation, understandable for a man who may have to perform a Caesarean operation without proper equipment. In any case, Nick and the reader have been given enough exposition to alleviate, temporarily, their curiosity. There will be no fuller explanation for now, and the door is closed on further questions, a fact structurally implicit in the way the passage begins and ends with Nick and the manner in which Hemingway inverts the identification tags from "Nick asked" to "said Nick," quietly providing visual brackets that close off the conversation.

The next three paragraphs depict the remainder of the journey to the Indian camp:

> [P5] [1] Across the bay they found the other boat beached. [2] Uncle George was smoking a cigar in the dark. [3] The young Indian pulled the boat way up on the beach. [4] Uncle George gave both the Indians cigars.
>
> [P6] [1] They walked up from the beach through a meadow that was soaking wet with dew, following the young Indian who carried a lantern. [2] Then they went into the woods and followed a trail that led to the logging road that ran back into the hills. [3] It was much lighter on the logging road as the timber was cut away on both sides. [4] The young Indian stopped and blew out his lantern and they all walked on along the road.
>
> [P7] [1] They came around a bend and a dog came out barking. [2] Ahead were the lights of the shanties where the Indian bark-peelers lived. [3] More dogs rushed out at them. [4] The two Indians sent them back to the shanties. [5] In the shanty nearest the road there was a light in the window. [6] An old woman stood in the doorway holding a lamp.

These paragraphs bring us to the location where the central events of the tale will occur. This sequence of action and the concurrent development of narrative suspense (termed by Roland Barthes the "proairetic" code and the "hermeneutic" code, respectively) establish verisimilitude through a specificity that compels the reader's participation in the journey/story. By the time we reach the shanty, we have been hooked.

Earlier, I quoted Chekhov's advice to writers about limiting details so that the reader can process them without slowing down. Frank O'Connor had another reason for restricting details: to enable the reader to participate imaginatively in bringing the story to life. The warning he offered, by way of analogy, was the bad playwright who precludes the actor from exercising a reasonable degree of interpretive freedom.[33] Such readerly inference-drawing is inherent in written narrative. By contrast, in a painting, the artist chooses what scene to paint and how much of it to include. "Within that frame," Seymour Chatman observes, "the number of details explicitly presented is a stylistic, rather than a general structural question." Fiction, on the other hand, can never be "complete" in the manner of a visual representation because "the number of plausible intermediate actions or properties is virtually infinite." The reader "accept[s] the main lines and . . . fill[s] in the interstices with knowledge . . . acquired through ordinary living and art experience."[34] In a movie or performed play, if a man walks into a room, he must be dressed in certain clothes and possess unique physical features. In narrative prose, the writer can merely say: "A man walked into the room" or "an elderly man in a faded blue suit burst into the room." From these clues the reader imaginatively fills in the necessary amount of detail to create the living scene. In Hemingway's texts, the details are typically few but carefully chosen, and the reader's imagination is engaged.

Roland Barthes observes that any series of actions is "the unfolding of a name."[35] The "name" is what folds into itself the myriad smaller actions that it represents, and, in reading, we "unfold" that name or signifier into the sub-actions it contains. For instance, in the seventh paragraph, after the dogs rush out, we read: "The two Indians sent them back to the shanties." But what we *picture* while reading is always something more, perhaps something like: "The two Indians yelled at the dogs. The dogs closest to them halted, one of them baring his teeth while several dogs in the rear continued to bark. One of the Indians motioned with his arm and the dogs backed up. They retreated to the shanties, tails down, glancing back at the intruders." This may be an example of over-reading, and what each reader envisions will differ. But whatever a reader pictures, it is certainly something more detailed and vivid than "Indians . . . sent . . . dogs . . . to shanties." That sentence is not a picture, but it evokes a picture; in a successful story, it must, for fiction cannot be experienced abstractly. The entire sequence of action (all of which can be subsumed under the signifier/name "journey") that "unfolds" over these first seven paragraphs does so in the manner I have just described, from the two Indians waiting at the shore (perhaps the younger one is impatient and taps his foot while the older one stands silently with his arms crossed) to the old woman (her face is leathery and wrinkled, and her hand trembles slightly from the weight of the lamp).

The pace of the narrative also makes demands on the reader's imaginative abilities. Throughout these paragraphs the relationship between the duration of the action (fabula time) and the amount of prose employed to represent that action (narrative time) continually changes. In the paragraphs before the dialogue, narrative time more closely approximates fabula time than in the last three paragraphs, especially the sixth paragraph, which is a much condensed summary. In the dialogue, there is virtual temporal reality (fabula time and narrative time are roughly equal). Between the paragraphs, indeed between the sentences and even within the sentences, there are ellipses in which fabula time passes but is not represented in the text. For example, between the young Indian pulling the boat way up on the beach and Uncle George giving the Indians cigars there is unstated action, probably the young Indian rejoining the group. These are instances of what I term an *implication omission* in which what is omitted is clearly implied.[36]

The lengthiest ellipses, however, occur between the paragraphs and help to separate passages whose relation to temporal reality (fabula time) differs greatly. After the passage of dialogue, for example, the rest of the trip across the lake is left out. Because Hemingway has already represented enough of that action sequence, the reader is not surprised, in the following paragraph, to find the other boat already beached and the two men waiting. Later in the story, the birth of the baby is omitted. This ellipsis takes place between a brief paragraph that radically condenses the time of the operation and a passage that approaches complete temporal reality.[37]

In addition to a shifting relationship between fabula time and narrative time, ranging from narrative time equaling fabula time to narrative time eliding fabula time altogether, as we pass from one paragraph to another the length and cadences of the sentences, the camera angle, and the reader's psychic distance from the characters also change. Short sentences slow down the pace of a narrative as the reader unconsciously pauses for an instant when a sentence ends, and also because the breaks between sentences force the reader to concentrate in order to grasp the transitions from one sentence to another. That is why short sentences are effective in a paragraph that tries to approach temporal reality, as in the third paragraph of this story. On the other hand, lengthy sentences help to convey continuity of action, as in the first sentence of the second paragraph, and condense the duration of action. Thus, in the sixth paragraph, which summarizes a very lengthy sequence of action, Hemingway employs long, flowing sentences that focus on the specific actions of "walking," "going," and "following." The transitions between these sentences are so slight that the first two and the last two sentences could feasibly be joined together.

At the same time, the narrator pulls away from Nick, his focalizer, in order to present a panoramic perspective of the action of paragraph 6. This shift in camera angle, evident in three uses of the third-person plural pronoun, briefly establishes physical distance from the characters so that their long sequence of action can be quickly summarized by describing it from afar (a pan shot). But as soon as they come around the bend, Hemingway sends a barking dog at them to re-immerse the reader in the immediacy of Nick's experience by returning to him as the focalizer. In other words, in order to get the characters through the woods to the camp as quickly as possible without jarring the reader, the narrator pulls back and sights his characters from a physical distance, but before this physical distance can turn into a troublesome psychic distance, he puts the narrative camera back in Nick's head. This is a risky, though necessary tactic that works because Hemingway uses it with restraint and because the forward movement of the story compels the reader into the next paragraph where not only the focalizer reappears, but also a number of specific events take place to seize the reader's attention.[38]

All of these aspects of an action sequence—inference drawing, unfolding action signifiers, changes in narrative pace, filling in the unstated action of ellipses and summaries, shifts in both the camera angle and focalizing distance—force even the dullest of readers to participate in the construction of the story. These techniques make demands on readers' imaginative abilities to which they will respond as long as the writer does not fall into a series of blunders that disturbs the fictional dream, a dream that is the joint creation of both writer and reader. But there is still another requirement that must be met if readers are going to go through all of this effort; the story must arouse their curiosity. It must raise a series of immediate questions that it promises to answer somewhere along the way. All fiction does this, even a Harlequin romance. In great fiction, however, there are also larger, more universal questions that emerge. Often, these will go unanswered, but they will nevertheless be dramatized, within the context of the story, in a meaningful way.

The "hermeneutic code," Barthes's term, includes those elements by which the enigma in a story "can be distinguished, suggested, formulated, held in suspense, and finally disclosed[.]" The hermeneutic code is akin to a "'well-made' sentence; it contains a subject (theme of the enigma), a statement of the question (formulation of the enigma), its question mark (proposal of the enigma), various subordinate and interpolated clauses and catalyses (delays in the answer), all of which precede the ultimate predicate (disclosure)."[39] The disclosure, I should add, is never full, except perhaps as to the whys and wherefores of the action, for at the heart of the ultimate predicate in a great story, as we will see later in our reading, there is always a mystery of human life that is insoluble.

Eudora Welty observes that "the finest story writers seem to be in one sense obstructionists" and that "if we look for the source of the deepest pleasure we receive from a writer, how often do we not find that it seems to be connected with this very obstruction." To Welty, fictional art, like all beauty, is "not a blatant or promiscuous or obvious quality; indeed, it is associated with reticence, with stubbornness, of a number of kinds."[40] It derives mainly from the deeper meanings of a work of fiction, which are linked to mystery and insolubility. But along the way there are many kinds of obstruction, of storytelling reticence, that comprise the hermeneutic code, and that contribute to the story's beauty by determining how the narrative reveals itself.

Barthes further points out that "every narrative obviously has an interest in delaying the solution of the enigma it poses, since this solution will signal its own death as a narrative[.]"[41] (The "solution" he refers to pertains to the questions the text raises and eventually answers, not to the mystery that is ultimately insoluble.) The hermeneutic code structures "the enigma according to the [reader's] expectation and desire for its solution." It functions as a component of the "static dynamics" of the text:

> [T]he problem is to *maintain* the enigma in the initial void of its answer; whereas the sentences quicken the story's "unfolding" and cannot help but move the story along, the hermeneutic code performs an opposite action: it must set up *delays* (obstacles, stoppages, deviations) in the flow of the discourse; its structure is essentially reactive, since it opposes the ineluctable advance of language with an organized set of stoppages: between question and answer there is a whole dilatory area whose emblem might be named "reticence[.]"[42]

The proairetic (action) code and the hermeneutic (suspense) code function together to engage the reader, and often share elements of the narrative. For instance, implicit in action are questions of motivation that are evaded, for a time, until the author is ready to reveal them. The hermeneutic code raises these questions, but also simultaneously keeps the reader at bay in a number of possible ways. Chief among these, Barthes cites: "the *snare* (a kind of deliberate evasion of the truth), the *equivocation* (a mixture of truth and snare which frequently, while focusing on the enigma, helps to thicken it), the *partial answer* (which only exacerbates the expectation of the truth), the *suspended answer* (an aphasic stoppage of the disclosure), and *jamming* (acknowledgment of insolubility)."[43] The hermeneutic code, then, teases the reader into reading the story by sustaining the expectation of an answer, and simultaneously, paradoxically, delays that answer.

In "Indian Camp," the hermeneutic code operates from the start. If we had access to the reader's consciousness, we would see something like the following questions emerge as he or she reads: Where are we? At what lake shore? What other rowboat? Who are these Indians? Why are they here? Whom are they waiting for, and why? Who are Nick, his father, and Uncle George? What are they doing here? Why are they going off with these Indians? Where are they all going? Why does the older Indian take Nick and his father in the Indians' boat while the younger Indian takes Uncle George in the camp rowboat? Why does Uncle George give cigars to the Indians? Where is the Indian camp? Is it much farther? Where did these dogs come from? Who is this old woman? Paragraph 4 provides an interesting "equivocation," to use Barthes's term. The Indian lady is not, technically speaking, "sick"; she is having a difficult childbirth and needs medical attention. The answer is a mixture of truth and snare. The reader assumes

that Uncle George or Nick's father is either a doctor or else has some sort of medical skills and that he is going to aid an ailing person, not to deliver a baby.

As these questions propel the reader into the story, the progress toward the Indian camp (where we expect our questions to be answered) is further aided by a perfect use of light imagery. "Indian Camp," as Welty observes, comes "wrapped in an atmosphere."[44] But it is an atmosphere of light and dark and shades of gray; there are no colors. The journey starts off "in the dark" and "in the mist." Then, there is a faint light on shore, Uncle George's cigar. They follow another light, the Indian's lantern, up the beach across the meadow and into the woods. The light increases again, on the logging road, so that the Indian can blow out his lamp. It must therefore be a moonlit night, obscured on the lake, beach, and meadow by mist or fog, and on the wooded road by the trees. But with the timber cut down on the logging road, they can now see by moonlight. (How very much Chekhov would have admired the indirection and suggestiveness of this scene. In a statement on such techniques, Chekhov wrote, "you will get the full effect of a moonlight night if you write that on the mill-dam a little glowing star-point flashed from the neck of a broken bottle, and the round, black shadow of a dog, or a wolf, emerged and ran, etc.")[45] In paragraph 7 they reach the camp. There are lights in the shanties. In the shanty to which they are heading there is a light in the window. In the doorway, an old woman holds a lamp. Like moths, we have been drawn to our destination.

Before proceeding, I must address another code that operates throughout the text. The "cultural code" consists of a body of knowledge that the writer assumes he or she has in common with the reader. Barthes calls this the code "of culture as it is transmitted by the book, by teaching and, more generally, by the whole of sociality[.]"[46] The "knowledge" the cultural code calls upon is not necessarily "true"; it is more accurately described as "beliefs" than as "knowledge," but it must be pervasive enough, or hegemonic, throughout the culture that the writer can draw upon it freely without worrying about being misunderstood (or, more likely, not understood). Such knowledge is, in fact, so taken for granted that most readers do not even notice that it is being accessed. Similarly, the writer is probably often barely aware when drawing upon this "knowledge" because it seems so commonplace. The cultural code is particularly important to a short story because it provides fullness of connotation and depth in a shorthand manner, allowing the writer to draw upon a fund of images and ideas in a few words. It is a major element in the technique of suggestiveness.[47]

One of the chief cultural codes in "Indian Camp" draws upon literary and cultural stereotypes of Native Americans. The two Indians serve as guides, first rowing the white men across the lake, then leading them to the camp through a natural landscape violated by loggers employed by white companies. Indian society is traditionally viewed by whites as elder-oriented, so perhaps it is no accident that the older Indian takes Dr. Adams, who is the essential person they have come for, in his boat, or that the younger Indian has the menial task of carrying the lantern as they cross the land. But the Ojibwa nation, by the early twentieth century, is also economically impoverished, robbed of their land, and unassimilated; the Indians of "Indian Camp" have been undermined and demoralized by their contact with white civilization. Fundamental to the story is that the Indians have to seek the help of a white medical man to deliver one of their babies. This suggests (and only suggests, for the symbolism of cultural codes is not heavy-handed) that the Indians now depend upon white civilization for their biological survival. When Uncle George gives the two Indians cigars it suggests the sort of barter exchange that historically has characterized economic dealings between the two cultures. Significantly, as Joseph M. Flora shrewdly points out, the "cigars offered by the white man rather than a pipe by the Indian hints at the changed position of the Indian in the white world."[48] In light of future events, it also represents the imposition of a white custom, a father passing out cigars upon the birth of his child, but here Uncle George appropriates the role of the father. Both the birth and the custom associated with it derive from white culture. As Thomas Strychacz poignantly observes, the story is filled with archetypal elements: "the narrative reenacts a . . . history of dispossession, annexation, betrayal, and death" as the doctor and Uncle George revisit "a form of Manifest Destiny upon the Indian camp"[49] When they come to the logging road the white loggers have denuded of timber, they no longer need the Indians as guides. There is additional symbolic resonance when the young Indian then extinguishes his lantern. Descendants of a once proud people, these Ojibwas are now "bark-peelers" living in shanties. They do menial work for white companies and are as domesticated as the dogs they peel away from their colonizers.

The next paragraph sets up the second part of the story by providing a good deal of delayed exposition:

> [P8] [1] Inside on a wooden bunk lay a young Indian woman. [2] She had been trying to have her baby for two days. [3] All the old women in the camp had been helping her. [4] The men had moved off up the road to sit in the dark and smoke out of range of the noise she made. [5] She screamed just as Nick and the two Indians followed his father and Uncle George into the shanty. [6] She lay in the lower bunk, very big under a quilt. [7] Her head was turned to one side. [8] In the upper bunk was her husband. [9] He had cut his foot very badly with an ax three days before. [10] He was smoking a pipe. [11] The room smelled very bad.

The passage is culturally rich but aesthetically problematic. In order to convey necessary information economically, Hemingway possibly endangers his adherence to Nick's point-of-view and twice breaks into the scene with what seems to be omniscient exposition. More important, however, he gets away with it.

The paragraph can be divided into two similarly structured parts. Sentence 1 introduces the pregnant woman; sentences 2 through 4 inform us of her incapacity and the responses of others to it; and sentences 5 through 7 describe her action in the narrative present. Sentence 8 introduces her husband; sentence 9 explains his incapacity; and sentence 10 describes his action in the present. The introductory sentences, 1 and 8, are in the passive voice, mimetically conveying the inertness and helplessness of the wife and husband. The explanatory sentences, 2 through 4 and 9, are narrated in the past perfect progressive and past perfect.[50] Of the sentences on their incapacity, three describe the wife and one describes the husband. The same is true of the sentences on their actions in the present, because at this point in the story the wife's situation is what the characters focus on and seems to be, to the reader, what the story is "about." In terms of the hermeneutic code, however, this will prove to be a "snare."

The passage continues to draw upon white cultural codes pertaining to Native Americans, *some* of which is factually accurate. The whites had stopped following the Indians once the party reached the logging road; here, the white men take the lead as they precede the Indians into the shanty. In the white imagination, tribal society is organized according to carefully delineated and strictly observed gender roles. In addition, according to these white cultural codes, Indian men scorn activities within the woman's sphere. Indian men, again according to white codes, are also proud of their ability to endure pain and are insensitive to the suffering of others. Attending a birth is clearly, in the codes the text draws upon, "woman's work." The Indian man's only roles regarding children are to help conceive them, to provide for them, and, in the case of male children, to initiate them into manhood. The old women serve as midwives while the Indian men move out of range of the sounds of the pregnant woman's agony and engage in the male ritual of smoking. The husband, because of his injury, is not only unable to join the other men, but, even more humiliating, he is left in the shanty, surrounded by women, and exposed to his wife's ordeal. The ax injury therefore slightly suggests a sort of symbolic castration, and the Indian husband, although abandoned by the other men, smokes his pipe in a vain effort to maintain his "maleness."[51] Once again, however, my two earlier caveats bear repeating. First, the analysis I am here performing pertains to cultural codes that Hemingway draws upon, partly consciously and partly unconsciously, that he assumes he shares with his readers, and makes no claim to accuracy regarding Ojibwa or any other tribal culture. Cultural codes are a body of beliefs, not a sociological warehouse.[52] Second, the cultural codes embedded in a text operate with the greatest subtlety. If what I have said here about the Indian husband's symbolic castration seems, as it somewhat does to me, like the worst sort of psychoanalytic criticism, it is only because the symbolism of cultural codes, when explicitly stated, inevitably seems overstated.

Hemingway also uses these cultural codes to characterize Uncle George and establish that character's relation to the story in an extremely subtle fashion. When we read that the Indian men "sit in the dark and smoke" we recall that at the shore Uncle George was "smoking a cigar in the dark" and that he "gave both the Indians cigars." Although he serves a necessary function in the plot, George's relation to the events of the fabula is peripheral; the Indians have come for Dr. Adams, whose brother and son come along, so to speak, for the ride. Nick can, within the narrative, justify his presence as the focalizer and, ultimately, as the protagonist of the story. But Uncle George has no such role. The transaction with the cigars and the similarity of description regarding smoking "in the dark" suggest his desire to be with the Indian men and not in the shanty, and perhaps reveal his own attraction to the white cultural code's representation of Indian men as hyper-masculine. Like the Indian husband, he is trapped in a female space where he is emotionally uncomfortable and does not wish to be. In addition, his identification with the Indian men, in the context of the white cultural codes the story employs, helps to characterize him as insensitive to the pain of others, something that Hemingway went to great lengths to demonstrate in the original opening of the story. What makes his use of Uncle George in "Indian Camp" effective, especially when compared with his earlier attempt, is that here he is able to transmute his personal dislike for his real-life uncle in such a way that it contributes to, rather than interferes with, the narrative.

As noted, however, the paragraph is not without problems regarding its focalization. In paragraph 6, Hemingway shifted the camera angle to establish physical distance in order to compress the walk to the camp. A side effect of this technique was a brief, concomitant appearance of psychic distance as well. Before this psychic distance could turn into a problem, however, it was dispelled by the first sentence of paragraph 7: "They came around a bend and a dog came out barking." The sentence displays with syntactical symmetry a scenic collision of intentionality (the people and the dog) that reestablishes psychic immediacy. And yet, the camera angle, though much less distant than in the previous paragraph, still seems somewhat off to the side. We view the group from close range, but are we really seeing events through Nick's eyes?

In paragraph 7, the answer to this question is probably yes. Assuming that Nick knows that these Indians peel bark from felled trees for a living, there is nothing in the paragraph that undercuts his role as focalizer. But the material of paragraph 8 raises several questions. The sentences that describe the action sequences are not troubling: Nick can see the Indian woman in the bunk and hear her scream as they enter the shanty; he can observe her position in the bunk and see the man in the upper bunk smoking; and he can smell the bad odor in the room. Also, Hemingway presents Nick's observations in the same sort of short sentences he used during the boat trip, thus underscoring their random, unfocused nature. Each sentence in the narrating present contains only one sensory perception: [1] the woman's presence, [5] her scream, [6] her appearance, [7] the position of her head, [8] the man's presence, [10] his smoking, and [11] the room's smell. These are not the kinds of observations we would get with either Dr. Adams or Uncle George as the focalizer. The former would have been preoccupied with imminent medical procedures, and either man would have placed these sensory impressions in a structured context. The only question is how Nick would know that the Indian in the upper bunk is the woman's husband.

The real problem with focalization, however, emerges from the explanatory sentences (2 through 4, and 9). If we rearrange the exposition from these sentences chronologically (in the order of the fabula and not that of the plot), the following sequence emerges. Three days ago, the Indian husband cut his foot very badly with an ax. The next day his wife went into labor. For the past two days the old women have been trying to help her. During that period of time, the other men have probably avoided the shanty and are currently gathered in the distance smoking out of range of the woman's screams. If this were a first-person narrative, the reader could assume that Nick is interpolating information he learned later, because a first-person narrator describes past events from the vantage point of the narrating present. But in a third-person fixed internal focalization the character serving as the central consciousness exists in the past and only the narrator can speak retrospectively. Thus these sentences of exposition are an omniscient narrative intrusion: in such a strictly focalized story, a technical blunder.

This exposition, however, is vital to the story, and it was impossible for Hemingway to have conveyed it in another manner without creating even bigger problems. Had he placed it earlier in the story it would have lessened the sense of mystery engendered by the journey to the camp, weakened the hermeneutic code, and diminished the impact of the opening scene in the shanty. If, on the other hand, he had allowed it to emerge subsequent to that scene, it would have been anticlimactic and also would have interfered with the main action sequences of the second part of the story. Furthermore, whatever solution he chose, there would remain the problem of getting the information to Nick to prevent compromising the point-of-view. In practical terms, this means that either the exposition would have to be conveyed to Nick in action that he could observe or in dialogue that he could hear, or some combination of the two. Plausibly, Nick could have seen the men in the distance smoking and Hemingway could let the reader infer their motives. In the same way, he could have Nick observe the old women attending to the pregnant woman. But the information in sentences 2 and 9 (the duration of the labor and the date of the ax injury) could not have been observed. That information could only be known by the Indians. The most likely way to convey it would be for Dr. Adams to inquire about the labor and the ax injury and for Nick to overhear the response. But this would dilute the compression of the paragraph and undercut its impact. More important, it would give the reader a chance to hear one of the Indians speak, something that Hemingway went to extraordinary lengths to avoid throughout the narrative. In fact, with the possible exception of Dr. Adams's statement of self-praise, made after the operation to no one in particular, nowhere in the story do we hear any of the Indians or whites speak to each other. Although we must assume that somewhere along the way they do converse, we are never allowed to hear it, and this silence emphasizes the separation of the two cultures while also contributing to the aura of mystery that pervades the story.

Confronted with these options, Hemingway finessed a difficult situation and, I should add, succeeded admirably considering that many millions of people have read this story over the past eight decades and no one, until now, has even mentioned, let alone been terribly bothered by, any problems in this paragraph. As Flannery O'Connor states: "It's always wrong of course to say that you can't do this or you can't do that in fiction. You can do anything you can get away with" (she then quickly and coyly adds, "but nobody has ever gotten away with much").[53] The two main challenges Hemingway encountered are that he had to break the rules that govern a strict adherence to focalization in a third-person limited point-of-view narrative and he had to provide exposition without it seeming intrusive. How, then, did he pull it off?

First, by the time we get to this paragraph the fictional dream is so well established through sensory detail, suggestive prose, compression, and the hermeneutic code that we are thoroughly engrossed in the story and not inclined to see it disrupted. Second, Hemingway hides the sentences of exposition among sentences of action that are carefully narrated from Nick's point-of-view. Third, the explanatory sentences are narrated with the simplicity of language that we already associate with Nick, which further disguises them, obscuring the obvious fact that it is not really Nick's observations we are getting here. For instance, Hemingway uses the phrase "had been trying to have her baby" instead of "had been in labor." Furthermore, sentences 2 and 3 employ the past perfect progressive tense indicating an ongoing action, so they give the impression that Nick can somehow observe these actions when he can, in fact, only observe some of them. That is, he can observe the old women trying to help and he can observe the pregnant woman, but he would not know that she's been in labor for two days. Sentence 4 is in the past perfect, but the action completed here is the Indian men's act of moving off up the road; they are, in the narrative present, still sitting and smoking in the distance. Sentence 9 is purely explanatory and a completed past action, but Hemingway does not linger on it; instead, he quickly follows with a visual image that puts the camera angle squarely in Nick's mind and follows this with a sentence that is easily identified as being from Nick's perspective: "The room smelled very bad."

With Nick now firmly reestablished as the focalizer, his father steps forward to demonstrate his authority through a display of professional competence. He will dominate the second and third parts of the story, the operation and its aftermath, and during this time become the principal object perceived by his son.

> Nick's father ordered some water to be put on the stove, and while it was heating he spoke to Nick.
>
> "This lady is going to have a baby, Nick," he said.
>
> "I know," said Nick.
>
> "You don't know," said his father. "Listen to me. What she is going through is called being in labor. The baby wants to be born and she wants it to be born. All her muscles are trying to get the baby born. That is what is happening when she screams."
>
> "I see," Nick said.
>
> Just then the woman cried out.
>
> "Oh, Daddy, can't you give her something to make her stop screaming?" asked Nick.
>
> "No. I haven't any anæsthetic," his father said. "But her screams are not important. I don't hear them because they are not important."
>
> The husband in the upper bunk rolled over against the wall.
>
> The woman in the kitchen motioned to the doctor that the water was hot.

This passage of dialogue is framed by two related actions: Dr. Adams's order to heat the water and the woman's signal that the hot water is ready. The passage seems to function as a means for conveying information. Normally, the use of dialogue to provide direct exposition would be a mistake because it slows down the pace of the narrative and can also seem artificial. But in this passage neither of these two objections pertains. First, there is a genuine break in the main action sequence; Nick's father has time on his hands while waiting for the water to boil. Second, it is entirely believable that he would use this time to explain the situation to his son in very simple terms.

But is the dialogue really being used to convey information that the reader needs to know, or does it serve an altogether different purpose? Dr. Adams's statements about the woman's condition tell us nothing of which we are not already aware. The only new information we get is that he has no anesthetic, which prepares us for the later revelation that the operation was performed with fishing equipment. That information will suggest to the reader (who has, of course, not read the discarded original opening of the story) that Nick, his father, and his uncle were on a fishing excursion when they were initially summoned. It will also explain why Dr. Adams brought his son along, although not, I believe, why he would allow the child to witness such an incomprehensible event. In any case, it is not mere information that is being imparted in this passage. Instead, much is revealed about the character of Nick's father and his relationship with others, particularly with his son. Unlike the way such characterization was performed in "Three Shots," it will not come in undigested pieces of character description but will be revealed within the context of actions and events inseparable from the development of the plot.

When he orders the water to be heated, Nick's father asserts his authority as a doctor and also takes command of the narrative. With a break in the action, he now becomes aware of Nick and has time to explain things to him. In his first statement he seems paternally condescending (as before, he refers to the woman as a "lady"), telling Nick something that the boy already realizes. Nick's reply that he knows is characteristic of a small child trying to impress an adult, or at least trying to fit into an adult situation; he is anxious not to appear in the way. His father cuts Nick short by telling him he does not know and demands his attention ("Listen to me"). Dr. Adams explains "being in labor" and connects it to the woman's screams. His three successive repetitions of "born" depict intentionality, on the part of the baby, the woman, and the woman's muscles, underscoring a question connected to the hermeneutic code that was implicit in the previous passage (Will the baby be born?) as well as other related questions (Will the baby be born healthy? Will the mother survive?). Nick replies "I see," meaning "I understand." But does he see? And what does he see? He understands his father's explanation of being in labor and that this condition is related to the woman's screams, but he does not understand why she is screaming. He does not know that being in labor is painful. Nor does he understand why birth should be so difficult. He cannot comprehend these questions without a fuller explanation by his father, but there is no time for such explanations, neither in the fabula nor the plot. Still trying to act like an adult, Nick does not raise any questions. Instead, he responds as he did before, with a dubious claim that his curiosity is satisfied.

But this time the sequence of the identification tag has been reversed. In Nick's first reply, the speech was tagged "said Nick." When the verb of a tag precedes the speaker, it suggests the intention of finality, on the part of the speaker, to what he has spoken. It was this suggestion that was countered by Dr. Adams's insistence that Nick did not know. Here, in Nick's second reply, the verb follows the speaker in the tag, a subtle indication that the speech "opens out" or leads into what follows, that it is not visually bracketed as it was, for instance, at the end of the passage of dialogue during the boat trip. In Dr. Adams's first speech of this passage, when he tells Nick that the woman is going to have a baby, the tag opens out because he is trying to draw Nick into a conversation and expects a response. In Nick's reply a closed tag was used, but Dr. Adams opened it. Now, Nick says he understands, but the tag is left open and what follows is the woman's scream.

Writers' manuals address the use of identification tags from a purely practical perspective: how to tell the reader who is speaking without cluttering up the page with a plethora of "she saids" and "he saids." Literary critics ignore the function of identification tags as, I suppose, being something beneath them. I pay attention to them on the assumption that that no element of a text is neutral; every word has an effect. This is especially true for a writer like Hemingway who chooses his words so deliberately and uses so few words at all. He also often uses identification tags even when they are unnecessary for the pedestrian purpose of identifying the speaker (as we'll see in "A Canary for One"), and such a conscious craftsman would not do so without reason. Whether or not to use a tag, whether to place it before or after the speech, how to identify the speaker (e.g., Nick's father, the doctor, he), the order of the speaker and the verb, the nature of the verb selected (e.g., he said, he replied, he reasoned, he intoned)—these are all choices a writer makes in composing dialogue. And they all come with consequences.

Some of these consequences are fairly obvious. When a writer omits tags, the dialogue has more verisimilitude and complete temporal reality. The text reads more quickly because it is uninterrupted, but the risk, in the absence of tags or in the case of a long dialogue with tags only in the first few speeches, is that the reader will become confused about who is speaking and will have to go back and sort it out. Sometimes, as perhaps in one of the dialogues in Hemingway's "A Clean, Well-Lighted Place" that has spawned something of a heated debate in critical journals, the question of who is speaking is not clear.[54]

In modern fiction, some choices are no longer available. A tag in which the verb precedes a pronoun (e.g., "said he" or "quoth she") is now antiquated and can only be used for comical or satirical effect. It will always draw attention to itself. The same is true of a tag that precedes the speech, in which the speaker must now always precede the verb; otherwise it would sound ridiculous (e.g., "Said Nick, 'All right.'"). Therefore, if a writer chooses to put the tag before the speech, he or she must choose an open tag. But this kind of open tag does not have the full effect of an open tag that follows a speech because what it opens out onto is that same speaker's speech and not what comes after it.

The most open identification tag is the open tag that follows a speech and is immediately followed by a period. Take, for example: "'I see,' Nick said. / Just then the woman cried out." Here, both the period after "said" and the end of the paragraph signal the reader that Nick's speech is over. But the form of the tag, "Nick said," leads the reader into what follows because these words, in daily use, make the auditor expect that something will come after them. "'I see,' said Nick," on the other hand, brings the speech to a full stop before the reader goes on to what follows. The most halting, non-continuous way to render pure dialogue is to use a closed tag at the end of each speech and to have that tag end the speech, the sentence, and the paragraph.

The Indian woman's scream, strategically placed by the author, is an implicit comment on the inadequacy of Dr. Adams's explanation, just as that explanation was a comment on Nick's earlier assertion that he "knew." The scream signifies pain, a specific physical phenomenon that undercuts Dr. Adams's practical and medical, but non-experiential, knowledge of being in labor. The scream punctures whatever comfort and assurance Nick might have drawn from his father's explanation and thoroughly unnerves him. Nick drops his attempts to act adult and desperately pleads with his "Daddy" to give the woman "something to make her stop screaming." He does not understand how extreme the woman's pain is because no one has explained it to him, and, even if someone had, he could still hardly be expected to comprehend. He only knows that the woman's screams frighten him. In the egocentricity of childhood, he does not ask his father to relieve her pain, only to stop her from screaming. Because his father's professional competence and paternal authority, in the mind of his son, translates into omnipotence, he wants his father to demonstrate that power by ending the screams. The identification tag is reversed ("asked Nick"), which suggests the conflict in Nick's consciousness; he is asking a question but also insisting on a specific action. Nick's question and his father's reply that he has no anesthetic are part of the hermeneutic code, a "partial answer" that responds to Nick's immediate question but that also raises another question in the reader's mind (Why is there no anesthetic?). Having answered Nick's question to no one's satisfaction, the doctor must now address the screams and the pain they signify.

To whom is Nick's father speaking in the second part of his reply?—"But her screams are not important. I don't hear them because they are not important." Not to his patient or her husband; he says nothing to them during the entire ordeal. Uncle George, the one person capable of comprehending what Dr. Adams means, is absent from the scene, so he is not the intended listener. The conversation is ostensibly between Nick and his father, but how could Nick possibly understand his father's statement? How can the screams that fill the room be unimportant? How can his father say he does not hear them, especially since he earlier tried to explain them? The reply, to the extent that it is meant for Nick, is cryptic at best. Dr. Adams cannot do anything about the woman's pain; he cannot explain the biological reasons for her pain to a young child; and he cannot answer, to himself or anyone else, the metaphysical question of why childbirth should be so painful. His authority is utilitarian; he can and must ignore the woman's pain in order to deliver the baby. His speech is therefore not a reply to Nick, but a self-referential articulation of his resolve to do what he must by blocking from his consciousness everything extraneous. The doctor's authority does not extend beyond the sphere of his medical competence.

This dedication and the mental concentration it requires are understandable and even commendable, but his reply does bring into focus several questions pertaining to character. First, it underscores his preoccupation with the task ahead, a preoccupation that has made him emotionally oblivious to those around him. In his own way, he has been as insensitive to the feelings of his child as has Uncle George. During the journey to the camp, he did not bother to explain the impending procedure to Nick. This makes his thoughtlessness in allowing Nick to attend the operation even more astonishing. Although he will later show concern that his son not see the dead husband, to a small child the brutal and noisy Caesarean operation performed with a jackknife and no anesthetic is much more frightening and confusing than the silent suicide. Nick could have been told to wait outside the shanty. On a practical level, Hemingway could not allow this because then there would have been no story, at least not with Nick as the focalizer. But Dr. Adams's paternal irresponsibility, within the story, is incredible, and perhaps an indictment not only of him but of fathers in general, including Ernest Hemingway himself, who had recently missed his own son's birth, and Dr. Clarence Hemingway, the super-competent but humanly flawed real-life model for Dr. Adams.

In Dr. Adams's first speech, the identification tag was open because he was trying to elicit a reply from his son. Nick replied that he "knew," which provoked his father's second speech that denied Nick's assertion. In that second speech, the tag was closed, suggesting that Dr. Adams intended his reply to have an air of finality. Nick responds accordingly, saying that he "sees," but the woman's scream, the first significant action of the passage, gives the lie to Nick's response, for he immediately requests that his father stop the screaming. In Dr. Adams's third speech (his second reply), he asserts that the screams are unimportant. But the identification tag is open, and this leads into the second significant action of the passage—the Indian husband rolls over against the wall, implicitly giving the lie to Dr. Adams's evaluation of the screams. They *are* important, both to Nick and to the Indian husband. In terms of the hermeneutic code, Dr. Adams's statement about the screams is a snare, "a kind of deliberate evasion of the truth." Incidentally, if it seems as if I am reading too much into Hemingway's use of identification tags, then I should point out that not one of the tags in this passage is used for the commonplace purpose of identifying a speaker. By contrast, in the final extended passage of dialogue in this story, the author, after identifying each speaker once, drops all further tags from the passage.

The Indian husband is observed three times in the story. The first time, he has been left behind in the shanty and is smoking, which symbolized his attempt to maintain his male identity. Here, he has stopped smoking and rolled over, suggesting some kind of "giving up" (as in, for example, Ole Andreson turning to the wall in "The Killers"). The next time he is noticed will be after the operation, when we discover he has killed himself. These three actions comprise a logical, if mysterious sequence, and all are performed silently, in contrast to his wife's actions. The first two actions foreshadow the final one, quietly planted in the narrative to keep us aware of the husband's presence, but in such a way as to relegate him to the periphery of our consciousnesses until his final action when he emerges as the ultimate enigma of the third part of the story. Then we will look back at his earlier actions in order to figure out why he took his life, and they will assume an importance they did not possess the first time we read them. He will become the hypothetical gun in Chekhov's advice to playwrights: if a gun appears in the first act then it had better go off by the final act.[55] But for now he seems, unlike Chekhov's gun, something of a stage prop that we barely notice in light of more pressing concerns.

From the moment he ordered the hot water, Nick's father assumed center stage in the story, with the shanty as his operating theater and the others his assistants. Like a football player, a comparison Hemingway will later make, he has put on his game face. After the woman motions to him that the water is hot, and he is referred to, for the first time in the text, as "the doctor," he puts on a display of technical competence that is matched by the prose that describes it. Whenever a character demonstrated competence in action it always seemed to draw out the best in Hemingway's former journalistic skills—keen observation and perfectly precise prose. In this story, written so early in his career when his main accomplishments were still those of a reporter, the depiction of Dr. Adams's actions is particularly noteworthy.

Nick watches his father go into the kitchen and pour half the hot water from the kettle into a basin. Then the doctor unwraps "several things" from a handkerchief (likely the jackknife, needle, and gut leaders) and puts these in the kettle. To no one in particular he announces: "These must boil." Throughout this passage, he evolves from Nick's father into Dr. Adams, a transformation symbolized in the description of his hand washing. In three successive sentences, we see him "scrub his hands" and then: "Nick watched his father's hands scrubbing each other with the soap. While his father washed his hands very carefully and thoroughly, he talked." In the second of these sentences, the one attributing the observation directly to Nick, the hands are personified, a synecdoche that represents how the man has become his professional function. As he washes, the doctor offers his son another perfunctory explanation about childbirth, that when babies are not born head first "they make a lot of trouble for everybody." For the first time he mentions the possibility of an operation: "Maybe I'll have to operate on this lady." This speech evidences both calculation and involuntary self-revelation. As a father, he wants to prepare his son for what might take place. But as a doctor, he is preoccupied with what he must do and thus unable to address what Nick needs to know. His role as doctor then fully supplants his role as father when, immediately following his speech, we read: "When he was satisfied with his hands he went in and went to work." Literally, he is satisfied that his hands are clean enough to perform surgery. Figuratively, however, he signals his approval of the synecdoche that represents him as a surgeon. With the necessary attention to detail and commanding presence of the virtuoso, he orders Uncle George to pull back the quilt: "I'd rather not touch it."

The next paragraph, devoted to the birth, is framed by lengthy ellipses; Hemingway radically foreshortens the duration of the action, as he previously did in the walk to the camp. But this time, he increases neither the camera distance nor the psychic distance; instead, he holds tenaciously to Nick's point-of-view:

> [1] Later when he started to operate Uncle George and three Indian men held the woman still. [2] She bit Uncle George on the arm and Uncle George said, "Damn squaw bitch!" and the young Indian who had rowed Uncle George over laughed at him. [3] Nick held the basin for his father. [4] It all took a long time.

This brief paragraph is all we get of the operation that, at this point, still figures as the story's central event. The passage is deliberately unfocused, and the main action is omitted. The ellipsis before the operation is accounted for by the word "later." The bulk of the operation is compressed into the sentence: "It all took a long time."

The key to understanding this paragraph is to recognize Nick's function as the focalizer. What he literally sees, reconstructed from the action depicted but, more importantly, from what is omitted, is a pregnant, screaming woman being pinned down by four men while his own father cuts open her stomach with a knife that Nick has previously watched him use to gut fish. The woman and bed are covered with blood, surely more blood than Nick has ever seen. His father's meticulously washed hands are dripping with blood. The woman bites Uncle George (severely enough, it turns out, to break the skin), and one of the Indians laughs. During this unbearable period of time, Nick is forced to watch because he must hold the basin for his father. What Nick sees, therefore, is ghastly beyond words and, to him, his father's preceding explanation notwithstanding, totally incomprehensible. What is therefore reported from his point-of-view is limited to the few scattered details that he can comprehend. His father's role is subsumed under the abstract phrase "when he started to operate" which recasts the words his father had used earlier: "Maybe I'll have to operate on this lady." After his father starts, however, there is no further reference to the actual operation except to say that it took a long time. Hemingway wants to omit the details of this central action in order to show the effect they are having upon Nick, and he can omit them because the reader can supply them imaginatively (a process that also makes for a more powerful depiction). That is why the passage, despite its brevity and omission, works. It perfectly demonstrates Hemingway's theory of omission: "Anything you can omit that you know you still have in the writing and its quality will show. When a writer omits things he does not know, they show like holes in his writing."[56] It is a tribute to Hemingway's craft that this passage does not create a "hole" in the narrative.

It is another sign of his craft that he not only refrains from depicting the operation, but also, using external focalization, from directly exploring Nick's consciousness even though technically he has access to it in this third-person fixed internal focalization. The presentation is entirely dispassionate, yet it amply conveys, in ways that a subjective presentation never could, Nick's state of mind. It does so through the details it reports impressionistically from Nick's point-of-view and by drawing upon the terms of the already established cultural code. The main focus of the narration, what Nick perceives and the narrator reports, is Uncle George. Hemingway purposely uses the full name "Uncle George" four times in two sentences. The first two times this is unavoidable, but the third time he could have used a pronoun, and the fourth mention is unnecessary since we already know that the "young Indian" rowed Uncle George over. In terms of space, the words "Uncle George" occupy 8 words in a 56-word paragraph, or one-seventh of the paragraph. They also take up more than one-fifth of the first two sentences, the part of the paragraph in which all of the reported violence takes place.

An adult in Nick's place would find the operation nauseating, but would understand the situation (consider how this passage would read if reported from the doctor's, the old woman's, or one of the Indian men's points-of-view). To Nick, it is not only sickening, but the violence of the scene must seem surreal. Read completely out of context, the passage would be an apt description of a gang rape: the men pinning the woman down, the woman resisting and screaming, Uncle George's sexist epithet, the young Indian's heartless laughter, and Nick, too young to be actively involved, holding his father's basin like an apprentice at a satanic sexual initiation rite, and watching until what happens goes beyond his ability to acknowledge it.

Although the violence of the actual operation is not directly depicted, it is conveyed by means of displacement, with Hemingway again drawing upon cultural codes. Uncle George calls the woman a "bitch," literally a female dog, thus equating her and the other Indians with the dogs of the camp. His meaning is made even more apparent in the way he modifies "bitch" with "squaw." To an Indian, this is a fairly neutral word; it derives from the Narragansett word for a woman—"*eskaw.*" But to a white man, the term is an epithet meaning something less than a woman, something connoting property. We have seen how Uncle George has symbolically tried to link himself to the Indian men in an effort to perform his own masculinity. The sexism revealed in his curse is not particularly offensive to the young Indian; it may even be a view shared by him. But Uncle George's reaction to pain differentiates him from the Indians who, according to cultural code stereotypes, are stoic in the face of suffering, their own as well as others. Uncle George's racism is offensive to the young Indian, and his exclamation of pain gives that character a chance to exult. His laughter is aimed at Uncle George's frailty, expressing the young Indian's contempt for the white man who has attempted fraternity with him and been humiliated, and it underscores Uncle George's separateness from the Indian men. Although the violence conveyed in the scene is physical, the cruelty, on the part of Uncle George and the young Indian, is verbal. Together, they function to characterize indirectly Nick's experience of the operation as cruel and violent.

Nick's experience of the operation is defamiliarizing, the sort of psychically disorienting incident in which a person feels as though he is watching himself as he participates in an event. During such an experience, it is natural to search for and focus upon that which is familiar as a way of getting reoriented. Nick cannot focus on his father because what his father is doing terrifies him. So he looks at Uncle George, the only other familiar character. But Uncle George's behavior offers no solace, and thus the rest of the scene goes unreported as Nick, the focalizer, enters into a kind of fog. The unfamiliar aspect of the scene is further enhanced by the third Indian who shows up in the first sentence. The third Indian, although needed to secure the woman's fourth limb, is not really necessary to the story, representing an unaccounted-for element in the narrative, one that functions by being gratuitous. He resists systemization and, in so doing, contributes to the story's verisimilitude because such people do show up in real life. Details like this are a story's way of reminding us that there is much more going on in the fabula than what finds its way into the plot, or that we can presume to know.[57]

After a lengthy ellipsis, the next passage begins with the baby already born:

> His father picked the baby up and slapped it to make it breathe and handed it to the old woman.
>
> "See, it's a boy, Nick," he said. "How do you like being an interne?"
>
> Nick said, "All right." He was looking away so as not to see what his father was doing.
>
> "There. That gets it," said his father and put something into the basin.
>
> Nick did not look at it.
>
> "Now," his father said, "there's some stitches to put in. You can watch this or not, Nick, just as you like. I'm going to sew up the incision I made."
>
> Nick did not watch. His curiosity had been gone for a long time.

The action of the first sentence—the slap and the baby's omitted but implied subsequent crying—captures Nick's attention through a sensory impression whose function is similar to that of the barking dog in paragraph 7. Snapped out of his fog, he once more focuses on his father. The doctor, however, remains oblivious to his son's sensibilities, his previous preoccupation now turning to exhilaration upon the completion of the dangerous operation. He points out that the baby is a boy, a fact likely not evident to Nick who has perhaps just seen his first naked woman. Now both the fathers in the shanty have sons, and perhaps Nick is wondering if he himself once looked like this baby and whether his own mother went through a similar experience when he was born. Dr. Adams, who can only see that the operation has been successful, asks Nick the astoundingly thoughtless question about how he likes being an intern, implying that Nick had some choice in the matter, while also suggesting that he might someday follow in his father's footsteps. Nick's reply is decidedly unenthusiastic, but Hemingway follows it with a quasi-explanatory clause that is unnecessary ("so as not to see what his father was doing"). Nick's discomfort is made abundantly clear by his reply, and the author would have done better either to eliminate the sentence or else have Nick stare at something specific that would serve as an objective correlative of his inner state. His father is unaware that his son is deliberately not watching. In his moment of triumph, his conversation turns chipper. As he places the afterbirth in the basin Nick holds, he does not bother to explain, even in a cursory manner, this grotesque item to his bewildered intern.

In the doctor's next speech, it's apparent that he feels not only relief, but also pride in his admittedly difficult achievement. The way he starts each speech with an exclamatory word displays his elation ("See"; "There"; "Now"). The first two exclamations point to something he has already done. The third refers to something he is about to do, and he tells Nick he can watch or not, whatever he likes. Perhaps he senses that his son is not reveling in his father's accomplishment (here, unlike in his second speech, the identification tag is open), but still he remains indifferent to his child's feelings. The words "you like" were first used in regard to Nick's being an intern, something he was compelled to do. Here, they represent an actual choice for Nick, but it is a little late to be giving him some say in the matter. In the final sentence of the speech, the doctor twice uses the first-person singular pronoun. The first is appropriate, but the second is unnecessary and suggests his self-absorption. What other incision is there but the one he made? Nick, who chose not to look at the baby or the removal of the afterbirth, chooses not to watch his father close the incision.

Again Hemingway adds a sentence explaining why Nick does not watch, but this time it is effective because the phrase "a long time" repeats the same phrase used at the beginning of the preceding passage. "A long time" provides a frame for the two passages and gives the impression that Nick's curiosity has been gone since the first time the phrase was used, near the beginning of the operation. This is somewhat reinforced by the incidental rhyme of "took" (in the earlier passage) and "look" (used twice in this passage). For as long as it "took," Nick did not "look." In the last instance, Nick did not "watch." Earlier, he "watched" as his father "washed," but he has watched very little since then. In this passage, like the previous one, Nick is completely the focalizer. Hemingway is very careful to adhere to his point-of-view even down to the detail of calling what his father puts in the basin "something" rather than "the afterbirth." But although Nick sees more here than he did during the operation, his interest has vanished.

Nick's mental withdrawal sets up the third part of the story—the operation's aftermath. In this section, Hemingway will de-emphasize Nick's presence by having Dr. Adams and Uncle George dominate the action. Nick is neither seen nor mentioned except at the very beginning and at the end, after the suicide is discovered. Hemingway wants the reader to assume, with the operation successfully concluded, that the story's main event is over and the hermeneutic code is complete. He also wants to build Dr. Adams's hubris to a high pitch in order to maximize the deflating effect the suicide will have on him. And he wants us temporarily to forget about Nick so that when the suicide is discovered, the reader as well as Dr. Adams will suddenly remember him. All of this serves the Poesque purpose of making the discovery of the suicide as emotionally powerful as possible. By de-emphasizing Nick, Hemingway takes two slight risks that might compromise the text's fixed internal third-person focalization. Yet the story is, by now, so strong and the ensuing disclosure so shocking that the reader does not notice these risks.

> His father finished and stood up. Uncle George and the three Indian men stood up. Nick put the basin out in the kitchen.
>
> Uncle George looked at his arm. The young Indian smiled reminiscently.
>
> "I'll put some peroxide on that, George," the doctor said.
>
> He bent over the Indian woman. She was quiet now and her eyes were closed. She looked very pale. She did not know what had become of the baby or anything.
>
> "I'll be back in the morning," the doctor said, standing up. "The nurse should be here from St. Ignace by noon and she'll bring everything we need."
>
> He was feeling exalted and talkative as football players are in the dressing room after a game.
>
> "That's one for the medical journal, George," he said. "Doing a Cæsarian with a jack-knife and sewing it up with nine-foot, tapered gut leaders."
>
> Uncle George was standing against the wall, looking at his arm.
>
> "Oh, you're a great man, all right," he said.

They disengage in order of status: first the doctor, then the other four men, and last the lowly intern. Nick carries the basin holding the afterbirth into the kitchen and then, judging from his next appearance in the story, probably stands by the doorway between the kitchen and the main room. He watches as Uncle George looks at his arm and the young Indian smiles.

This reminds him of the incident during the operation, which is now carried into the present like the remembered fragment of a nightmare. Uncle George's injury will enable Nick's father to continue playing his doctor's role. It also reminds the reader of the cultural codes upon which it draws, implying that one of the reasons for Uncle George's impending resentment of his brother is George's humiliation in the eyes of the male Indians. Following the operation, Dr. Adams is figuratively whirling about the room like a football player celebrating a victory, filled with energy engendered by his feelings of accomplishment. From the start of the story, he has been identified either as Nick's father or with the third-person pronoun, and only once referred to as "the doctor," when the woman signals him that the water is hot. During this third part of the story, however, once Nick removes to the periphery, he will be identified either as "the doctor" (four times) or with a pronoun, and never in relation to Nick. That is because Nick is out of the reader's (and his father's) sight, and because Dr. Adams forgets his paternal responsibilities as he basks in the glow of his professional triumph.

In fairness to Dr. Adams—toward whom I have been, and will continue to be quite critical—I should note a valuable context illuminating his medical feat. Linda Lizut Helstern observes that the first Caesarean in America was performed in 1894, "but the procedure remained highly controversial for another two decades" and it "was never used in home births." The Caesarean in "Indian Camp," which would have occurred in the first decade of the twentieth century, is therefore arguably unique, and the lack of proper equipment makes it a truly stunning achievement. As Helstern concludes, "Dr. Adams's Caesarean—Hemingway's much-commented-upon spelling [Cæsarian] follows the standard spelling utilized in early medical textbooks describing the procedure—is, indeed, one for the record books."[58]

His continued role as doctor is evident from the start of the post-operation scene. Although he forgets about Nick, Dr. Adams does notice George's wounded arm and offers to treat it. Then he bends over the inert Indian woman to ascertain her condition. The description of her is from Nick's somewhat distant point-of-view, but the last sentence of the paragraph, although clearly an observation that Nick would make ("She did not know what had become of the baby or anything"), tells us nothing that is not already implied in the paragraph. Even though the style of the sentence mimics that of a young child, especially the phrase "or anything," the sentence is not particularly effective and adds nothing. The "satisfied" doctor announces that he will return and, in what will prove to be an ironic statement in light of subsequent events, says that the nurse will "bring everything we need." The next sentence, stating that he "was feeling exalted" and containing the "football players" simile, serves no purpose; it is technically the only real mistake in the story; and it is an excellent illustration of why Hemingway would later punningly refer to similes as being "*like* defective ammunition" (italics mine).[59] The sentence is an unnecessary authorial intrusion not demanded by the story, unlike, for instance, the required explanatory sentences of the first scene in the shanty. Hemingway has already amply depicted the doctor's state of mind through his speeches and actions, and the narrator is not supposed to have access to the doctor's consciousness. This momentary flirtation with variable internal focalization indicates a brief loss of artistic control.

Fortunately, the ensuing dialogue quickly re-captures the reader's attention. Through the doctor, Hemingway reveals to the reader just how difficult the operation was, enough so that we may slightly forgive him for his obnoxious post-operative behavior. The doctor craves some recognition of his remarkable feat and turns to his brother, the one character capable of appreciating it. But Uncle George's response is the same as before; he continues to look at his arm. The sentence is narrated in the past progressive, indicating that he has been looking at his arm this whole time, perhaps wondering if his brother has forgotten about it. The doctor wants to be properly appreciated and applauded by Uncle George, and Uncle George wants his wound, symbolic of his humiliation, treated. His reply to the doctor drips with sarcasm; Uncle George tells him the exact words he wants to hear ("you're a great man") but not in the way he wants to hear them. The addition of the phrase "all right" echoes Nick's earlier reply to the doctor about how he liked being an intern. Neither his son nor his brother shares the doctor's enthusiasm.

I should note here that Dr. Adams craves more than just an appreciation of his professional virtuosity and that his disappointment in Uncle George's rebuff has much in common with Uncle George's own feelings of humiliation. In *Hemingway's Theaters of Masculinity,* Thomas Strychacz reads both this scene and the entire story in light of his book's main thesis, in which, "Masculinity in Hemingway can be seen more profitably as a trope that must be negotiated into meaning by means of a changing structural relationship between character, masculine code, and legitimating audience." In other words, "Hemingway's narrative art constantly represents masculinity as temporary and subject to abrupt change rather than stable and permanent; as relational and contingent rather than self-determined; as the function of insubstantial codes and evaluating audiences rather than the sole possession of code heroes; as negotiated and constructed rather than constitutive of an essential identity." From the operation's preparation through its aftermath, as Strychacz demonstrates, the doctor has sought to turn the shanty into both an operating theater *and* a manhood theater in which he can demonstrate his authority, competence, and masculinity, but lacking an appreciative audience he is unsuccessful at the latter despite the impressiveness of his medical accomplishment.[60]

This passage shows each of the characters either responding to different events or else responding to the same event differently (i.e., Nick, Uncle George, and the doctor to the operation; Uncle George, the doctor, and the young Indian to Uncle George's wound). There is no commonality of interest as each stands in relation to the others' needs as unaware, insensitive, indifferent, or malicious. By the end of the passage, Nick is absent, the doctor is vainglorious, and Uncle George is resentful. The male Indians and the old woman have faded from our awareness; the Indian mother is asleep; and we have forgotten about the Indian husband, who is now the Indian father. The reader's alertness has been subdued somewhat by the relative inaction and the lack of focus in the passage, the hermeneutic code lies dormant, and we have been set up for the subsequent revelation. The discovery of the suicide will shock the reader, reactivate the hermeneutic code, and reorient the story; it will command the focus of the three main characters and change their relations to one another; and it will prepare us for the denouement.

The next passage begins with the doctor's speech:

> "Ought to have a look at the proud father. They're usually the worst sufferers in these little affairs," the doctor said. "I must say he took it all pretty quietly."

The doctor's words are a direct response to Uncle George's rebuff in the preceding passage. Up to this point, the doctor has shown no interest in the Indian husband who, he assumed, was resting stoically silent in the upper bunk during his wife's ordeal. He was never even curious, as we might have expected him to be, about the Indian's injured foot: Who treated it? Was it properly treated? How is his recovery progressing? But now, with neither his son nor his brother able or willing to give him the approval he craves, he chooses to attend to the Indian husband and hold off on treating his unappreciative brother's wounded arm. Perhaps he hopes the Indian will show him some respect.

The tone of the doctor's speech is one of self-satisfied affectation. In the first sentence he omits the first-person pronoun, which is probably unnecessary since he has been talking about nothing but himself since the end of the operation. The phrase "to have a look at," in its cavalier verbosity, is similarly affected in a way that, say, "to look at" or "to see to" would not have been. The term "proud father" draws on a cliché from white civilization's cultural code. The next sentence combines another white cliché (the suffering expectant father) with a jocular understatement ("these little affairs") that is insensitive considering the nature of the operation. The tone of the final sentence is, like the entire speech, breezy and condescending. In response to Uncle George's ridicule, the doctor's speech is an attempt at self-validation and self-glorification. It implicitly asserts that he is a conscientious doctor and father, and that he himself has reason to be proud. The words "ought" and "must" imply that he feels compelled by his medical responsibilities to look in on the Indian. The second sentence, cliché-ridden though it be, and the third sentence are judgments offered from his years of medical experience and, one may assume, from his own experience of fatherhood.

This story shows two cultures that view each other with mutual disdain and incomprehension. But because the Indian husband is now a father, there is a bond of identity between him and the doctor, one much more genuine than the bond of masculinity that Uncle George tried unsuccessfully to establish with the male Indians. The doctor's speech, the subject of which is ostensibly the Indian father, is oddly self-referential in its comments on fathers. When the baby was born, the doctor told his son: "See, it's a boy, Nick." Now he will "have a look at" his own counterpart.

The phrase "proud father" has two meanings. On the literal level it refers to the Indian, but in another sense it is the doctor who has been "the proud father" ever since the baby was born. The entire sentence has an ironic second meaning, one unintended by the doctor, that is to say, Nick's father indeed "ought" to have a look at himself. These ironic double meanings continue in the second sentence. The use of the third-person plural pronoun, while consistent with proper usage in the generalization the doctor offers, nevertheless can be seen as referring to both the Indian and the doctor. Like "proud father," the phrase "worst sufferers" also has two meanings. "Worst sufferers" can mean "those who suffer the most" as well as "those who are the worst at suffering." The Indian fits both descriptions; he will prove to have suffered the most emotionally and to have been the most incapable of bearing his suffering. But at least he takes his suffering "pretty quietly." The insufferable doctor, on the other hand, is also a "worst sufferer"; he is disappointed by his unappreciative audience and anything but silent about it. Even the term "little affairs" has multiple meanings; it is an understatement for the operation, a platitude for the baby, and a metafictional reference to the story itself. This little affair has affected the two fathers very differently; for one it may have been the cause of ultimate despair and self-negation, while for the other it has been the cause of exultation and self-affirmation.

But then the doctor makes his grisly discovery:

> [1] He pulled back the blanket from the Indian's head. [2] His hand came away wet. [3] He mounted on the edge of the lower bunk with the lamp in one hand and looked in. [4] The Indian lay with his face toward the wall. [5] His throat had been cut from ear to ear. [6] The blood had flowed down into a pool where his body sagged the bunk. [7] His head rested on his left arm. [8] The open razor lay, edge up, in the blankets.

This paragraph, deceptively simple, is told almost entirely in short declarative sentences of action and description. Each sentence leads perfectly into the next but stays in the moment and does not get ahead of itself in anticipating what will follow (we see here something Hemingway learned from Gertrude Stein and adapted to his impressionist technique).[61] For instance, sentence 5 reports the discovery of the Indian's cut throat, but does not anticipate the obvious assumption—once the facts are processed—that he committed suicide. In fact, by putting the sentence in the passive voice, Hemingway not only impressionistically represents *exactly* how the discovery would have felt to the doctor at the precise moment he made it, he also suggests the socially environmental forces that have sapped the Indian of his autonomy and victimized him. (Here we glimpse the influential legacy of such literary naturalists as Zola, Crane, Dreiser, and London in their philosophical emphasis upon environmental determinism.) In this way, by dispassionately presenting what Hemingway would later term "the sequence of motion and fact which made the emotion,"[62] the passage employs delayed decoding (how a character makes full sense of a sequence only in retrospect) to depict the moment-by-moment impressions of the doctor's discovery and convey that quality of immediacy to the reader.

The paragraph contains 80 words: 67 are monosyllabic; 11 have two syllables; and only 2, necessary uses of the word "Indian," have three syllables. The words selected would all be found in the vocabulary of a small child. In rendering this scene, Hemingway was determined not to let anything, whether a complex word (which would undermine the focalization) or a subjective one (which would undercut the impressionism and external focalization by accessing a character's consciousness), stand between the reader and the object being perceived. It would be difficult to find a passage of prose more precise or more completely dispassionate than this one.

The Indian, we may assume, took his life during the operation. The story's two key events thus took place simultaneously; it is the characters' and the reader's awareness of them that is separated in time (they are simultaneous in the fabula but separated in the plot). The sequence of action that began with the operation and ends with the discovery of the suicide is therefore chronological yet implicitly cyclical. The latter quality is indicated by the use of the past perfect tense in sentences 5 and 6, which describe actions that took place during the operation. The paragraph devoted to the operation was the most durationally foreshortened passage in the story, but in each succeeding action between that passage and this last paragraph, the duration of the narrative has increasingly slowed down and approached temporal reality (fabula time). This paragraph, with its drum roll of short direct sentences (each of which is a small separate discovery), forces the reader to slow down in order to absorb each succeeding impression and make sense out of the larger discovery slowly being revealed. This gives the passage the feel of complete temporal reality, which in turn heightens the emotional impact of the discovery.

The character upon whom the Indian's suicide has the most revealing effect is the doctor. His speech immediately prior to the discovery made manifest his unconscious sense of identification with the Indian who, like him, is a father. The discovery will subtly suggest another link between the two men. While the doctor was successfully performing surgery in the lower bunk in order to bring forth life, the Indian, directly above him, was operating in an equally successful effort to end life. The assumption of the Caesarean is that life, no matter how painful and difficult, is worth the effort. The assumption of the suicide is that it is not. (These two assumptions not only form the metaphysical frame of the story, but also anticipate the antipodal shift in Hemingway's own existential perspective during the next three and a half decades.) It is the assumption of the suicide, acted upon by the character to whom he feels some tie, that emotionally unnerves Dr. Adams. Not only does the suicide deny the values that define the doctor, but the very process by which he discovers it, which imitates a birth, serves to humiliate him further. In this mock birth, the upper bunk sags like a womb from the weight of the Indian's body and is filled with blood. The doctor pulls back the blanket to reveal the Indian's head and stands on the edge of the lower bunk, lamp in hand, to look into the upper bunk. The Indian lies dead, like a stillborn baby, and the metaphor is extended even to the point of narrating sentence 5 in the passive voice, which seems to strip his death of the aspect of volition. (Compare the doctor's earlier statement—"The baby wants to be born"—with the passive depiction of the father's act that suggests—"The father wants to die.") Between the personification of the surgeon's "hand," in sentence 2, and the surgical instrument, the open razor in sentence 8, lies the dead Indian. The doctor's hand is separated from the instrument by five sentences describing the dead Indian. The doctor stands on the "edge" of the bunk staring at the "edge" of the open razor, staring not only at the implement of death, but of a death that implicitly negates his sense of worth and meaning. In that shocking moment, his feelings of accomplishment and power vanish, and he is reduced to mortal dimensions.

In this story of birth and fatherhood, in which white cultural customs (the passing out of cigars) and practices (the Caesarean) have displaced Indian ones, it is significant that the Ojibwa father takes his life with a product from white commodity culture. While the doctor initiates his son into white medicine, perhaps hoping that the young "intern" will someday follow in his footsteps, the despairing Indian bark-peeler leaves his own son a bitter legacy. His dead body presides at his son's entrance into the world; his suicide hovers over his son's birth like a curse.

Both fathers in this story fail their sons. The Indian father's action not only humbles the doctor, it also "peels" away the "bark" of his professional persona (there is now nothing more he can do as "doctor") and reminds him of his duty as "father." It reminds him of this because the Indian's disregard for his son's needs is of a kind, although obviously much more extreme, with the doctor's insensitivity toward his own son's needs. Upon making his discovery, and the unconscious self-discoveries that arise from it, the doctor's first thought is of Nick, who has been absent from the minds of both the doctor and the reader throughout the passage:

> "Take Nick out of the shanty, George," the doctor said.
>
> There was no need of that. Nick, standing in the door of the kitchen, had a good view of the upper bunk when his father, the lamp in one hand, tipped the Indian's head back.

This is the third command we hear the doctor give. The first two, ordering the hot water and telling Uncle George to pull back the quilt, were carried out to the doctor's satisfaction. But here, whether or not Uncle George obeys his brother's order, the purpose behind it cannot be fulfilled; Nick has already seen the dead Indian. The first two commands derived from the doctor's medical authority. This order, however, stems from his paternal concerns, even though the speaker is identified, for the final time, as "the doctor." The doctor's newfound concern for his son, his unsatisfiable order, and his no longer required professional abilities transform him from "the doctor" back into "Nick's father." With this transformation, Nick reenters the narrative.

But before he does, there is an authorial intrusion ("There was no need of that"), one that in terms of neither style nor content adheres to Nick's point-of-view, and that is rendered superfluous by the exposition that immediately follows. (It is also a rather silly sentence; would it have been better to allow Nick to continue to stare at the gruesome sight?) All the narrative required in terms of exposition could have been accomplished by eliminating the sentence and beginning the next paragraph with the word "But." The sentence thus seems like an accusation by the author; to wit, why did the doctor not have Nick removed from the shanty long before this? Embedded in a passage otherwise scrupulously devoid of all authorial comment, in which even the Indian's cut throat was not directly explained as having been by his own hand, this sentence stands out. In the absence of any possible narrative purpose, we might conclude that it gauges the depth of the author's complex and often accusatory feelings toward the real-life father upon whom he based the character of Dr. Adams. Moreover, there is just enough of a sense of pity in the narrator's voice, which is so unlike the rest of this dispassionate prose, to make us wonder if Hemingway is giving way, for just an instant, to self-pity as well.

The final sentence of the passage depicts Nick's view of the dead Indian and should raise a question. Who was the focalizer when the suicide was discovered? Earlier in the third part of the story, Nick was on the periphery of the scene, but could have easily observed the action and heard the dialogue. The discovery paragraph, though, seems perilously close to being focalized through the doctor. Yet there are sound reasons for why this had to be. First, the most effective way to present the scene was through the sequence of observations that the doctor makes as he discovers the dead Indian. Second, the character most directly and immediately affected by the suicide is not Nick, but his father. Last, Hemingway wanted Nick to remain vaguely absent in order to maximize the effect when his father shifts back into his paternal role and orders Uncle George to take his son away. In other words, he wanted the reader to be shocked by the discovery first, and then suddenly to realize, along with Dr. Adams, that Nick has seen it too.

It is once again a mark of Hemingway's art, however, that this challenge to maintaining fixed internal focalization is so well finessed; as in the first scene in the shanty, he figures out ways to keep the reader from being jarred, and we do not stop to ask how a small boy can observe the precise details being reported in an upper bunk that must certainly be above his eye level as well as somewhat in the distance. As noted, the vocabulary of the discovery paragraph is exceedingly simple. The camera eye may be Dr. Adams, but the language is Nick's. In the next paragraph, the author directly states that Nick "had a good view of the upper bunk," which sounds reasonable, though not very likely upon reconsideration. He then repeats exactly a phrase from the discovery paragraph ("the lamp in one hand"). This subtly links Nick's view to the focalization of the discovery paragraph. Significantly, the detail he chooses to repeat is one that suggests the upper bunk was well lit. Last, he adds one small piece of exposition, that "his father . . . tipped the Indian's head back." This powerful image, which logically would and should have taken place in the discovery paragraph between sentence 4 (where the Indian is facing the wall) and sentence 5 (where his cut throat is revealed), is a part of the doctor's sequence of action in that paragraph, but was removed and relocated to the next paragraph in order to give the impression that Nick was able to observe the entire sequence. In this manner, by employing what I term his technique of *sequence displacement,*[63] Hemingway manages to focalize through the doctor—reaping the dramatic benefits enumerated above—while still making it seem as though he is focalizing through Nick.

By the end of the third part, the hitherto arrested enigma in the hermeneutic code of the story has been redefined. The penultimate enigma has nothing to do with a lady who is sick or with a woman who needs a Caesarean operation; it concerns the Indian father's suicide. With this latest shift of the enigma, the final part of the story must serve as a denouement by addressing it in a meaningful way, and this will lead to the ultimate enigma on which the story ends: Nick's encounter with ontological shock. The narrative concludes with one of the finest scenes Hemingway would ever write—a sentence locating the action and then a perfect passage of dialogue that will be followed by two equally perfect paragraphs of descriptive prose:

> It was just beginning to be daylight when they walked along the logging road back toward the lake.
>
> "I'm terribly sorry I brought you along, Nickie," said his father, all his post-operative exhilaration gone. "It was an awful mess to put you through."
>
> [Q1] "Do ladies always have such a hard time having babies?" Nick asked.
> [A1] "No, that was very, very exceptional."
> [Q2] "Why did he kill himself, Daddy?"
> [A2] "I don't know, Nick. He couldn't stand things, I guess."
> [Q3] "Do many men kill themselves, Daddy?"
> [A3] "Not very many, Nick."
> [Q4] "Do many women?"
> [A4] "Hardly ever."
> [Q5] "Don't they ever?"
> [A5] "Oh, yes. They do sometimes."
> [Q6] "Daddy?"
> [A6] "Yes."
> [Q7] "Where did Uncle George go?"
> [A7] "He'll turn up all right."
> [Q8] "Is dying hard, Daddy?"
> [A8] "No, I think it's pretty easy, Nick. It all depends."

This passage follows a lengthy ellipsis because Hemingway wants to juxtapose it with the suicide discovery scene. Some of the unstated action can be inferred by the reader: Dr. Adams must have informed the Indians of the husband's death; he probably made arrangements, perhaps with Uncle George, to report it to the authorities; and he started home with Nick. Uncle George's absence, revealed later in the passage, is left unexplained. He may have stayed behind to relate the events to the nurse from St. Ignace. But he has already served his function in the story and will henceforth make his final contribution only through his absence. By using an ellipsis, Hemingway eliminates action unnecessary to the plot so that he can go directly to the dialogue about the significant action just completed.

These kinds of major ellipses are essential to the modern short story, the only alternative being summary sentences that account for the passage of time, like, for instance: "His father came outside the shanty where they were waiting and spoke with Uncle George. Then Uncle George went back inside and his father took Nick and headed away from the camp." Major ellipses are, of course, used in novels as well, especially in picaresque novels, and for much the same reason as we see it used here. For example, many of the most dramatic moments of *Adventures of Huckleberry Finn* are placed at the ends of chapters, with significant ellipses between chapters, so that the power of the dramatic moment can reverberate without commentary or extension (e.g., chapters 14, 15, 23). Through such ellipses, Mark Twain uses silence to its full effect, knowing that more words are mere words that drain the moment of its power.

But the ellipsis is especially important to the modern short story because it enables compression. Nothing is more compressed than something implied but entirely omitted. The well-placed ellipsis is a writer's way of terminating an action sequence abruptly, alerting the reader that what has just happened is significant, and giving that reader time to ponder it before moving on. It also enables significant juxtapositions, serving much the same purpose as do the dashes in the poems of Emily Dickinson. The major ellipses in this story have all served such functions. The ellipsis following the depicted portion of the boat trip across the lake contributed to the mystery of the journey. The ellipsis before they entered the shanty focused our attention on the preceding image of the old woman with the lamp whose appearance marked the end of the journey. The ellipses before and after the operation and following the removal of the afterbirth were used to avoid unnecessary action and also served to underscore Nick's experience of the stated action as taking "a long time." This latest ellipsis also eliminates unnecessary segments of the proairetic code while commenting upon, through silence, the effect of what Nick, his father, and the reader have just seen. These sorts of ellipses are examples of what I have termed Hemingway's technique of *implication omission.*

In the first sentence of the above passage, Hemingway again draws upon a birth metaphor. Nick and his father must have left the shanty in the dark, since the daylight is just starting when they get to the logging road. The word "daylight" is used literally, but it also resonates as a comment on Dr. Adams, who is now beginning to see the light. The suicide has stripped him of his feelings of power, forced him to recognize that there are things beyond his control, and made him aware of his son's needs and his parental responsibilities. When they reach the road, which will lead them from the dark, unfamiliar world of the Indian camp back to their "normative" world of white civilization, they are figuratively reborn. But their own relatively safe world can never again be the same; the events they have witnessed and participated in have marked them.

In his first speech, Dr. Adams admits his mistake. His use of the diminutive "Nickie" suggests a concern for Nick's anxieties (he used the same diminutive in the original opening when entering the tent after Nick fired the shots). But in trying to comfort his son he betrays his own feelings of guilt. His apology is not for Nick's having seen the dead Indian (which could not have been anticipated), nor for his thoughtlessness in having Nick attend the horrifying operation (which was his only irresponsible act). Instead, he apologizes for having brought Nick along in the first place, though he had no other option, which undercuts the apology by passing over his one truly unconscionable action. (I might also add that nowhere in the story does he seem to notice that his child has just gone a night without sleep.) What he had earlier termed a "little affair" (the operation), he now calls an "awful mess"—an understatement that covers everything that Nick has seen and experienced (including his father's paternal inadequacies) and, by its imprecision, continues to diminish the apology. The phrase about his "post-operative exhilaration" being gone is, of course, gratuitous and should have either been eliminated or else replaced with a specific detail to suggest the doctor's deflation. The last phrase of the statement shows Dr. Adams looking at these events from Nick's perspective ("to put you through") in order to console him, but his feelings of guilt are manifest in his use of an inert construction; a more honest admission of culpability would have been: "I put you through an awful mess." By his need to assuage his own guilt, then, the doctor's apology is involuntarily self-revelatory; he is still mainly concerned with his own needs, not his child's.

If the doctor's initial seventeen-word speech is revealing, the ensuing eight questions and answers are a marvel of indirection, miscommunication, suggestiveness, and compression. Nick has conflated all of the events he has witnessed and therefore asks about the operation, although, by the end of the passage, it will become clear that what he really wants to know about is the probability of death (either his father's or his own). His father, however, is obsessed with the suicide and so, for all his newfound sensitivity toward his son and Nick's careful attention to his father, the two characters miscommunicate throughout the conversation.

Nick's first question ("Do ladies always have such a hard time having babies?") elicits a somewhat detached response from his father, whose thoughts are elsewhere. Dr. Adams can draw upon his medical knowledge to answer the question; the repetition of "very" and the understated "exceptional" give the impression of a considered, dispassionate reply. Nick's second question, however, directly presents the mystery at the heart of the story: "Why did he kill himself, Daddy?" The use of "Daddy," which Nick previously employed when frightened by the woman's screams, suggests the anxiety beneath his outwardly composed demeanor. (In the first scene on the lake, when Nick genuinely was calm, he called him "Dad.") But his father does not notice Nick's anxiety, and he cannot, in any case, satisfactorily answer the question. His profession has equipped him to answer medical queries, not psychological ones. He replies honestly—he does not know. But he also senses that his response is not enough to satisfy his son, so he adds an explanation that is strategically vague ("He couldn't stand things, I guess"). On a conscious level, this reply is somewhat evasive; yet, on an unconscious level it is self-revelatory, even self-reflexive. He consciously means to say that the Indian was emotionally unable to go on living, but he employs an idiom with the word "stand," reminding the reader of the Indian's injured foot, which prevented him from joining the men outside the shanty and forced him to be a silent witness to his wife's ordeal. The Indian father's injury is a sign of his helplessness, and perhaps functions in Dr. Adams's speech as a subtle indication of the helplessness that the story's other father now feels.

When Nick asks about the suicide, the dialogue takes a notable turn. The suicide revealed that his father was not omnipotent. Now, compelled to reply to his son's question, he must confess that neither is he omniscient. The words "I don't know," coming from so proud a man who has performed with such competence under duress, resonate with the doctor's deep sense of confusion, guilt, and deflation. For the rest of the conversation, Nick will focus on death and suicide, asking questions that either cannot be answered or that his father is not in the mood to address.

His father's inability to answer these questions, and the shock he feels over what has happened, will force him back into the self-absorption he displayed during the operation. And yet, although his answers to his son's questions will be brief and somewhat perfunctory, they will have an oddly soothing effect on Nick, relieving his son's anxiety. As Joseph M. Flora observes: "The questions are profound, beyond the comprehension of the questioner ultimately, and so are the answers. Yet the answers, if uncomprehended, carry authority and assurance."[64] Although the characters miscommunicate, the failure to communicate has an ironically successful result.

Nick's questions are relentless. With a small child's curiosity and unerring ability to ask precisely the questions that an adult does not wish to discuss, he pursues his interrogation. When he catches his father in an inattentive reply, as in the answer to question 4 about the frequency of women's suicides, he immediately issues a follow-up question ("Don't they ever?") that reveals his dissatisfaction with his father's response. Other times, he jumps from one question to another, catching his distracted father off guard. His father's preoccupation can be glimpsed in the laconic, indefinite nature of his replies ("Not very many"; "Hardly ever"; "sometimes"; "He'll turn up"; "It all depends"). He answers Nick's questions, but just barely, and he makes no effort to address the anxieties that obviously lie beneath them. His sixth reply is particularly revealing. Nick says, "Daddy?" just to get his father's attention, and his father replies "Yes." Technically, a question mark should follow his reply, but the punctuation indicates that his father's inflection is declarative rather than interrogative; Nick has gotten his attention, but he remains lost in his own thoughts. When Nick then asks about Uncle George, a subject that his father is especially not interested in, the reply is again unspecific ("He'll turn up all right"). The addition of the phrase "all right" resonates with the two times the expression was previously used in the story: Nick's response to his father's post-operative inquiry about how Nick liked being an intern, and the sarcastic remark George made about Dr. Adams being a "great man, all right[.]" Nick's use of the expression was intended to satisfy his father but revealed his lack of enthusiasm. George's use both intended and revealed his resentment of his brother. Here, Dr. Adams wishes to satisfy his son, but he unintentionally reveals his own lack of enthusiasm for answering any more questions as well as his own resentment toward George, whose earlier sarcasms anticipated the doctor's present feelings of inadequacy.

Many able critics addressing this story (and, I suspect, most readers as well) have found this to be a touching passage of dialogue that demonstrates a warm, close father-son relationship. For instance, Philip Young calls it "a calm discussion of suicide," and Arthur Waldhorn describes Nick's questions as "curious rather than searching" and characterizes his father's answers as "wisely brief, honest, and comforting."[65] But Dr. Adams's evasiveness and self-absorption preclude this from being a discussion of any kind, and his words are neither wise, nor notably honest, nor intentionally comforting. Like Dr. Clarence Hemingway, he is a man of great competence and good intentions, but one who seems to exist in a very private world. When caught outside the sphere of his professional duties, or the camaraderie of outdoorsmanship, he is awkward in his relations with others. Perhaps this passage of superb dialogue writing has, in a way, affinities with the awful passage from the discarded opening when Dr. Adams, after the shots were fired, responded tepidly to his brother's cruel comments about Nick. It is also more than possible that both scenes have something to do with Ernest's own lifelong efforts to gain his father's approval, and, when he could not, to try to get Dr. Hemingway's attention by any means possible. (As in having an order for *in our time* sent to his parents, knowing that his father would be outraged by the vignettes.) As for Dr. Adams, his earlier insensitivity toward his son could be excused because he was concentrating on the operation. But his abdication of parental responsibility in this scene, after a brief acknowledgment of that obligation, makes his paternal shortcomings all too clear. The very least he could do, after what he has put his son through, would be to hold him or establish some sort of physical contact, actions more intimate and comforting to a small child than abstract discourse. That Nick eventually does derive comfort from this conversation and the subsequent action on the lake testifies to the remarkable resilience of children and not to his father's wisdom.

Nick, of course, cannot comprehend death. He can only feel it as absence. His first glimpse of death was in the context of the Indian father's withdrawal from life. Therefore, the anxieties he expresses in the passage concern absent fathers. The four questions he asks ending with "Daddy?" (2, 3, 6, and 8) make manifest the subject of these anxieties (including his sixth question, which is intended to bring his mentally absent father back into the conversation). In his second question he asks why the Indian baby's father killed himself and receives an uncomforting but honest reply.

What he really wants to know, however, is whether he is safe from suffering the same fate as the Indian baby boy. So he continues his inquiry by a more circuitous route. His next two questions, about the frequency of male and female suicide, are unconsciously self-referential—he wants to know about his own father and mother—and the responses are comforting. But the real point of the last three questions is revealed only in their juxtaposition. The sixth question is about Nick's sense of his own father's mental absence; the seventh question is about Uncle George's physical absence, foreshadowed by his brief disappearance during the first boat trip and here serving as a displacement of Nick's anxiety over his own father's mortality; and the eighth question ("Is dying hard, Daddy?"), read in the above context, is about the *probability* of Nick's father's death. Ironically, his father solipsistically assumes the question to be, in light of his own concerns, about whether the act of dying is difficult to face, and his answer is unintentionally chilling: "it's pretty easy." Even more ironically, however, the words that confirm Nick's anxieties about his father's mortality do not matter, for, as the doctor says, it all "depends."

Just what it depends on becomes clear in the final two paragraphs of the story, the second of which reiterates the images of the first:

> [1] They were seated in the boat, Nick in the stern, his father rowing. [2] The sun was coming up over the hills. [3] A bass jumped, making a circle in the water. [4] Nick trailed his hand in the water. [5] It felt warm in the sharp chill of the morning.
>
> [1a] In the early morning on the lake sitting in the stern of the boat with his father rowing, [1b] he felt quite sure that he would never die.

During the first boat trip, the older Indian was rowing, with Nick and his father in the stern. The trip took place in the dark and was enveloped in suspense. Nick's one comfort was his father's arm around him. Now it is daylight and they are returning to the familiar world. Nick is again in the stern, but this time his father is rowing—not only present but in control. The sensory presence of Nick's father is so strong that Hemingway can omit it and know the reader will feel it: the sight of his father pulling the oars, the sound (and perhaps smoke) of his breath as he rows, the steady surges of the boat along the water (as in the description of the first trip). That presence is, in fact, so strong that it counteracts both Nick's experiential sense of absence and his father's words about dying being easy, so that Nick no longer countenances the idea that his father could ever cease to be.

In this way, his father's tangible physical actions are far more comforting than his perfunctory words. These powerfully implied but omitted actions enable Nick to leave behind adult considerations of death and suicide, and to return to his state of youthful innocence.

The other sensory impressions of the paragraph, abundantly suggestive and not omitted, are also comforting, unlike those of the first trip. The scene is vibrant with life. The sun is just coming up, signaling the start of a new day and marking the end of the previous night's horrors. Nature is animated and, in yet another small metaphor of birth, a bass jumps up from beneath the water; life appears from nowhere. The word "hand," by now, has developed a good deal of symbolic significance. Earlier, his father's hands had been carefully scrubbed and even personified, but during the operation they were covered in blood, and later his hand came away from the upper bunk "wet" with blood. The lake water both cleans Nick's hand and also links him to the impressions of life going on all around him. The water feels warm in the sharp morning chill, suggesting that this scene feels warm in the sharp chill of what has gone before. In the midst of all this palpable "being," it is impossible for Nick to imagine "non-being."

The form of the paragraph helps the reader to experience its meaning. It consists of five short sentences that slow down the reader's pace as he or she takes in the sights and sounds of the lake, the living sensations that impress themselves upon Nick. As with the passage depicting the earlier trip, the paragraph scans as iambic and anapestic, mimicking the motion of the boat as it crosses the lake. The only double stresses, either spondees or else iambs followed by trochees or dactyls, are: "bóat, Níck"; "úp óvĕr"; "báss júmped"; "Níck tráiled"; "félt wárm"; and "shárp chíll." The first of these is neutralized by the comma; the second underscores the appearance of the sun and the new day; the third contributes to the surprise of the fish's sudden appearance and links it to the emergence of the sun; the fourth prosodically connects Nick to the thematics established by the "new" sun and the "newly emerged" fish; and the final two double-stresses juxtapose the contrasting sensations of warmth and cold, heightening the effect of the former in a wonderfully tactile image of life.

The final paragraph is then narrated in one sentence. In the first part of this sentence, Hemingway employs what I term his technique of *recapitulation with variation* as he gathers up the scattered impressions from the preceding paragraph and restates them in a continuous manner to convey both their literal simultaneity and their processing, in retrospect, in both

Nick's and the reader's consciousnesses.[66] As the images from the previous paragraph are processed or integrated within the mind, they are repeated as variations (e.g., "the sun coming up" above the "water" becomes "the early morning on the lake"). Only the phrase "his father rowing" is repeated exactly, just as the phrase "the lamp in one hand" from the discovery paragraph was repeated exactly in the next paragraph linking the discovery to Nick's observation of it. In both cases, the repeated words emphasize Nick's focus on his father's hands, which are the engines of the action sequences. This phrase, "his father rowing," narrated in the past progressive to indicate an ongoing action, further links the final two paragraphs.

In a letter written five years after composing "Indian Camp," Hemingway told fellow author Owen Wister: "I know . . . how damned much I try always to do the thing by three cushion shots rather than by words or direct statement. But maybe we must have the direct statement too."[67] Until the last part of the final sentence, these two paragraphs have been three-cushion shots; by the suggestiveness of specific sensory images that form an objective correlative, they have impressionistically conveyed to the reader Nick's state of mind.[68] They have also prepared the reader for the direct statement that comprises the second part of the final sentence. This statement is appropriate and effective because Hemingway has access to Nick's consciousness, and because the statement functions not as an explanation, but as an articulation and further confirmation of what has already been implied. In this sense, it expresses Nick's feeling that the world of the Indian camp is not his world. His is the world depicted in this scene in which his father is in control and he is free from responsibility, where the sun comes up and fish jump and the water feels warm in the morning chill. This bountiful natural world asserts its reality and erases the nightmare of the dark and bloody Indian camp with its silent Indians, dying fathers, and screaming mothers. Immersed as he is in the natural world, it is altogether believable that Nick would have "félt qúite súre" (the three consecutively stressed syllables emphasizing the certainty of his feeling) "thăt hé wŏuld névĕr dié" (the iambic float-off ending).[69]

But the final sentence is much too complex to be viewed simply as an affirmation. The first part of the sentence, an objective correlative for Nick's sense of immortality, placed in juxtaposition with Uncle George's absence and the story's other signifiers of death, does indeed triumph over them, yet ambiguities and ironies compound. If the antecedent to the final "he" is Nick's father, a less likely possibility but one that Hemingway purposely leaves open, then all the miscommunication between the two and his father's disquieting responses have inadvertently comforted Nick. On the other hand, if the antecedent is Nick, the much more likely possibility, then another irony is created by the disjunction between Nick's sense of his own immortality and the reader's knowledge that it is otherwise.[70] Moreover, it is the final turn in the screw of the passage's indirection, for it indicates that what Nick was really asking about all along concerned his anxieties about his own finitude, not his father's. Therefore, the entire conversation is about Nick's anxieties over his own death, and the story has not been "about" the Caesarean operation, the Indian's suicide, or the probability of Dr. Adams's death, but Nick's first encounter with ontological shock, the numbing realization of his own mortality. Hemingway omitted this from the story when he discarded the opening pages with their "silver cord breaking," only to treat it at the end by, characteristically, having Nick deny it. If the visible part of the iceberg is Nick's denial of his own mortality, then the seven-eighths lying beneath the surface are that he must have, at some point during the story, experienced, however fleetingly and inchoately, an existential recognition of his eventual non-being. Even in his "direct statement" Hemingway operated by three-cushion shots. And all of these matters are compressed into just a few "simple" sentences of enormously suggestive dialogue in which two characters thoroughly miscommunicate in such subtle ways that most readers of the passage, for the past eight decades, seem to have assumed that the two are communicating clearly.

There is, of course, more beneath the surface than a child like Nick can perceive or process. The reader, whose comprehension is much greater than that of the story's central consciousness, knows that the world of the Indian camp is no different from Nick's world, or from any other (significantly, no article appears in the title), and that the fact of human finitude and the mystery of non-being cannot simply be denied. Nick's feeling is qualified by the mood of the conditional sentence that states it, with the auxiliary "would" indicating the subjunctive. Nick can feel he *would* never die under the following conditions: that it is early morning, he is on the lake, he is sitting in the stern of a boat, and his father is rowing. This is what the sentence literally states. What it means is that Nick's feeling is contingent upon his innocence. And the reader knows that this beautiful innocence must die (even Hemingway's pet word "quite" is effective, appealing as it does to the reader's ironic perspective on Nick's surety). "*Beauty plus pity*" is how Vladimir Nabokov defined art. "Where there is beauty there is pity for the simple reason that beauty must die: beauty always dies, the manner dies with the matter, the world dies with the individual."[71] How aptly that definition fits the reader's emotional response to this story.

Hemingway's strict adherence to Nick's point-of-view makes this possible, for the pity arises out of the ironic disparity between what Nick feels and what the reader knows. The narration also makes possible the final twist in the hermeneutic code. Because Hemingway has worked so hard to have us watch events unfold through Nick's eyes (even and especially in those passages in which he had to finesse the focalization), we have seen the enigma subtly shift throughout the four parts of the story. At turns, we believed it concerned a sick woman, then a brutal Caesarean, and then a silent suicide, but in the very last word of the story the real enigma is revealed: Nick's unstated encounter with, and innocent denial of, ontological shock. The other enigmas have turned out to be snares, a series of indirections that hold sway until the final word. With this word, the hermeneutic code's puzzle is complete and the story immediately concludes.

There is, however, another kind of mystery, one that is different from the matter of "suspense" as embedded in the hermeneutic code, what Flannery O'Connor refers to as the "ultimate mystery."[72] Nick innocently states the ultimate mystery of "Indian Camp" by asking: "Why did he kill himself, Daddy?" When his father answers that he does not know (and then, in a very human fashion, speculates that he "couldn't stand things, I guess"), his reply explains nothing about the reasons for the suicide but it also tells us all we can possibly know about it. Although Hemingway provides us with hints about the Indian's motivation through the cultural code (e.g., he cannot stand and join the other Indian men in their performance of masculinity; his role as father has been co-opted by the white men), and through the proairetic code (e.g., he turns toward the wall after the doctor calls his wife's screams "unimportant"; he kills himself during the operation), nowhere does the author state why the Indian kills himself nor does he even imply that he himself knows. Hemingway respects the mystery of the Indian's suicide and thereby displays his understanding that the reasons why a person chooses self-annihilation are always unknowable, no matter how much we, like Nick's father, feel compelled to speculate, and even to pass off our assumptions as knowledge. The hints Hemingway gives us are no different from the clues we receive retrospectively about anyone who has taken his or her own life. Even if we knew more about the Indian, could we ever really know why? If he were a close friend, would we know then?

The Indian's suicide, like any suicide, is an explicit epistemological mystery (why did he kill himself?), an implicit ontological mystery (what is non-being?), and an implicit ethical mystery (why must being cease?). Our most meaningful response to the story arises from these mysteries. If we were to remove the element of mystery from the Indian's suicide, the story would be greatly diminished. Flannery O'Connor, who placed the representation of mystery at the center of her fictional vision, addressed this matter in words that are remarkably relevant to "Indian Camp":

> I often ask myself what makes a story work, and what makes it hold up as a story, and I have decided that it is probably some action, some gesture of a character that is unlike any other in the story, one which indicates where the real heart of the story lies. This would have to be an action or a gesture which was both totally right and totally unexpected; it would have to be one that was both in character and beyond character; it would have to suggest both the world and eternity. . . . It would be a gesture that transcended any neat allegory that might have been intended or any pat moral categories a reader could make. It would be a gesture that somehow made contact with mystery.[73]

Nick's feeling that he will never die is just such a gesture: totally right and totally unexpected; suggesting both the world and eternity; transcending easy categorization; and making contact with the larger mysteries implicit in the Indian's suicide.

Stripped of this mystery, "Indian Camp" would lose much of its power. But in all of the voluminous scholarship written on this story, I can find only one critic who acknowledges that we do not know why the Indian husband took his life. Everyone else who has commented on the reason for the suicide—including some of our finest Hemingway scholars and two of the world's greatest storywriters—has assumed that the Indian took his life either because of his wife's screams or because he could not endure the humiliation of the operation—either her pain or his. Each of these readers takes their assumptions for granted, stating the causal connections as though they are perfectly obvious.[74] These misreadings are themselves mysterious. Perhaps the disparity between Nick's and the reader's awareness causes readers to assume that they can fully understand all the events of the story. Perhaps readers resist finding themselves in the same position as Nick's father when he says that he does not know. Or maybe we have become uncomfortable with the idea of ultimate mysteries; we have been trained as critics to explain everything, and the inexplicable makes us feel ignorant. As Flannery O'Connor observes: "a generation . . . has been made to feel that the aim of learning is to eliminate mystery. For such people, fiction can be very disturbing, for the fiction writer is concerned with mystery that is lived. He's concerned with ultimate mystery as we find it embodied in the concrete world of sense experience."[75]

Hemingway himself once noted: "there is a mystery in all great writing and that mystery does not dis-sect out. It continues and is always valid."[76] The purposes of literary criticism are to understand, to illuminate, to appreciate, and to evaluate, but in the face of ultimate mystery these related functions may seem at odds. I hasten to add that they need not be, for to understand mystery one must first appreciate that it is mysterious; otherwise one understands nothing. It may be that these readers are doing nothing more than what people do in real life when they encounter the mysterious; like Mr. Compson in Faulkner's *Absalom, Absalom!* they acknowledge their own epistemological limitations, but then they find themselves compelled to insist on the very explanations they have already acknowledged to be inadequate.[77] Yet, just as in life there must be some humble admission, despite our need to make sense of things and our resultant assumptions that quickly metamorphose into convictions, that some things, as so many writers have tried to show us, are "past finding out," so too in literary criticism we must display more negative capability and less arrogance. It's easy to read "Indian Camp" smugly, merely to disapprove of Dr. Adams's hubris while we pity and yearn for Nick's innocence. But it is much too great a story to be read in this fashion. We should not be so proud or innocent ourselves as to deny the story's mystery or to believe that its most disturbing implications apply only to a world other than our own. Rather, we ought to affirm the truth of Herman Melville's timeless statement: "It is with fiction as with religion: it should present another world, and yet one to which we feel the tie."[78]

There is one final aspect of "Indian Camp" I should address—its complex unity. Some of that unity is manifest: unity of place (from lake to camp to lake); unity of time (from night to dawn); and unity of action (a Poesque causal consistency directed toward a single end). In addition, the strict adherence to a central consciousness automatically produces a certain degree of coherence. A fixed internal focalization, whether in first- or third-person, holds even the most seemingly unstructured narrative together, for even in a stream of consciousness narrative there is, no matter how chaotic it may seem, a strong coherence.

Various patterns of plot and action also provide a unified structure for this story. The two lake scenes frame the main action in the shanty. From the beginning of the story to the end of the operation, the characters share a common intention—to help the woman have her baby. After the birth, this centripetal focus is removed and the characters' personal concerns reassert themselves: Nick's father looks for appreciation and approval; Uncle George worries about his bite wound; Nick tries to deal with what he has witnessed; the Indian mother lapses into unconsciousness; and the young Indian enjoys Uncle George's discomfort. The Indian husband, of course, is now in a realm far removed from finite human concerns. After a brief pause in the flow of events, the discovery of his suicide acts as a centrifugal force; the characters are again implicitly united in their concerns by an event, but that event sends them in different directions. The Indians must bury their dead; Uncle George must make arrangements with the authorities; the Indian mother, once she awakens, must deal with her loss; Nick's father needs to remove his son from the scene; and Nick must confront ontological shock. This shifting centripetal and centrifugal dynamic among the characters is reflected in the addition and subtraction of characters present in the story. In the very beginning there are two, then five, then at least nine (four additional characters are specifically mentioned but it is implied that there are more), and finally two again (although a different two).

This pattern of movement is intertwined with the use of light imagery. The darkness of night in the beginning gives way to the dawn at the end, but along the way the light increases by increments. These stages are marked by Uncle George's cigar, the young Indian's lantern, the moonlight on the logging road, the lights of the camp, the old woman's lamp, the light in the shanty, and the lamp held by Nick's father as he peers beneath the dead Indian's blanket. There is light, but there is no color except as the reader infers it; despite Hemingway's fondness for colors, especially elemental ones, this is a story narrated like a nightmare, in shades of gray. The incremental emergence of light accords with the gradual unveiling of the hermeneutic code; the light increases literally at the same time as it does so metaphorically. As the light increases, the reader's comprehension of the events in the story grows. Nick's confusion also gives way to a sense of surety, but the reader recognizes that Nick's clarity at the end is a false light possible only in the dawn of life. The light imagery thus serves as a counterpoint to Nick's journey toward an illusion. The story begins with the two Indians waiting and ends with Nick feeling quite sure that he will never die. But death is implicitly waiting beyond the story, as it does in every story, for "all stories," as Hemingway would write, "if continued far enough, end in death, and he is no true-story teller who would keep that from you."[79]

In his study of *A Farewell to Arms,* Michael Reynolds discusses three important techniques Hemingway employs to provide that novel with "ordered tightness." The first of these is foreshadowing. Second, there is the use of an "echo scene" in which Hemingway runs a particular scene past the reader for a second time. In the second or echo scene, Reynolds observes, "the emphasis of the scene will have shifted slightly so that the reader is invited to make a comparison between the two scenes. The result of such a comparison is frequently irony." This device "achieves both foreshadowing and irony while at the same time serving to bind the action into unity." The third technique is role reversal, a complex device that combines both foreshadowing and echo scenes, which Hemingway uses "to tighten his action and to make covert commentary on the action[.]"[80] These techniques are certainly more complexly realized in a novel like *A Farewell to Arms* than they could ever be in a story, but even in a short narrative such as "Indian Camp" all three are present and contribute to the story's unity.

The most important of these techniques in "Indian Camp" is foreshadowing. "The soul of any function is," according to Roland Barthes, "its seed, what allows it to sow the narrative with an element which will ripen later[.]" "[A]rt," he adds, "does not acknowledge 'noise'" and "there is never a 'wasted' unit[.]"[81] We have already demonstrated, in our close reading, the truth of this statement—how every element of the story contributes to the effect of the narrative, what Hemingway meant when he told his publisher that "the alteration of a word can throw an entire story out of key."[82] But two particular "seeds" should be further elucidated, each of which is a kind of foreshadowing.

The first is what Gérard Genette terms the "advance notice," which *explicitly* alerts the reader to something that will happen later on.[83] These advance notices include the first conversation between Nick and his father when we are told that there is a woman who is sick, the first shanty scene when we find out she is in labor, the doctor's statement that he has no anesthetic, his elaborate hand washing, his statement that maybe he'll have to operate, and his announcement that he will have a look at the proud father. Each of these advance notices points to a specific action that will take place. There are also three advance notices pointing to actions that will occur after the narrative is over: the doctor's announcement that he'll return in the morning, his statement that the nurse will arrive by noon, and Nick's feeling that he will never die (which, to the reader, points to the inevitability of Nick's death). There are also what I term *retrospective notices,* which allude to something that has already happened which the reader, at the time, did not know.[84] Such notices include the information that the operation was performed with a jackknife and fishing gut leaders, and the discovery of the Indian's suicide.

Genette terms a second kind of seed the "advance mention," which is "only an 'insignificant seed,' and even an imperceptible one, whose importance as a seed will not be recognized until later, and retrospectively."[85] The advance mention is what we customarily term foreshadowing. These kinds of seeds contribute a great deal of resonance by the end of a story, more so upon each new reading. The advance mention and what it points to affect each other mutually, creating a symbolic web that helps hold the story together. In "Indian Camp," these advance mentions include the details of the first lake scene that characterize it as confused, foreboding, dark, and cold; Uncle George's first brief disappearance; Uncle George smoking in the dark and passing out cigars (pointing to the Indian husband smoking his pipe and the Indian men smoking in the dark); the lantern carried by the young Indian (pointing to the lamp held by the old woman and the lamp held by Nick's father); the woman under her quilt (pointing to her husband under his blanket); the husband's foot injury; the woman's screams and her husband's silence (pointing to her producing life and his taking it); the doctor's scrubbed hands (pointing to his hand later coming away wet with blood and Nick's hand in the water); and the doctor's accomplishment and exultation (pointing to his subsequent deflation and sense of powerlessness).

There is also an echo scene, of sorts, that suggests a slight role reversal—the boat trips that frame the story. In the first scene, there are two boats; the Indians row; Nick and his father sit in the stern, his father's arm around Nick, and are carried across; it is dark and cold; the conversation between Nick and his father is brief, direct, and commonplace; and they are headed toward birth and death. The images of the scene seem random, mysterious, and slightly disturbing. In the echo scene, there is one boat, suggesting that something is gone. Nick remains in the stern but his father rows, a spatial separation implying a new emotional individuation for the child. It is light and although it is still cold, the water in which Nick trails his hand feels warm. The conversation is awkward, indirect, and exceptional. Nick's father leads his son away from the scene of birth and death, but also toward a new scene of birth and death as the images of renewal suggest rebirth and the last sentence reminds us of Nick's mortality. Unlike the scattered, impressionistically reported images of the first scene, the natural images of this scene are harmonious, clear, and affirming. In the first scene, the doctor was sure of himself and Nick was confused. Here, this state of affairs is reversed; the doctor is unnerved and Nick is self-assured. Nick's father controls the boat but knows that there are things he cannot control; Nick is perfectly under control and senses no limitations.

One last aspect of the text's unity comes from its *illustrative stamp,* my term for a striking set of sensory impressions that seems to embody a story.[86] In "Indian Camp," I believe the stamp is the image of Nick in the final sentence, sitting in the boat in the early morning feeling quite sure that he will never die. It is a stamp of innocence, not unique in Hemingway's stories (e.g., "A Day's Wait"), but certainly rare. Much more typical is a stamp in which a character stares at something in anger, incomprehension, fear, or despair. Perhaps its rarity makes the stamp of "Indian Camp" stand out even more for the Hemingway reader, who is well aware that even as his father leads Nick away from the camp and back to the rest of his life he is leading him to future stories that must inevitably destroy the innocence he maintains in this one. This quickly becomes apparent to the reader who reads "Indian Camp" at the beginning of *In Our Time* or *The Nick Adams Stories* and watches Nick's fall from grace.

Coda: Coming Full Circle in "Fathers and Sons"

> Mice: What is the best early training for a writer?
> Y.C.: An unhappy childhood.
>
> —Ernest Hemingway (1935), "Monologue to the Maestro: A High Seas Letter," in *By-Line*, 219

The final Nick Adams story to appear during Hemingway's lifetime, "Fathers and Sons," was published in 1933, nine years after "Indian Camp." Written subsequent to Dr. Clarence Hemingway's suicide by gunshot in 1928, it is a powerfully moving story in which a son reveals his ambivalent love for his dead father. Nicholas Adams, now thirty-eight years old and a writer, drives through a seemingly deserted town with his own small son sleeping by his side. In a lengthy reminiscence, Nick recalls his father's remarkable eyes, how he could see like an eagle, and how he taught him about hunting and fishing and gave him a love for the outdoors.

But his father was very nervous and sentimental, and "like most sentimental people, he was both cruel and abused."[87] He "died in a trap," betrayed by those around him (the cause of his death is omitted). His father was also very "unsound" in advising Nick about sex, and there is a long interlude in which Nick recalls the innocence of his own initial sexual encounters with an Indian girl named Trudy. These memories remind him of his father's dark side. Nick hated the very scent of him, and especially hated to wear his father's undergarments because they smelled like him. He remembers the time he threw away the clothes and lied about it, and how his father whipped him for lying. Afterwards Nick sat in the woodshed with a shotgun, loaded and cocked, watching his father on the porch and wanting to kill him. Later, he went into the Indian camp to visit his girlfriend and get rid of his father's smell. "After [Nick] was fifteen he had shared nothing with him." And yet, "his father had the finest pair of eyes he had ever seen and Nick had loved him very much and for a long time." The memories plague him. In the fall or early spring the sight of nature always reminds him of his father and of just how much a part of Nick he remains. The memories of even the happier early times are not good for him. He wants to get rid of them by writing about them, like throwing away the clothes. But he cannot: "it was still too early for that."

Nick's own son asks, "What was it like, Papa, when you were a little boy and used to hunt with the Indians?" Nick, self-absorbed in his memories, is startled: "He had not even noticed the boy was awake. He looked at him sitting beside him on the seat. He had felt quite alone but this boy had been with him." Very much an Adams father, Nick's response to his son's question is "I don't know." His son persists in asking questions and Nick answers as best he can. Then the boy asks what his grandfather was like and Nick replies, "He's hard to describe." Nick remembers the good things about his father, that he was "a great hunter and fisherman" and "had wonderful eyes." His own son wants Nick to claim that the grandfather was not a better shot than Nick, but Nick replies: "Oh, yes he was. He shot very quickly and beautifully. I'd rather see him shoot than any man I ever knew." He adds, "He was always very disappointed in the way I shot." The boy wants to visit his grandfather's tomb to pray and Nick makes excuses as to why they cannot. The boy will not relent until finally Nick, in an effort to placate his child, ends the story by saying: "We'll have to go. . . . I can see that we'll have to go."

With this reply, the Nick Adams saga, which always seemed, in one way or another, mainly concerned with father-son relationships, ends. There was no way for it to continue. Neither in his life nor in his art could Ernest ever come to grips with his feelings for Clarence. He would remain ambivalent until the day, thirty-three years later, when he followed in his father's footsteps and put a loaded gun to his head.

The final irony in the ending of "Indian Camp" is extratextual, but it resonates eerily and powerfully. The Hemingway reader can never forget that the day would come when the real-life models for Nick and Dr. Adams, like the Ojibwa father in the story, would each die by his own hand.

II

How Craft Readings Contribute to Understanding Stories

In the act of writing, one sees that the way a thing is made controls and is inseparable from the whole meaning of it. The form of a story gives it meaning which any other form would change, and unless the student is able, in some degree, to apprehend the form, he will never apprehend anything else about the work, except what is extrinsic to it as literature.

—Flannery O'Connor, "The Teaching of Literature"

2

Dueling Wounds in "Soldier's Home"

THE RELATION OF TEXTUAL FORM, NARRATIVE ARGUMENT, AND CULTURAL CRITIQUE

> If five or six or more good explainers can keep going why should I interfere with them? Read anything I write for the pleasure of reading it. Whatever else you find will be the measure of what you brought to the reading.
>
> —Hemingway, interview by George Plimpton

> If you're studying literature, the intentions of the writer have to be found in the work itself, and not in his life. Psychology is an interesting subject but hardly the main consideration for the teacher of English.
>
> —Flannery O'Connor, "The Teaching of Literature"

In the previous chapter, I performed an exhaustive reading of a Hemingway story in order to support the validity of three claims: that careful attention to articulated technique is necessary for fully understanding a short story's aesthetic *and* cultural dimensions; that the author is much more than merely a social construction through whom culture speaks without conscious human agency; and that the literary richness of a short story is closer to that of poetry than to most novels and will reward very close critical scrutiny. In this chapter, we will take a different tack and focus on how an examination of the formal properties of a short story can contribute in fruitful ways to scholarly debates about its meaning. In other words, by taking a story that has generated a great deal of biographical and cultural interpretation, and critical debate, and by explaining its textual form and methods of narrative argumentation, I hope to demonstrate how a craft analysis is essential to understanding a story's larger cultural significance.

Because it is both Hemingway's only story about a First World War veteran's homecoming *and* a story that portrays a conflicted mother-son relationship, "Soldier's Home" has been, along with "Big Two-Hearted River" and "Now I Lay Me," a highly contested text in the debate between critics who, following Philip Young, locate war trauma at the heart of Hemingway's fiction and other critics who instead emphasize the author's unhappy childhood (I have previously labeled these the "war-wound thesis" and the "childhood-wound thesis" respectively).[1] One early "war-wound" critic, Frederick J. Hoffman, speaking of the "unreasonable wound" Hemingway suffered in 1918 and his consequent repetition compulsion, sees the story as the "sharpest portrait" in 1920s fiction of the returning veteran. "In the absence of any clearly defined reasons for having fought," according to Hoffman, "the returned soldier felt hurt, ill at ease, uncertain of his future, 'disenchanted.'" Like other veterans, Hemingway's Harold Krebs is unable to "adjust to the life he had left" for the war; he no longer loves anyone and cannot "bring himself to enjoy or respect his family, his home." And so he must go away.[2]

Although Young did not address "Soldier's Home" in his book, in which his main interest was confined to stories about either Nick Adams or the "Hemingway code," nevertheless his war-wound thesis has echoed endlessly in Hemingway scholarship. For example, Robert Penn Warren observes that the "battlefields of *A Farewell to Arms*" explain young Krebs, "who came back to a Middle-Western town to accept his own slow disintegration." In accord with a conclusion drawn earlier by Sheridan Baker, Richard Hasbany states that Nick Adams's trauma in "Big Two-Hearted River" can be better understood in light of Krebs's wartime experiences. Leo Gurko declares that "Hemingway's particularly bad case of postwar jitters was described with special delicacy and insight" in "Soldier's Home." Arthur Waldhorn sees Krebs as having been "shocked into psychic disorientation . . . by the demands of a society whose values" he rejects. Krebs's "silence is a wordless metaphor expressing outrage against the chaos of the universe and the isolation of the individual." Scott Donaldson contrasts Krebs's world as formed by his wartime experiences with the world of his hometown, and concludes that his "world was full of unreasonable pain and unconscionable suffering and inexplicable violence." James R. Mellow calls the story "a classic in the literature of alienation following World War I, a definition of a generation returned from the war, dissatisfied with the goals and values of American life." And Joseph DeFalco asserts that Krebs's war experiences have made him unable to accept the old norms: "Church, family, and society no longer command allegiance from the individual who has experienced the purgatorial initiation of war."[3]

The principal "childhood-wound" critic, however, considers Krebs's wartime experiences barely worth noting. Instead, Kenneth S. Lynn sees the story as a transmutation into fiction of Hemingway's own troubled postwar response to his family and as an attack by the author on his mother, akin to the one in "The Doctor and the Doctor's Wife," in which Hemingway's home town of Oak Park, Illinois, has been changed to a "town in Oklahoma." Observing that Krebs's last name derives from Hemingway's comrade, Krebs Friend, "who had married a woman fully old enough to be his mother" (but ignoring in his analysis of the story that Friend was also a shell-shocked veteran), Lynn focuses on the "portrayal of Mrs. Krebs's tyranny" that he regards as the story's triumph. He concludes with this assessment:

> Soldier's Home" is the story of a young man's struggle to separate from home, and Hemingway packed it with a lifetime of revulsion and outrage. Nevertheless, the utterly unrelenting, utterly unqualified characterization of Mrs. Krebs as a monster revealed that the author was in fact still in thrall to her flesh-and-blood counterpart.[4]

Although Lynn's relatively more recent perspective has influenced fewer critics of "Soldier's Home" than has Young's, it has been followed by a number of non-war-wound interpretations. Hemingway's most perceptive biographer, Michael Reynolds, observes that "far beneath its surface" the story is, among other things, "about Hemingway's anticipation of his parents' inability to accept his fiction." J. Gerald Kennedy and Kirk Curnutt make an excellent argument that the story may also represent, perhaps consciously, Hemingway's effort to declare his literary independence from his maternal surrogate and mentor, Gertrude Stein, whose recent experimental *Geography and Plays* he deliberately signifies on in a sentence about the Rhine not showing. And J. F. Kobler unpersuasively attempts to question the extent of Krebs's combat experience in order to view the story as Hemingway's "carefully constructed *mea culpa* for the lies he had told and for the truths he had allowed the press to distort regarding his own role, duties, and injury on the Italian front in 1918."[5]

As these conflicting interpretations demonstrate, "Soldier's Home" is a complex story. But it is also a structurally divided one as well: bifurcated into two nearly equal parts of summary exposition and scenic development in which the war-wound interpretation (here manifested in the theme of a veteran's postwar alienation) derives from the first half of the text and the childhood-wound interpretation from the second half. Therefore, unless one is foolish enough to insist on a predominant meaning, both interpretations have merit. I cannot fault Hoffman; anyone writing about literary responses to the war would be remiss not to see this story as a dramatization of postwar disillusionment and alienation. Nor can I blame Lynn for searching out the biographical relevance of the text (he is, after all, writing a biography), even if the use of fiction as biographical evidence can lead to a misunderstanding of that fiction *qua* fiction (e.g., how can the characterization of Mrs. Krebs be "utterly unqualified" unless we regard her *only* as a non-fictional depiction of Grace Hall Hemingway?).

On the other hand, no story can be satisfactorily interpreted by de-emphasizing half of its text. By neglecting the story's form and instead selectively strip mining it for cultural and biographical content, critics have missed the manner of Hemingway's narrative argument as well as the considerable art that underlies it, for *what* "Soldier's Home" really means depends on *how* it means. Despite the story's neat division into summary exposition that points to one interpretation and scenic development that points to another, there must exist the relationship that normally obtains between these two elements of a realist text (certainly, at least, of a non-postmodernist text). That is, exposition provides us with the informational context necessary to understand development, and development illustrates and formally flows from exposition. Were this not so, then one or the other would be gratuitous and the story would make no sense.

If we divide the story into its constituent halves, making it, in effect, two separate stories, it becomes clear how each needs the other. The first part would be like "Mr. and Mrs. Elliot," a story consisting of pure summary: undramatized, unconvincing, and, lacking the verisimilitude that scene contributes, unsatisfactory as a narrative. Such a story would be but a profile of a character, an extended passage of complex cultural codes without specific actions or a hermeneutic code. The entire piece would unfold in the past progressive tense: what Krebs generally "was doing" and "was thinking" over a period of time. On the other hand, the second part of the text by itself would recall Frank O'Connor's objections to "Hills Like White Elephants," which he found in want of "the familiar element" (by which he meant that "Hills" needed more exposition).[6] Although I strongly disagree with this assessment of "Hills"—which in *Art Matters* I analyzed as a successful experiment by Hemingway of having exposition emerge from his innovative constructive dialogue techniques—nevertheless O'Connor's general point is well taken.[7] The second part of "Soldier's Home," standing alone, does not contain enough exposition to make its scenes work, and thus the reader would correctly conclude that necessary information was being withheld. How could the reader properly assess whether Krebs, or his mother, is being reasonable or not? How would we know where our sympathies should lie? Is the story about a lazy young man and his concerned loving mother? Is it about an emotionally disturbed veteran and his insensitive, uncomprehending mother? There would be no way to tell.

Any adequate interpretation of the story must therefore take into account both of these elements—exposition and development, summary and scene—because each is an indispensable part of how the story functions: its particular structure, its narrative argument, and its terrain of potential meaning. In other words, the "either/or" attitude that critics have brought to this story needs to be replaced by a "both/and" reading that subsumes the war-wound and childhood-wound interpretations within a more inclusive perspective that engages the aesthetic form and cultural implications of the *entire* text.

I

Unlike scene, especially scene that is mostly dialogue, summary exposition inherently foregrounds epistemological questions—how reliable is the narrator? This is particularly true when exposition is lengthy and unsubstantiated by scene, which, by convention, is generally considered reliable when presented in the third-person. Because exposition, or *diegesis,* is by its nature less convincing than scene, or *mimesis,* and because it raises these epistemological questions, Hemingway employs narrative strategies to make the often dubious exposition more convincing and also to raise questions about the reliability of the scenes. Through craft, he thereby balances the story's conflicting exposition and scenic development, as well as the interpretations that derive from them.

This equilibration of meaning begins in the deliberate ambiguity of the story's title. With Hemingway's penchant for symbolic, allusive, and intertextual titles—as opposed to neutral, descriptive ones (e.g., "Krebs's Home")—he begins his narrative argument by specifically categorizing Krebs as "soldier" rather than as son, student, former Marine, Oklahoman, American, or just plain Krebs. "Soldier" points to the exposition and the war trauma thesis, "Home" to the scenes and the conflicted mother-son relationship. The two words, and the interpretations they signify, are linked by an apostrophe and an "s." But the nature of this construction is purposefully ambiguous. If it indicates the possessive case, then the title can be restated as "Home of the Soldier," which emphasizes the home. But if it is merely a contraction, then the title could be rewritten as "Soldier Is Home," highlighting the soldier. And there is also a third possibility to increase the ambiguity; in the United States the term "soldiers' home" (often misspelled as "soldier's home") has been, since the Civil War, a common vernacular expression for a chronic care facility for physically or emotionally incapacitated veterans.[8]

Throughout the story, Hemingway's sympathies are with Krebs, but he disguises this in the exposition in order to hide his bias from the reader, making the exposition, and the disillusioned war veteran interpretation that derives from it, more persuasive. In the first three paragraphs he adopts a seemingly "objective," reportorial narrative voice in which he appears to be presenting just some "facts" in a random fashion:

> Krebs went to the war from a Methodist college in Kansas. There is a picture which shows him among his fraternity brothers, all of them wearing exactly the same height and style collar. He enlisted in the Marines in 1917 and did not return to the United States until the second division returned from the Rhine in the summer of 1919.
>
> There is a picture which shows him on the Rhine with two German girls and another corporal. Krebs and the corporal look too big for their uniforms. The German girls are not beautiful. The Rhine does not show in the picture.
>
> By the time Krebs returned to his home town in Oklahoma the greeting of heroes was over. He came back much too late. The men from the town who had been drafted had all been welcomed elaborately on their return. There had been a great deal of hysteria. Now the reaction had set in. People seemed to think it was rather ridiculous for Krebs to be getting back so late, years after the war was over.[9]

A war-wound critic could make much of these two snapshots. In the prewar photograph, Krebs is pictured in a male social organization and no women are present; he attends a denominational educational institution; and he fits in easily, his conformity implied by the collars that mark the fraternity brothers as indistinguishable. The second photograph pictures him quite differently in a way that suggests the changes he has undergone during the war. The first sentence of the second paragraph presents a fairly common image: two soldier-buddies on the Rhine with a couple of German women. But the next three sentences quickly undercut that image.

Although he is in uniform, it fits him less well than did the clothing of the prewar photograph. This suggests that he has become more individualistic and, since he is too big for his uniform, that he has "grown" in some sense as a result of his wartime experiences. The presence of the German women implies a sexual involvement that was lacking in the earlier picture. However, the women are not beautiful and the Rhine does not show. Like a man who is trying to recall a pleasant dream upon awakening but who is fighting a losing battle with the dreamwork of his psyche, Krebs is trying to hang onto the good feelings he once had as a soldier in Europe: what it was like to have enjoyed soldierly camaraderie, to have been with a woman, and to have won a war. But the photograph makes these memories elusive by problematizing the referent to which they are attached. Continuing this line of inquiry, we could speculate that if there were a third photograph, one taken in the story's present, it would show Krebs casually dressed, sitting by himself on his mother's front porch, and watching the young women walk by on the other side of the street. He would be a part of no social organization (college fraternity or military); he would have no woman (his sisters and mother would be the only females in his life); and he would be on a street in his home town. What emerges from this hypothetical picture is that he is isolated and inert, without function or goal. His wartime experiences, both good and bad, have therefore in some way incapacitated him; he feels alienated from the homefront, and this has somehow vitiated his energy.

What this exposition says is fairly clear, and one must assume that Hemingway wants the reader to believe it because a third-person narrator perceived from the start as duplicitous (in the manner of, say, Gogol or Hawthorne) would wreck this story. Therefore, what is most significant from a technical viewpoint is not what the exposition says, but the strategies of narrative argumentation that the author employs to get us to believe it. The emotional distance and apparent disinterestedness of the prose in the first two paragraphs give the reader no cause to suspect that the narrator has hidden motives. The device of the two photographs further supports this matter-of-fact exposition, so that the reader will not stop to think that Hemingway is deliberately choosing which pictures to present as well as what details to report. Moreover, the first paragraph seems disjointed, as though the narrator is merely listing a number of facts: information, a description of a picture, and some additional information. But one of these facts, which readers today would likely glide over but that readers in 1924 would have immediately recognized, is that Krebs served in the renowned Marine Brigade of the Second Division. As Steven Trout points out, this unit was one of the earliest to arrive in France, and it "saw more combat than ninety percent of the A.E.F." (American Expeditionary Force). Trout further observes that of the twenty-nine American combat divisions that fought on the Western Front, each at full strength containing 27,000 men, "the Second suffered the highest number of casualties—approximately 18,000 wounded and 5,000 killed—and received the highest number of replacements—more than 35,000 men."[10] By merely mentioning Krebs's unit, then, Hemingway gets the contemporary reader to sympathize with him. But if Hemingway is planning something more, it is not immediately discernible.

The third paragraph, which introduces the first explicit evidence of the disillusioned veteran theme, seems narrated in an equally dispassionate manner, even though the narrator makes a number of highly dubious statements. Because of the seemingly objective presentation, however, the reader accepts the following "facts": the drafted men were elaborately welcomed on their return home; this hysterical greeting of heroes subsequently led to a reaction against further celebrations; Krebs returned much too late for a hero's welcome; and the townspeople thought it ridiculous for him to have come back so late. From these facts the reader infers that drafted men returned before enlisted men. The passage also strongly implies, in the way it singles out Krebs, that his late return resulted from his having enlisted and that enlisting was unusual.[11]

But let's take a closer look at the "logic" employed in the third paragraph. According to the text, Krebs returned to the United States with the Second Division in the summer of 1919, which would be seven to nine months after the Armistice of November 1918. In fact, this date can be fixed precisely; Steven Trout informs us that "the official order of battle for the A.E.F. confirms that the Second Division arrived in Hoboken [New Jersey] on 3 August 1919."[12] Yet, if "years" really have passed between the end of the war and his return to his hometown, then he did not come home for at least a year after his return stateside. If he was mustered out upon his arrival in the United States, then he chose to remain away from home for another year. Even if, having enlisted, he still had another year to serve—and this is a virtual impossibility, given the almost complete demobilization of the A.E.F. between the Armistice and the summer of 1919[13]—certainly he would have had a furlough coming to him before that. Moreover, the implication that men who were drafted came home before those who volunteered is ludicrous, as is the suggestion that enlisting was unusual. In the First World War, 42 percent of America's soldiers were enlistees.[14]

If the last sentence of the third paragraph were literally true, and Krebs returned "years after the war was over" (which would place the date of the story's fabula closer to the 1924 date of its narration than to 1919), then both the alienated veteran thesis and the unhappy son thesis could use this as supporting evidence by asking why he stayed away and coming up with different answers to this question. But it would be an act of extreme bad faith for an author to leave such critical information out of his exposition. It would not be an example of Hemingway's technique of omission, making readers feel something more than they understand, but of the suppression of vital information—highlighting a discrepancy in dates in the opening paragraphs and then letting it remain an inexplicable (and unexplorable) mystery for the rest of the story. Such a clumsy use of omission might have served as a trick to contribute to the hermeneutic code, but it would have been completely atypical for Hemingway who, whenever he erred in employing omission, which was seldom, inevitably erred on the side of subtlety and not of heavy-handedness. Therefore, the last sentence *cannot* be read literally. Instead, it must be viewed as the narrator's representation in free indirect speech of Krebs's own sense of the townspeople's indifferent response to him. In free indirect speech, also known as free indirect discourse, the voices of the narrator and the character merge. The result is a combination of the narrator's words and the speech, feelings, and/or thoughts of the character. Free indirect speech is the polar opposite of the external focalization we usually associate with Hemingway, which is why this story is unusual in the Hemingway canon and also perhaps why critics have so easily accepted these opening three paragraphs at face value.[15]

Because I will later argue that elements from the story's 1924 time of narration found their way into the text, it is necessary to establish beyond a doubt that Krebs returns home in 1919, and that the sentence about him "returning years after the war was over" is indeed his own hyperbolic feeling narrated in free indirect speech and not literally true. Although an airtight case could be made for dating Krebs's return home in 1919 by examining the story as fictionalized autobiography, I will abstain from such an approach because it would merely echo the excellent work of Hemingway's biographers. Besides, Krebs's war experiences, unlike those of Nick Adams, are completely different from Hemingway's and, furthermore, there is plenty of internal textual evidence for a 1919 date. For example, in the fourth paragraph we read: "His town had heard too many atrocity stories to be thrilled by actualities." This is elaborated upon in the next paragraph, in which the townspeople's "patriotism" causes them to believe stories about "German women found chained to machine guns[.]" Such home-front credulity still existed in 1919, but by 1924 this sort of wartime propaganda had been thoroughly discredited and forgotten. Later on, we read: "He did not want to leave Germany. He did not want to come home. Still, he had come home. He sat on the front porch." The segue from Germany to the front porch, like the prose in which it is reported, seems straightforward enough and, since we know that Krebs arrived in the United States in August 1919, there seems no reason to believe that it took him five years to find Oklahoma. Two paragraphs later, Krebs is devouring a book on the war, reading about the battles he fought in, "the most interesting reading he had ever done." Given this level of interest, are we to believe that for five years it never occurred to him to read a book about the war? The text continues: "He looked forward with a good feeling to reading all the really good histories when they would come out with good detail maps." Such books existed by 1924, but not in 1919. In short, then, the third paragraph and the above evidence only make sense for a story set in 1919; if the story, written by a writer who prided himself on getting the details right, were set later there would be no way to account for any of these statements.

Hemingway's use of free indirect discourse also occurs earlier in the third paragraph, in such overblown phrases as "the greeting of heroes" and equally subjective, vague phrases like "welcomed elaborately" and "a great deal of hysteria" that should signal us that we are beginning to shift from the carefully dispassionate voice of the narrator that controlled the first two paragraphs into the consciousness of his unappreciated protagonist.[16] When we then read that "[p]eople seemed to think it was rather ridiculous for Krebs to be getting back so late," the question that should occur to the careful reader is, "seemed to whom?" Surely, Hemingway is not suddenly employing omniscient narration (which he abhorred), nor is he focalizing through the townspeople, but through Krebs, as the Jamesian use of "seemed" (i.e., "seemed [to Krebs] to think") makes clear. In addition, if these sentences were fully in the narrator's voice and if Krebs literally did return years later, then "who had been drafted" could easily have been replaced by "who had returned earlier," and the sentence would no longer be historically inaccurate. Instead, Hemingway merged the voices of Krebs and the narrator in free indirect speech. The questionable suggestions as to why Krebs missed out on the celebrations show just how strongly Hemingway identifies with his protagonist. The lengths to which he went to disguise that identification demonstrate how important it was for him to make the exposition convincing enough to hold its own with the later scenes.

Even if we were inclined to wonder about this exposition, to step back for a moment and examine Hemingway's attempts to persuade us, the next paragraph, which discusses how Krebs was compelled to lie about his war experiences in order to be heard, begins with some further expository information that is effectively tossed into the story by way of an inertly constructed, nonrestrictive clause—"At first Krebs, who had been at Belleau Wood, Soissons, the Champagne, St. Mihiel and in the Argonne did not want to talk about the war at all." These were among the bloodiest battles in which American troops fought; in 1924 this list would evoke in the reader an immediate visceral sympathy for Krebs. At Belleau Wood alone, in which the final German offensive nearly managed to reach Paris, many Second Division units lost more than 50 percent of their men.[17] A similar list from the Second World War might read: Salerno, San Pietro, the Rapido River, Monte Casino, and the advance from the Anzio bridgehead through Rome.[18] The purpose of both the dispassionate presentation and the grim list of battles is to get the reader to sympathize with Krebs, and to establish the credibility of the exposition well enough so that the reader will not look too closely at how this effect is being accomplished.

Once Hemingway gets the reader past the third paragraph, the rest of the exposition unfolds with an impressive tightness of argument. Every one of the five main sections of exposition leads smoothly into the next, often with the first sentence of each providing a graceful transition. The first three paragraphs establish Krebs's background and introduce the theme of a veteran's alienation. The second section shows more specifically how the townspeople's failure to understand him produced this alienation. Forced to lie to the insensitive townspeople about his wartime experiences by attributing to himself the experiences of other soldiers, "Krebs acquired the nausea in regard to experience that is the result of untruth or exaggeration" (note how Hemingway again tries to establish distance between the narrator and Krebs here by employing an uncharacteristically elaborate verbosity rather than by simply saying that "lying made Krebs nauseous").

Krebs is compelled to pose, and in "this way he lost everything." The third section focuses on Krebs's daily activities and illustrates the behavior of a man who has lost everything. The reader believes that Krebs's passive, desultory behavior has resulted from the process of alienation described in the previous section.

Before the war, Krebs was not allowed to use his father's car; the third section ends, "Now, after the war, it was the same car." This suggestion about how his rights to the car have not changed leads to the lengthy fourth section of exposition, which begins, "Nothing was changed in the town except that the young girls had grown up." In this section, we see Krebs's desires for the "young girls" wax as he contemplates them and wane as he thinks about the effort he would have to expend to get them. Completely eschewing Hemingway's trademark use of external focalization, his narrator makes full use of his access to Krebs's consciousness as the free indirect speech of the passage approaches interior monologue. Krebs rationalizes his passivity, but because the exposition is so firmly established by this point, the reader attributes that passivity to a veteran's alienation and buys Krebs's rationalizations. The section concludes with Krebs deciding that the hometown women are not worth the effort. "Not now when things were getting good again." This sentence leads into the fifth and final section of the exposition, in which Krebs is reading about the war. He is learning what happened to him, and this makes him feel better. The exposition thus leaves off with Krebs still fighting his demons, the inner conflicts caused by the war.

However persuasively the exposition argues the disillusioned veteran thesis, a childhood-wound critic could point out that Hemingway deliberately offers a prewar photograph of Krebs at college in Kansas and avoids showing us any image of the soldier at home before he was a soldier. Our knowledge of his prewar experiences in his home must therefore be deduced from the scenes presented later in the story—scenes that appear to demonstrate Mrs. Krebs's unsuitability as a mother and the ease with which she can manipulate and infantilize her son. Three gestures from the climactic breakfast scene capture the nature of Krebs's relationship with his mother, a relationship that surely had a long foreground before the war. In the first gesture, Mrs. Krebs removes her glasses after asking him if he has made a decision about his future. On the one hand, this gesture seems to imply that she either cannot, or does not want to "see" him, even though she seems "worried" and does not ask him questions "in a mean way." From another perspective, Mrs. Krebs's removal of her glasses can be viewed as an attention-getting, dramatic gesture in which she aggressively pins her emotionally wriggling and sprawling son with her gaze and formulated phrases—"Have you decided what you are going to do yet, Harold?" and "God has some work for every one to do[.]"[19] A few lines later, after his mother has spoken about God's Kingdom, revealed her worries about the "temptations" he must have been exposed to during the war ("I know how weak men are"), and stated that she prays for him "all day long," he makes his own significant gesture: "Krebs looked at the bacon fat hardening on his plate." The hardening bacon fat is an objective correlative of Krebs's feelings toward his mother. The image is especially effective because it is associated with the act of a mother feeding her son; Mrs. Krebs's nourishment is unnurturing. The food is good but the "nipple," as psychiatrist Harry Stack Sullivan would put it, is "bad."[20] There is also an interesting comic undertone to this notion that Mrs. Krebs's nourishment fails to nourish. Having entered the room with a "superbreakfast" of eggs, bacon, buckwheat cakes, and a jug of maple syrup, she peppers her hungry son with annoying questions that can only be responded to, if at all, with lengthy explanations, and she will not shut up long enough for him to eat anything.[21] The fact that the bacon fat is in the process of "hardening" rather than already hardened indicates, on the literal level, that poor Krebs is watching his food grow increasingly cold and unappetizing as he endures his mother's verbal bombardment. The breakfast, by the way, never does get eaten.

The final significant gesture occurs after Krebs's statement that he does not love anybody causes his mother to cry. She refuses to accept his explanations and buries her head in her hands. First he holds her, then kisses her hair. She puts her face up to him and reminds him of how she held him next to her heart when he was a baby. He feels "sick and vaguely nauseated," calls her "Mummy," and promises to "try and be a good boy" for her. Having thoroughly infantilized him, she then manipulates him into kneeling beside her on the floor while she prays for him. These three gestures, then, seem to characterize their relationship: her inability to see him for who he is and her visual/verbal assault on him, his resentment of her, and his inevitable capitulation to her demands. As Krebs has only been home for a month, it would appear that this is what their relationship has been like for a long time, an assumption borne out by such sentences as "Krebs felt embarrassed and resentful *as always*" (italics mine).

In order that the exposition and the scenes might be equally convincing, rendering it impossible for a reader to make either the alienated veteran interpretation or the unhappy son interpretation paramount, Hemingway found ways to make the former more persuasive; he also worked to undermine the latter, mainly by bringing his sympathies for Krebs out into the open where no reader could miss them. The presence of the narrator's sympathy for his protagonist is pervasive in the scenes, but rather than engage in a full-blown explication of these passages I will merely point out two instances where the narrator intrudes with unnecessary diegetic commentary that decreases the mimetic effectiveness of the scenes.

The first of these comments occurs after Mrs. Krebs says that everyone is in God's Kingdom. To this point, Krebs has responded to her speeches with either silence or else unenthusiastic monosyllabic replies. But here the response is an observation by the narrator: "Krebs felt embarrassed and resentful as always." After her next speech, the response is: "Krebs looked at the bacon fat hardening on his plate." Although the first response is appropriate since Hemingway has rejected external focalization in this story and instead chosen to employ his legitimate access to the mind of his central consciousness, the second response renders it superfluous. The second employs an objective correlative to show Krebs's feelings with a perfectly selected detail; by contrast, the first merely tells about it. A psychobiographer might call this a slip and conclude that Hemingway's hatred of his mother caused him to intrude, but from a technical perspective the sentence, whether or not an unconscious slip, serves the purpose of slightly decreasing the effectiveness of the scene by directing the reader's attention away from Krebs and toward the narrator. Another such sentence occurs a page later. After his mother tells Krebs how she held him next to her heart when he was "a tiny baby," the response is: "Krebs felt sick and vaguely nauseated." As before, this directly stated commentary is unnecessary (the entire scene is already making the reader feel sick and vaguely nauseated) and it again turns the reader's attention toward the narrator. With the narrator's sympathies for his protagonist now out in the open, the identification between narrator and character is complete. The denouement is Krebs's decision to go away, and the free indirect discourse of the story's final passage fully merges the narrator's and Krebs's voices.

If Hemingway's second diegetic comment is, as I believe it to be, deliberate, so too is his use of the word "nauseated," the key verbal clue that links the scenes with the exposition. Krebs feels nauseous because his mother "made him lie" about his feelings. In the second section of the exposition, lying about his war experiences gave him "nausea." Moreover, in the fourth section of exposition, the reason why he does not actively seek one of the hometown women is because he "did not want to tell any more lies," which would logically lead, although Hemingway skillfully omits directly stating it, to more nausea:

> [1] Vaguely he wanted a girl but he did not want to have to work to get her. [2] He would have liked to have a girl but he did not want to have to spend a long time getting her. [3] He did not want to get into the intrigue and politics. [4] He did not want to have to do any courting. [5] He did not want to tell any more lies. [6] It wasn't worth it.

This passage follows one in which the young women are introduced as a "pattern" that he likes: their good looks, youth, "round Dutch collars above their sweaters," "silk stockings and flat shoes," "bobbed hair and the way they walked" under "the shade of the trees" on the other side of the street. In that passage, the word "like" is repeated six times and then countered by a sentence in which he "did not like them." In the second passage (quoted above), he at first "wants" one of these women, but this is followed by four uses of "did not want." The second sentence of the above passage reiterates the first, but expands it through a deliberate and awkward verbosity that mimics the "chore" of having to get a woman. That bloated sentence then collapses into four progressively shorter declarative statements leading to the free indirect, "It wasn't worth it." (The final sentence could also be an example of "immediate speech," Krebs's exact thoughts in his own words.)[22]

In these two passages, the one describing his attraction to the young women, the other his repulsion at the effort of getting a woman, Krebs's alternative feelings are conveyed by Hemingway's use of "like" and "did not want." As the fourth section of exposition proceeds, he wavers between these opposing feelings more and more rapidly until, at the end of the section, his ambivalence at last turns maddening:

> He would like to have one of them. But it was not worth it. They were such a nice pattern. He liked the pattern. It was exciting. But he would

> not go through all the talking. He did not want one badly enough. He liked to look at them all, though. It was not worth it. Not now when things were getting good again.

Like T. S. Eliot's hollow men, Krebs finds that "Between the idea / And the reality / Between the motion / And the act / Falls the Shadow[.]"[23]

The shadow that renders Krebs incapable of action and that constitutes the crux of the story is stated in three sentences of free indirect speech that follow immediately after his first statement that the young women are not worth it: "He did not want any consequences. He did not want any consequences ever again. He wanted to live along without consequences." Buried in the exposition, placed between the passage that describes his ambivalence toward the women and a passage in which he rationalizes that ambivalence, these three sentences underlie Krebs's thoughts and actions throughout *both the exposition and the scenes,* and thus form the main thread that unites the two parts of the story. His desire to avoid consequences is his single overriding motivation. He fondly recalls the French and German women because relationships with them were uncomplicated and without consequence: "That was the thing about French girls and German girls. There was not all this talking. You couldn't talk much and you did not need to talk. It was simple and you were friends." He wants the hometown women yet does not act on these desires because these young women are too complex and not worth the consequences: "But here at home it was all too complicated." He is attracted to his little sister because he can shrug off her demands and she will still love him. But his mother repels him because her demands are difficult and unavoidable. His father he avoids altogether. He lies because it is the easiest way to avoid complications, but his lies consequently make him nauseous by alienating him from his own experiences and thereby cause him even more complications.

In college and in war Krebs did not have to think or make decisions; he merely did "the one thing, the only thing for a man to do, easily and naturally[.]" At home he wants to create a similar kind of world, one without complications and consequences, but he cannot. So he tries to disappear into his bed, or a book, or the sports pages, or the internal rhyme of "the cool dark of the pool room." Yet, just when "things were getting good again[,]" reality impinges and flushes him out. When things get too complicated, "Hare"—his sister Helen's nickname for him—bolts; the road to Kansas City is the path of least resistance. The story ends with a *float off*[24] in free indirect speech in which Krebs's voice is a stronger presence than that of the narrator's with which it merges:

> There would be one more scene maybe before he got away. He would not go down to his father's office. He would miss that one. He wanted his life to go smoothly. It had just gotten going that way. Well, that was all over now, anyway. He would go over to the schoolyard and watch Helen play indoor baseball.

The illustrative stamp of the story will take place after the narrative is over. It consists of the poignant image of Krebs, in his futile attempt to escape life's complications, halting just long enough to peer into a world from which he is irrevocably cut off, the seemingly simple world of childhood. This is the point to which both his wartime experiences and his filial experiences have brought him, the logical denouement of his story, beyond which this text and its intrinsic interpretive terrain cannot go.

II

"Soldier's Home," then, is a tale about a disillusioned war veteran *and* a conflicted mother-son relationship. But it is also a great deal more. Having examined the story's form and argument, I would like to conclude with some additional analysis on how understanding its formal aspects and technical methods is essential to grasping its larger cultural significance. The two parts of the text are connected by Krebs's desire to avoid complications, but they are also linked through craft by a recurrent rhetorical strategy in which a "normal" popular image is presented and then immediately problematized. These images are found in both the exposition and the scenes, and speak to an important cultural issue—the ways in which fundamental social constructs and values seemed to be everywhere disintegrating in the mid-1920s. "Soldier's Home" thus expresses not only the "social reality" of veterans' 1919 postwar alienation and the personal reality of its author's resentment of his mother, but also represents what Raymond Williams has described as a "structure of feeling that is lived and experienced but not yet quite arranged"[25]—the "social experience" of a society that in the mid-1920s was perceived to be losing its coherence.[26] In other words, the approximately five-year difference between the time in which the story is set and the time in which it was written contributes to its deeper cultural implications. In "Soldier's Home," meaning is produced by the dynamic and recursive interplay between a narrator/author writing in 1924 and a fictional protagonist living in 1919.

To explain this, I need to coin a new critical term—*dialogical textualization.* I do not intend this term in a Bakhtinian sense—that all texts (especially novels) are in constant dialogue with previous and later texts, what we think of as intertextuality, and that there is a spectrum from dialogism (heteroglossic, polyphonous, and multivocal) to monologism (univocal). Rather, by a *dialogical text* I mean a text in which the gap between the time in which the narrative takes place (the fabula) and when it is written (the moment of narration) creates a sort of dialogue between the two time periods. In a dialogical text, elements of the present—Williams's "structure of feeling" that is felt but not yet fully understood—anachronistically and inevitably find their way into the narrative. Sometimes, this is intentional on the author's part. For example, in *The Scarlet Letter,* Nathaniel Hawthorne deliberately and often explicitly sets up contrasts between the mid-seventeenth and mid-nineteenth centuries. In *The Red Badge of Courage,* written by an author born in 1870, Stephen Crane represents the experience of fighting in the Civil War by drawing upon his observations of the experience of labor in a steel mill in the 1890s. That novella's verisimilitude derives from the fact that these two seemingly disparate experiences turned out to have much in common. In these examples, the authors set their narratives in a fabula they did not personally experience. Even though they thoroughly studied the "social reality" of those times in books they read, there is no way they could fully depict the "social experience" of periods in which they had not lived.

But you can also have a dialogical text in narratives in which the author experienced both the time of the fabula and that of the narration. For instance, Mark Twain lived through the 1840s, the period of slavery in which *Adventures of Huckleberry Finn* takes place, and the late 1870s and early 1880s, the post-Reconstruction decade during which he wrote the novel. The controversial ending of *Huck Finn,* although it takes place in 1845, is, because of its dialogical textualization, as much what I term a *symbolic historical representation* of the many failures of Reconstruction (e.g., the paradox of "freeing a free man," which is what Huck and Tom try to do in freeing Jim when he's already free, or the post-Reconstruction southern white concept of "gradualism" in allowing ex-slaves their full freedom, as embodied in Tom's evasion schemes) as it is a *reflection* on the situation of a fugitive slave in the antebellum South.[27]

The gap between the fabula and the time of narration in "Soldier's Home" is shorter than in *Huck Finn,* but not without its effect. Simply put, Hemingway and his culture were not the same in 1924 as they were in 1919, and his experiential knowledge in 1924 pervades his representation of 1919 in this story of a soldier's return home. Therefore, the story combines elements of Hemingway's retrospective depiction of "social reality" as it was in 1919 *and* his felt "personal/social experience" of the intervening half-decade. The popular cultural images that dissolve or are problematized in "Soldier's Home," which represent the social institutions that seemed to be disintegrating or in transition by the mid-1920s, derive from the text's dialogical perspective.

The photograph in the second paragraph presents one such popular image—two triumphant American soldiers in Germany with their *Fräuleins,* the symbolic fruits of military victory—but the image is immediately undercut as the women are not beautiful and the Rhine River does not show.[28] Analogously, the fruits of the war that President Woodrow Wilson disingenuously claimed was waged to "make the world safe for democracy" were proving equally illusory. Between the Armistice of 1918 and the spring of 1924, when Hemingway was writing "Soldier's Home," the United States turned its back on the League of Nations, France and Belgium invaded the Ruhr, bloody civil insurrections in Spain and Italy were followed by military coups, the Russian civil war led to an ominous treaty between Russia and Germany, and yet another savage Greco-Turkish War erupted. On the homefront during that same short span of time, the hypocritical Wilson's putative democratic ideals were mocked by the Volstead Act, the Red Scare, the Palmer raids, nationwide urban race massacres directed against peaceful African American citizens, the outrage of presidential candidate Eugene V. Debs being forced to campaign from a federal penitentiary for having criticized the war, several major government corruption scandals (including the infamous Veteran's Bureau scandal of 1923 in which government officials stole money that was supposed to provide for the needs of disabled veterans), the Black Sox scandal (the sports pages that provide Krebs with one of his few pleasures were, that summer, charting the course of Hemingway's hometown team on its way to throwing the World Series in the fall of 1919), the first half of a decade-long farm depression, the rise of the Ku Klux Klan to political power in the South and Midwest (which led to the collapse of civil government in Krebs's Oklahoma in the fall of 1923), pervasive xenophobia, the immigration restriction acts, and a torrent of religious fanaticism (so nicely captured in the character of Mrs. Krebs). In "Soldier's Home" and the change in Krebs from military conqueror to enervated son we see in miniature what Marc Dolan has identified as the "narrative transit of mood" that underlies the myth of the Lost Generation—a transit "from joy to dissipation" in a decade that "began with exhilaration and ended in deflation."[29]

Another qualified popular image is that of the "good-looking young girls" with their odd combination of the morally conventional (Dutch collars, sweaters, flat shoes) and the shockingly new (bobbed hair, silk stockings).[30] The appeal of this image is seen in Krebs's normal healthy desire for these young women, but the image is problematized by his anxious avoidance of them and his rationalization of his failure to act. Krebs returned from the war to find an incipient sexual and gender revolution taking place, and the "nice pattern" he silently observes is, as he suspects, a good deal more complicated than it appears to be. These young women, who had grown up while Krebs was in Europe, were on the verge of open rebellion against the society into which they had been born. They were a significant part of the workforce, eager to escape the stultification of small-town life, and openly questioning the imprisoning sex and gender roles to which Krebs's mother still clings. *Partially* aping the dress of their flapper sisters in the speakeasies of the big cities, this generation of what Mrs. Krebs calls "nice girls" would in the 1920s engage in hitherto unheard-of promiscuity and help to inaugurate a new era of widespread birth control, rampant venereal disease, and increased divorce rates.

Although their cultural codes elude Krebs—who cannot read the mixed signifiers of their attire and can only sense in them an intricate system of "already defined alliances and shifting feuds" that he does not possess the "energy or the courage" to penetrate (in any sense of the word)—nevertheless his attitude expresses the general male response to a phenomenon that surprised, excited, baffled, and frightened them. Furthermore, Hemingway's geopolitical language of "alliances" and "shifting feuds" links these women to the actions of European nations, both before and after the Great War, making Krebs representative of the United States in its ambivalent and confused response to European politics. Krebs, like his country in the 1920s and later in the 1930s, wavers between intervention and isolationism.

What is especially interesting about the description of the young women in "Soldier's Home" is their manifest dialogical textualization. It is not believable that young women in a town in Oklahoma in 1919, where reactionary social attitudes prevailed, would have bobbed their hair and worn silk stockings. Bobbed hair, according to Paula S. Fass, was the very "badge of flapperhood"—perceived as "a symbol of female promiscuity, of explicit sexuality, and of a self-conscious denial of respectability and the domestic ideal."[31] Such styles, though, were already appearing on college campuses, in big cities, and making their way into suburbs like Oak Park, the home to which Lieutenant Ernest Hemingway returned after the war. On the other hand, by 1924 these styles had spread to the hinterland, promoted by the proliferation of a whole new set of slick magazines that were, like so many other consumer items in this period, targeted at the young. The mixed attire of the young women of "Soldier's Home"—conventional dress from 1919 and flapper dress from 1924—can only be the product of a dialogical text, with the flapper dress (the bobbed hair and silk stockings) being an incongruous textual displacement: a projection across space (from Oak Park to a town in Oklahoma) and time (from 1924 to 1919) that endows the text's fabula and its protagonist with a preternatural sense of what was in the offing.

I should briefly note that when a much earlier version of this chapter appeared in *The Hemingway Review*, one reader objected that my above argument actually supported a 1924 date for the story's fabula. So perhaps I ought to offer one last word on why I insist that "Soldier's Home" takes place in 1919 and not later. For my interpretation of this story as a dialogical text—combining elements of its fabula (1919) with the social experience of its time of narration (1924)—to be wrong, *all* of the following would have to be true: when Hemingway named his fictional persona Harold Krebs instead of Nick Adams and moved him from Oak Park to Oklahoma, he changed the date of his return home too; this one town in Oklahoma was unique in that nearly all the soldiers were drafted, the men who enlisted were unaccountably detained on their way home, the patriotic fervor was so strong that people continued to believe atrocity stories five years after they were disabused of such beliefs by their returning veterans, the public library's history section was woefully inadequate, and the young women were the most bizarrely dressed women in America. Also, in this one text Hemingway occasionally abandoned minimalism for unnecessary verbosity and baroque prose, abstained in the third paragraph from the free indirect speech that pervades the rest of the story, and decided to mystify his readers by announcing, up front and in neon lights, that there was a crucial five-year period in his protagonist's life about which he would give them no clue. I find all of this difficult to accept.[32]

A third aspect of social experience in the story pertains to an especially cherished image—the American family. In Krebs's dysfunctional family, the father is absent, represented synecdochically by the car that stands outside his second-floor office, which itself represents the autonomy Krebs desires but absurdly can have only if he becomes an accomplice to his own infantilization. There is no small degree of irony in Mrs. Krebs's statement: "Your father does not want to hamper your freedom. He thinks you should be allowed to drive the car." This irony is compounded when she then adds: "If you want to take some of the nice girls out riding with you, we are only too pleased." Krebs's favorite sister, the only family member to show him unconditional love, is summarily dismissed by his mother before the breakfast confrontation that will cause him to leave home for good. The domestic breakfast scene, a wholesome centripetal image of family life, is in this story a scene of absence, dispersal, manipulation, resentment, capitulation, and passive-aggressive self-abnegation. The text, then, expresses the anxieties, pervasive by the mid-1920s, that the American family—for over a century an indispensable fortress of prevailing cultural values—was on the verge of collapse.[33] Moreover, this development was taking place in a society in which a culture based on production was giving way to a spectator culture based on consumption, and where a traditional ethos of self-denial was increasingly turning to self-indulgence, a fact evidenced by an alarming rise in alcoholism and drug addiction.

Krebs, in his own idiosyncratically situated, self-indulgent torpor, represents a larger cultural malaise that was gripping so many Americans during the 1920s and that formed a significant part of the social experience of the decade. Disappearing into a cool, dark pool room, reading newspapers and war books, and anxiously peering from his mother's porch at the young women whose social codes he does not understand, this awkward child of the new consumerist culture has become an uncertain spectator in a society in transition in which the disappearance of old norms precludes his participation. Caught between his parents' world that he senses is obsolete and the new world that he is not equipped to enter, all he can do is passively observe as he *practices* on (rather than "plays") his clarinet which, by its metonymic association with the "Jazz Age" and the new, he approaches and avoids as he drifts ever farther from his familial matrix. Significantly, this activity, like all others, devolves into lethargy and retreat: "In the evening he practised on his clarinet, strolled down town, read and went to bed." Like the yellow fog representing the buried self in T. S. Eliot's "The Love Song of J. Alfred Prufrock" that after its "sudden leap" curls once about the house and falls asleep,[34] Krebs's impulse toward action inevitably winds down into inertia.

From his vantage point in Europe, Hemingway, in one of the relatively few non–upper Michigan stories he would set on the United States mainland, sensed the larger social experience of his age and expressed it through a character whose more specific, preliminary problems were, by their biographical relevance, compelling enough to engage the attention of readers and critics for nearly nine decades. But "Soldier's Home" was one of many texts published in 1925—Scott Fitzgerald's *The Great Gatsby,* Willa Cather's *The Professor's House,* Anzia Yezierska's *Bread Givers,* John Dos Passos's *Manhattan Transfer,* Ellen Glasgow's *Barren Ground,* Sinclair Lewis's *Arrowsmith,* Theodore Dreiser's *An American Tragedy,* T. S. Eliot's "The Hollow Men," and, of course, Hemingway's *In Our Time* were others—that captured the experience of a people in painful transition: their failed institutions, their confused and often tragic attempts to hold onto past ideals and ideologies, and their inevitable failure. In the mid-1920s, Hemingway could allow his hero to escape to Kansas City, just as Nick Adams escapes to the Big Two-Hearted River, Jake Barnes to the bullfight arena, and Brett Ashley into hedonism. Escape was still possible then. But soon, all too soon, the bill would come due.

3

The "Pointless" Story

WHAT IS "A CANARY FOR ONE"?

> You know that fiction, prose rather, is possibly the roughest trade of all in writing. You do not have the reference, the old important reference. You have the sheet of blank paper, the pencil, and the obligation to invent truer than things can be true. You have to take what is not palpable and make it completely palpable and also have it seem normal and so that it can become a part of the experience of the person who reads it.
>
> —Hemingway to Bernard Berenson (1954), *Selected Letters*

There is no critical debate about the merits of either "Indian Camp" or "Soldier's Home." Both stories have been frequently anthologized and highly praised, and each is rich in interpretive possibilities and open to a wide range of critical methodologies. But "A Canary for One" is a different sort of story, one intended to be purely mimetic, and has proven unfertile ground for all but biographical approaches. It is especially unrewarding to criticism requiring some sort of thematic assessment. To understand, appreciate, and properly gauge this type of Hemingway story (which is exemplary of a number of his stories), we must examine it from another perspective—in terms of craft.

"A Canary for One" first appeared in the April 1927 issue of *Scribner's Magazine* along with "In Another Country"; "The Killers" had come out the month before in that same publication.[1] Sandwiched between these two indisputable masterpieces, it was overshadowed then and has been relatively neglected ever since. The few critics who have addressed the story have mostly focused on its biographical relevance, as a fairly straightforward representation of Ernest and Hadley's return to Paris in May 1926 to begin their separation. With the exception of Hilary K. Justice's superb biographical article, which views the story as a complex representation not only of the end of Ernest and Hadley's marriage but also of his impending marriage to Pauline Pfeiffer, these critics all make essentially the same points.[2] The only two substantial pieces of criticism that examine the text *qua* story are Scott Donaldson's extremely valuable genetic study of the manuscripts and Julian Smith's analysis of the story's theme, motifs, and symbols. The biographical aspects of the story have thus dominated the criticism of "A Canary for One," and the thematic content of the text is, by now, all too manifest. Much more interesting than what the story is *about*, however, are the questions of what the story *is* and *how it works*. These are the questions I shall here address.

"A Canary for One" opens within a compartment aboard a train speeding its way along the coast of southern France. For the first half of the story it appears to be a third-person narrative, and the only character seems to be a slightly deaf American lady who is afraid of a possible train wreck and who is returning to Paris with a canary she has purchased in Palermo, Sicily, for her daughter. Although the story will turn out to be a first-person narrative—a fact deftly concealed by the use of inert constructions ("outside the window were dusty trees") and by placing the actions of the American lady at the center of the narrative—the reader suspects nothing of the sort.[3] Inside the compartment it is hot and oppressive. The train pulls into Marseilles, and the lady takes a brief walk along the platform, fearful of straying too far because she was almost left behind at Cannes. The train leaves Marseilles at dusk, passes a burning farmhouse, and pulls into Avignon at night, where people get on and off and black soldiers are standing on the platform. All night the American lady lies awake fearing a train wreck. In the morning, with the train approaching Paris, she washes, breakfasts in the restaurant car, and returns to the *lit salon*. She removes the cloth from the canary's cage, and the bird begins to sing.

At this point the narrator steps forth by using the first-person pronoun and reveals to the reader that he is traveling with his wife. In the first of two conversations between the American lady and the narrator's wife, we discover that the American lady has mistaken the couple for English, that she recently terminated her daughter's love affair with a non-American whom the girl had met in Vevey, Switzerland, and that she believes foreigners to be unsuitable husbands for American girls. There is then a summarized conversation about how the American lady has her clothes made in Paris and sent to her in New York City. Following a description of the train entering Paris, the second dialogue takes place between the two women, an exchange in which both appear self-absorbed. The talk is about Vevey, where, we learn, the narrator and his wife had spent their honeymoon.

This conversation is cut short when the narrator points out a wrecked train they pass. Their train comes to a stop in the Paris station where the couple parts company with the American lady. They follow a porter who hauls their luggage until they get to the ticket taker. In the final sentence of the story, the narrator reveals a critical piece of information he has hitherto withheld: "We were returning to Paris to set up separate residences."

Some critics have taken Hemingway to task for hiding until the end any knowledge of the narrator's impending separation, considering this, as well as his disguising of the point-of-view, to be something of a cheap trick or, at least, an artificial device.[4] In this view, the ending is akin to the twist or "snapper" made famous by Maupassant's uncharacteristic "The Necklace" and popularized by the anecdotal stories of O. Henry. But although "A Canary for One" is a story with a surprise at the end, indeed literally at the end since it is contained in the last two words, nevertheless the story does not turn upon that twist and therefore is not dependent upon the anecdote in the manner of an O. Henry story. For one thing, although there is no way for the reader to know, or even suspect, that the American couple is returning to Paris to begin their separation, such a revelation is not at odds with the mood of the story or the emotions that the narrative evokes in the reader. Second, there is not even a reversal. Certainly, we would view the ending in a different light had Hemingway portrayed the Americans as a happy and loving couple. Third, unlike the surprise ending of the anecdote, this one does not draw our attention to itself per se, but instead compels us immediately to re-read the story searching for clues and depths that have eluded us. An anecdotal story can be read only once; subsequent readings bring disappointment, and sometimes indignation, if the reader feels he or she has been grossly manipulated. The surprise *is* the story, and the reader cannot be surprised a second time. This story, however, demands to be re-read, and with each new reading yields a deeper appreciation.

I

Let us now begin our inquiry by simply listing a number of objective points. Since these observations reflect specific decisions made by Hemingway, they are also implicitly questions. For instance, were I to note that the story takes place on a train, this leads to many questions. Why did

Hemingway set his story on a train? Why not a boat, a car, in a restaurant, a hotel room, on a fishing expedition, or on a street? And why does the story begin with a speeding train? He could have first introduced the American lady, or the narrator and his wife. Or he could have begun with the train pulling out of the Cap d'Antibes (where the Hemingways' real-life trip began) or entering Paris. The questions are endless and, to be sure, typically irrelevant to critics, who tend to take these elements of a story as given in their rush to glean larger significances. But any practicing story-writer will tell you that these are essential questions, and that a great deal of thought and effort goes into answering them in the decision-making process of how to construct a particular story. By listing the observations and then, throughout this chapter, answering the implicit questions, I will try to show what the story is and how it functions.

1. The theme of this story has something to do with the dissolution of a marriage, but Hemingway tells us nothing about the couple's marriage or their decision to separate. How long have they been married? Was this once a happy marriage? Was one of them egregiously at fault for the break-up? How do they feel about each other? When did they decide to end their marriage? Under what circumstances? The story provides no clues. For that matter, we know nothing about the narrator or his wife. What are their names? How old are they? Where are they from? What are they like? What do they do? Why are they in Europe? Do they have any children? If the theme of this story concerns the end of a marriage, then how can Hemingway tell us virtually nothing about the characters or their marriage? Is the theme of the story something other than what it appears to be? Is the question of theme irrelevant here? Or, to cover all possibilities, is this story badly flawed by its lack of exposition?
2. The story begins in the middle of the journey as the train hurtles at breakneck speed along the southern French coast. It ends, after several stops, in the Gare de Lyons station in Paris. It starts during the afternoon and concludes the following morning.
3. There are *five* extremely odd sentences in this story written by one of the greatest prose stylists in world literature. In the third paragraph we read: "There was no breeze came through the open window." The sentence is not, strictly speaking, ungrammatical, but highly irregular in

its elision of "that" between "breeze" and "came." At the Avignon station, tall black soldiers stand along the platform with their faces shining near the electric lights; the next sentence reads: "Their faces were very black and *they were too tall to stare*" (italics mine). On the outskirts of Paris, the narrator observes: "All that the train passed through looked as though it were before breakfast." A little later, coming into Paris, he reports: "Nothing had eaten any breakfast." If he is referring to the denizens of Paris whose houses he is passing, the use of the word "nothing" is curious. If he is speaking more generally, we note that the American lady has indeed just eaten breakfast. Last, as the couple leaves the train, the narrator says: "my wife said good-by and I said good-by to the American lady," a phrase that is utterly ambiguous. Is the author preparing us for the impending revelation about the separation by having the narrator and his wife say goodbye separately to the lady? Or is the wife saying goodbye to the narrator, after which he says goodbye to the lady? Or is there a third possibility?

4. The story appears to be a strict third-person fixed internal focalization with the American lady as the central consciousness, even to the point of accessing her feelings. At precisely midpoint in the narrative the narrator emerges by using the first-person singular pronoun.
5. There are four instances of direct speech. The first two occur before the narrator enters the picture. In these, the American lady speaks briefly to unidentified listeners about the canary she bought in Palermo. Just after the second speech, the narrator says: "For several minutes I had not listened to the American lady, who was talking to my wife." We now know of the narrator and his wife, and to whom the American lady has been speaking. The next sentence begins with the third piece of direct speech (the first conversation): "'Is your husband American too?' asked the lady." The final piece of direct speech (the second conversation) begins with the sentence: "'Americans make the best husbands,' the American lady said to my wife." In both dialogues, the first sentence of the conversation is spoken by the American lady and concerns "American husbands." Also, in both cases, just before the narrator/husband reports the dialogue, he has been looking out the window at the walls of the houses as they pass by and thinking about breakfast, or rather, about how everything seems before breakfast: "All that the train passed through looked as though it were before breakfast"

(preceding the first dialogue) and "Nothing had eaten any breakfast" (preceding the second dialogue).

6. In this five-page story, the American lady is referred to as "the American lady" 23 times, "the lady" once, "she" 15 times, "her" 7 times, and "herself" once. The narrator's wife is referred to as "my wife" 13 times, all in the second part of the story.

The theme of a story is its central or dominating idea, which can usually be stated as an abstractly definable condition. For instance, one might say that the theme of Herman Melville's "Bartleby, the Scrivener" is human isolation, and offer the following summary statement: "In a world in which people are walled off from one another, physically and spiritually, we are unable to respond to each other's needs, and the resulting isolation, in which each of us remains a mystery unto the last, leads to human alienation, societal fragmentation, and death." To give another example, a thematic statement drawn from Stephen Crane's "The Open Boat" could be: "Man's struggle for survival is unremitting and heroic, but inevitably doomed to failure since nature is mute and fate indifferent to human notions of justice."

Looking at these examples, and countless others like them, I am struck by the largeness of implication of thematic statements. They are not only grand assertions arising from the specifics of local narratives, assertions that genuinely are dramatized in the stories, but they are also applicable to much of the main body of work produced by the authors in question. As Scott Fitzgerald once confessed, writers "tell our two or three stories—each time in a new disguise—maybe ten times, maybe a hundred, as long as people will listen."[5] Nevertheless, as criticism of these two particular texts, the thematic statements seem surprisingly peripheral in their reductionist universalizing of our visceral responses to the stories. For instance, when we read "Bartleby," we are much more engaged by the narrator's self-justifying, confused, altruistic, incompetent, and even comical response to Bartleby's quiet pathos and autistic behavior, leaving us in a state of emotional unrest, sadness, and moral ambivalence, none of which are satisfactorily accounted for by the imposing thematic statement. Likewise, we experience the Crane story through its endless repetitions and descriptions of heroic human struggle, and through its alternating evocations of anxiety, weariness, hope, and despair. The end of the story brings both a release from this flux and a sense of tragic irony that no summary statement could possibly capture. Again, the thematic statement presented earlier is accurate; indeed much of it is explicitly stated in the narrative. Nevertheless, it seems far removed from what is most meaningful in the experience of reading the story. The same can be said of all such statements of theme.

What, then, is the purpose of theme? If all stories are, as I believe them to be, unique, and can only be fully appreciated when viewed in all of their specificity, still there is a need for categorizing what we read. Theme creates taxonomic sinews that enable us to discern the forest (or some sort of forest that we find satisfactory) but it carries the danger of obfuscating the trees. Theme provides a perspective that underlies our understanding of, say, such historical genres as, in the above cases, the romance or naturalism, in which similar attitudes can be used to group authors for study. In addition, theme is the ultimate paraphrase, to cite the *bête noire* of the New Critics, and it provides a means for discussing texts with other readers. But as Flannery O'Connor cautions:

> When you can state the theme of a story, when you can separate it from the story itself, then you can be sure the story is not a very good one. The meaning of a story has to be embodied in it, has to be made concrete in it. A story is a way to say something that can't be said any other way, and it takes every word in the story to say what the meaning is. You tell a story because a statement would be inadequate. When anybody asks what a story is about, the only proper thing is to tell him to read the story. The meaning of fiction is not abstract meaning but experienced meaning, and the purpose of making statements about the meaning of a story is only to help you to experience that meaning more fully.[6]

Furthermore, many of Hemingway's stories are particularly resistant to thematic summary in their Chekhovian emphasis upon mimesis and mood. Were I to hazard a thematic statement about "A Canary for One," the best I could do would be something like: "The dissolution of a marriage is an emotionally disorienting experience." So much, then, for the theme of "A Canary for One."

If this story is, as I have asserted, a success, then why is it successful and how does it succeed? To answer these questions we must try to figure out Hemingway's purpose: what was he trying to accomplish? The main action of the fabula has already taken place off-stage before the story begins, and it will resume after the story ends. Therefore, the story itself (what Hemingway has deliberately chosen to present), although continuous with events implicitly preceding and following, represents a period in time that is one of relative passivity in which actions and decisions, for the married couple, are either already made or to be made. The off-stage events of the past and future, the couple's decision to separate and the eventual consequences of that separation, though obviously important to them, are of no concern to the author or the story. Between these off-stage events we have the actual story, which attempts to make the reader *viscerally feel* the emotional state of the husband/narrator during the train ride to Paris.

I cannot state it too strongly—this is the *one and only purpose* of the text. Hemingway does not care whether the reader understands what happened to the marriage, who was at fault for the break-up, or even what will occur once the characters get to Paris. (Of course, he cares deeply about the real-life events behind the story, but that is another matter, one of the many differences between a professional author and a student in Creative Writing 101.) He does not even care about the main characters (the portrait of the American lady is almost Jamesian compared to the characterization of the American couple). Nor is he concerned that the reader "understand" the husband's emotional state. He only wants to convey impressionistically the texture of the narrator's feelings in a manner preliminary to any sort of conscious understanding on the reader's or narrator's part; as he would later put it, to "make people [readers] feel something more that they under[stand]."[7] That is why he provides such scant exposition. As Hemingway explained to his father, about eighteen months before he wrote this story: "I'm trying in all my stories to get the feeling of the actual life across—not just to depict life—or criticize it—but to actually make it alive. So that when you have read something by me you actually experience the thing."[8] As fodder for the cultural critic, then, "A Canary for One"—unlike "Indian Camp" or "Soldier's Home"— is slim pickings. But as a dramatization that enables a reader to experience the narrator's consciousness, it is a masterpiece, one which beautifully illustrates Flannery O'Connor's claim that "more happens in modern fiction—with less furor on the surface—than has ever happened in fiction before."[9]

In a different sort of literary analysis than the one I am here presenting, a critic might be quick to observe that the train in this story is an appropriate symbol of the American couple's marriage in particular, of the many failed marriages of the 1920s (including Ernest's and Hadley's), or of any failed marriage in general. The trip begins on the southeastern coast of France, a place where people go for holidays, and it ends in Paris, where the husband and wife will go their separate ways. The story begins with the train moving quickly in the sunlight and ends with it motionless in the dark. Furthermore, the train, like a love relationship, speeds up, slows down, and makes numerous stops; the stations on the way to Paris symbolize the landmark events in a declining marriage. The entire trip has about it the illusion of inevitability. Unlike an automobile, a train cannot run free but follows a pre-determined route ("the train . . . followed one track through many others into the station"). Just as a marriage, or any complex relationship, takes on a life of its own, operating according to an internal logic that is often beyond the control of the people involved, so a train, again unlike an automobile, is beyond the control of its passengers who cannot direct its movements. They can only choose, as in a marriage gone bad, to disembark if they do not wish to go where they cannot prevent the train from taking them. Last, this particular train is a *rapide* and therefore susceptible to wrecks, a fact that underscores both the passengers' powerlessness (akin to that which is felt by a couple in a failing marriage) as well as the potential dangers of marriage in general.

But whatever the critical legitimacy and value of viewing the train as a symbol, in this craft analysis I would prefer to examine it as a *device*, one whose qualities perform *technical functions* that serve the writer's purposes. Hemingway himself was not fond of the critical proclivity for discussing fiction in terms of symbols, noting of his own work, "I suppose there must be symbols since critics keep finding them."[10] This same attitude toward symbols (which critics love and authors tend to dismiss) was more fully delineated by Flannery O'Connor, who observes, "In good fiction, certain of the details will tend to accumulate meaning from the action of the story itself, and when this happens they become symbolic in the way they work." Addressing her character's wooden leg in the classic story "Good Country People," she states: "If you want to say that the wooden leg is a symbol, you can say that. But it is a wooden leg first, and as a wooden leg it is absolutely necessary to the story."[11] For Hemingway—who throughout his life was most fascinated with process—how something functions in fiction is much more important than how it can be viewed or what it might "mean."

From a writer's perspective, then, the first and most basic function of the train is that it provides the story with unity of place. The narrator, whose consciousness is the story's camera angle, does not leave his *lit salon* compartment until the end of the story. Although the relevance of the three classic unities of place, time, and action has always been a much debated question—and it was part of modernism's epistemological project to deconstruct these unities as being merely a socially determined aesthetics—nevertheless, in this story, which aims at a Poesque concentrated emotional effect, all three unities are present: the train compartment provides unity of place; the duration of the story is less than twenty-four hours; and the first-person narrator's consciousness as it experiences the journey creates a unity of action (mood). The train compartment has an additional advantage. Not only does it provide unity of place, but, because the train is moving over many hundreds of miles of terrain, the narrator can, by looking out the window, observe and be affected by whatever external scenes the writer chooses for him to see. Therefore, by setting the story aboard a train, Hemingway can both eat his cake and have it; he can maintain a strict unity of place and also move the story from place to place. Again, he could also have done this by using an automobile, but then the driver, either the narrator or his wife, would have been able to control where they were going, eliminating the element of passivity. It would also have removed the American lady from the story, thus forcing the narrator and his wife to talk to each other.

It is from this dual function of the train compartment setting that the story derives its fundamental structure. The narrator's compartment is on the left-hand side of the train. He is seated facing forward with his wife probably beside him, both of them across from the American lady who is facing the rear of the train.[12] As the train passes along the coast, the outside window of the compartment is on the narrator's left, facing south in the direction of the Mediterranean Sea. To his right there is "glass, then the corridor, then an open window." There are no compartments on that right-hand side of the train (typical in 1920s continental trains). Because of this spatial arrangement, the camera angle of the story (the narrator's consciousness) shifts back and forth between the events in the compartment (the American lady, his wife, the canary, the dialogue) and the landscapes that pass by on both sides of the train. These two locations, or sources of sensory impressions, that of the compartment and the passing scenery on either side, form the structure of the story. With this framework in mind, let us now fully examine the story as it unfolds. We shall see what it is, how it works, and what it is really "about."

II

"A Canary for One" opens *in medias res* with the train speeding along the coast and the narrator staring across the compartment through the corridor windows on the right-hand side: "The train passed very quickly a long, red stone house with a garden and four thick palm-trees with tables under them in the shade." He abruptly turns in the other direction and looks out the compartment window on the left: "On the other side was the sea. Then there was a cutting through red stone and clay, and the sea was only occasionally and far below against the rocks." This opening paragraph seizes the reader's attention because it tells us the train is moving quickly and makes us feel that movement by presenting so many images and then snatching them away. Although the story commences in the middle of the journey, the opening of the narrative still feels like a beginning since the train is just then ascending into the hills away from the sea. There is a good deal of disquiet implied as well. The house with the garden and shade trees, an image of domestic pleasure, disappears. The narrator turns to the sea, perhaps, given his marital status, unconsciously turning away from a domestic image, and it, too, disappears.

Before we can get our bearings, the American lady speaks, probably to the narrator's wife (judging from his limited involvement in future conversations), and tells how she purchased the canary in Palermo. This directs the narrator's attention back to the compartment: "It was very hot in the train and it was very hot in the *lit salon* compartment. There was no breeze came through the open window." The "hot" compartment is oppressive, a fact underscored by the narrator's exaggeration (no breeze coming through the open window of a speeding train?) and by his abridged syntax, a clue that his inner psychological state may be at odds with his outwardly calm demeanor. The American lady, whom we will come to see as the most unpleasant element in this stultifying compartment, then acts to remove any glimpse of the sea and to foreclose the possibility of a refreshing breeze: "The American lady pulled the window-blind down and there was no more sea, even occasionally." This action heightens our incipient awareness of the narrator's passivity, gleaned from his inert verbal constructions and his inaction in the face of physical discomfort. Deprived of the window on his left, oppressed by the compartment—its heat, the obnoxious American lady, her caged bird, the presence of his soon-to-be ex-wife (her absence from the first half of his narrative tells us much, in retrospect, about her presence in his consciousness)—the narrator turns to his one remaining outlet for relief, the open window across the corridor on his right through which he sees “dusty trees and an oiled road and flat fields of grapes, with gray-stone hills behind them.” Despite the visual appeal of this Cézanne landscape, in three brief paragraphs Hemingway has established his narrator’s suffering.

At this point there is a break in the narrative continuity, an ellipsis suggesting that the narrator’s discomfort has caused him to lapse into a reverie. The fourth paragraph begins: “There was smoke from many tall chimneys—coming into Marseilles, and the train slowed down and followed one track through many others into the station.” The sensation of slowing down and the sudden sight of smoke arrest his attention, snapping him out of his daydream (the ejaculation “coming into Marseilles” seems like a spontaneous attempt to locate himself in reality after having been rudely brought back to it). “The train stayed twenty-five minutes in the station at Marseilles” and he describes in some detail the movements of the American lady. She buys an English newspaper and a bottled water; she walks along the platform but stays near the “steps of the car because at Cannes, where it stopped for twelve minutes, the train had left with no signal of departure and she had gotten on only just in time. The American lady was a little deaf and she was afraid that perhaps signals of departure were given and that she did not hear them.”

This passage increases our growing awareness of the narrator’s passivity and his feelings of powerlessness. Of all the things Hemingway could choose to have him report, he has him dwell on the American lady’s concerns about not hearing the signals and being left behind, anxieties that are justifiable given her experience at Cannes and the vulnerability she feels due to her hearing disability. Like the narrator, she is prisoner to the whims of an increasingly personified train that acts to curtail her freedom (her buying the paper and water and strolling along the platform seem like small attempts to assert control). Throughout the story the train seems to have a mind of its own, and its stops and starts, as well as its resolute progress towards Paris, appear willful in contrast to the narrator’s passivity and the American lady’s anxiety. The narrator’s attentiveness to the movements of the American lady, a focus that is a product of his own unease, also suggests that there is something strange going on between him and his wife. Although at this point we are unaware of his wife's existence, or of the narrator's for that matter, in retrospect it is clear that he is avoiding his wife's presence and diverting his mind from her by following the movements of the American lady. The lady, then, dominates his consciousness for two reasons: as a conduit for the displaced expression of his own projected anxieties and, paradoxically, as a diversion from what is really on his mind.

The next paragraph describes the approximately fifty-mile stretch between Marseilles and Avignon, a journey that starts in early evening, takes place mainly in the dusk, and ends in darkness. The narrator seems composed and objective, but the facts he chooses to report, as well as his manner of relating them, further reveal his unrest:

> The train left the station in Marseilles and there was not only the switch-yards and the factory smoke but, looking back, the town of Marseilles and the harbor with stone hills behind it and the last of the sun on the water. As it was getting dark the train passed a farmhouse burning in a field. Motor-cars were stopped along the road and bedding and things from inside the farmhouse were spread in the field. Many people were watching the house burn. After it was dark the train was in Avignon. People got on and off. At the news-stand Frenchmen, returning to Paris, bought that day's French papers. On the station platform were negro soldiers. They wore brown uniforms and were tall and their faces shone, close under the electric light. Their faces were very black and they were too tall to stare. The train left Avignon station with the negroes standing there. A short white sergeant was with them.

When it leaves Marseilles, the train heads north away from the sea. For the first and only time in the story, the narrator looks back, perhaps betraying some sense of loss. He sees beyond the switch-yards and factory smoke to the pleasurable sights of the town: the harbor and the sunset reflecting on the water. Possibly, these pleasant connotations surrounding the sea have something to do with his memories of Vevey, the story's "great, good place," which lies on Lake Geneva. Later in the passage, Paris is mentioned for the first time. It will become the opposite of the coast and the sea, a place that the narrator anticipates with increasing dread as the train carries him ever nearer to it. The phrase used when Paris is first mentioned is "returning to Paris," a phrase that will be repeated in the story's powerful final sentence. It is one of the many recurring phrases that contribute to the story's unity.

The narrator's attention is riveted on the passing external scenes as he ignores the American lady and the compartment. But the scenery outside, as with the earlier scene of the American lady at Marseilles station, mirror and confirm the narrator's feelings of helplessness and so prevent him from experiencing any degree of psychological relief. The burning farmhouse is an objective correlative that contrasts with the pleasant, if fleetingly glimpsed domesticity of the red stone house from the first paragraph (the duration of the scene is also much more extended, either because the train is moving slower or else, more likely, because the scene makes a greater impression on the narrator's consciousness). This house is ablaze, its domestic entrails strewn across the field, and the people are powerless to save it. Worse, it is a source of casual interest to the onlookers, just as a marital failure, so devastating to the people involved, is often merely the stuff of gossip and entertainment to others. The narrator's mood is more than one of vulnerability and loss. He is also disoriented, a confusion made all the more striking by his efforts to seem composed and matter-of-fact.

The story employs a major innovative Hemingway technique—the use of external focalization in a first-person narrative, with the narrator refraining from directly expressing his feelings and instead revealing those feelings by the concrete details he reports, often through the use of objective correlatives. This is vintage Hemingway impressionism, to avoid depictions of the central consciousness's emotions and only give the external impressions viewed by that consciousness, letting the reader supply and feel rather than understand those emotions.[13] Hemingway also continues to convey the narrator's inner state by having him use inert or passive constructions wherever he can ("was not only"; "were stopped"; "were spread"; "was in Avignon"; "were negro soldiers"). His passivity is emphasized by juxtaposing these phrases with short, active declarative sentences ("[t]he train left"; "the train passed"; "[p]eople got on and off").

In this one paragraph we pass from dusk into darkness and confront two vastly different scenes, the picturesque Marseilles harbor and the burning farmhouse, before entering Avignon. Actually, we do not enter Avignon station—we suddenly find ourselves there—as again there is an ellipsis in the narrative continuity. The paragraph's first scene takes place in the waning light; the second transpires "[a]s it was getting dark"; and then, after the lacuna, this third scene occurs "[a]fter it was dark." The representation of Avignon station is cluttered and confused; it also lacks a unifying thread. Employing an element of the impressionism he learned from Stephen Crane, what Ian Watt terms *delayed decoding*, Hemingway depicts a distracted consciousness by reporting impressions as the focalizer becomes aware of them. Had he instead organized them coherently within the paragraph, it would indicate that the focalizer had already retrospectively processed them.[14] Thus, the observation of the sergeant comes as the train is leaving, rather than concurrent with the first notice of the black soldiers, since the narrator has been so focused on the soldiers that the sergeant's presence has not yet been recorded by his consciousness.

In addition to presenting the impressions of Avignon station in the random order of the narrator's awareness of them rather than through a structured composition, the passage also conveys its disoriented focalizer's consciousness by depicting the familiar, people going about their business in a train station, but in an unfamiliar and unsettling manner. For instance, why mention that the Frenchmen returning to Paris bought French papers? What newspapers would one expect them to purchase? Reporting that they bought French papers, in contrast to the English paper purchased earlier by the American lady, also underscores the narrator's keen awareness that the three of them are travelers in a foreign land. The tall black soldiers on the platform with their faces shining near the electric lights and their short white sergeant comprise another eerie image. The statement that they "were too tall to stare"—like the earlier unidiomatic sentence that there "was no breeze came through the open window"—gives the reader the feeling that the narrator is hypersensitive to every touch of the anomalous.[15] These observations stem from his emotional turmoil. Once again, we *understand* this upon re-reading the story, when we know it is a first-person narrative. On the first reading, we do not question the reliability of the narration, but we do *feel* the oddness of the sentences. The paragraph ends as it began, with the train leaving a station as it heads resolutely toward Paris.

From this surreal (to him) scene, in the next paragraph the narrator's attention returns to the compartment. It is night now; the porter has "pulled down the three beds from inside the wall and prepared them for sleeping" (a clue in the hermeneutic code that we probably miss on our first reading—aside from the American lady, who are the three beds for?); and there is nothing to see outside the windows. As he did in Marseilles station, the narrator focuses on the American lady, who again becomes an analogue of his inner state. "In the night the American lady lay without sleeping because the train was a *rapide* and went very fast and she was afraid of the speed in the night." The canary, a cloth covering his cage, is in the corridor that leads to the compartment washroom. The paragraph concludes: "There was a blue light outside the compartment, and all night the train went very fast and the American lady lay awake and waited for a wreck." The visual eeriness of the previous scene's black faces shining under an electric light continues into this scene with the blue light. The American lady becomes the means by which the narrator displaces his own anxieties, enabling Hemingway to omit having him directly express those anxieties while still making the reader feel them. She may very well have stayed awake all night waiting for a wreck, but he only knows this because he too must have laid awake, awaiting a different sort of wreck, one that was not a possibility but a certainty. The anxious insomnia inside the compartment is powerful enough to merit a concluding sentence that completely restates the phrases and images of the earlier sentence ("[i]n the night"—"all night"; "the American lady lay without sleeping"—"the American lady lay awake"; "the train was a *rapide* and went very fast"—"the train went very fast"; "she was afraid of the speed in the night"—"[she] waited for a wreck"). As we saw in the final two paragraphs of "Indian Camp," this is what I have termed Hemingway's technique of *recapitulation with variation,* a summarizing sentence that repeats or recasts phrases from earlier in the paragraph. In this passage, there is also a subtle shift between the two sentences as the train becomes the co-subject, along with the American lady, of the final sentence. Significantly, the narrator's wife is still textually absent; we have no idea what she is experiencing on this, their final night together.

Another ellipsis suggests that the narrator may have eventually dozed off. When he next speaks, the location of the train is foremost in his mind, perhaps because he's continued to think about it in his sleep, and he mentions Paris with far more concern than he earlier mentioned "coming into Marseilles":

> In the morning the train was near Paris, and after the American lady had come out from the wash-room, looking very wholesome and middle-aged and American in spite of not having slept, and had taken the cloth off the birdcage and hung the cage in the sun, she went back to the restaurant-car for breakfast. When she came back to the *lit salon*

> compartment again, the beds had been pushed back into the wall and made into seats, the canary was shaking his feathers in the sunlight that came through the open window, and the train was much nearer Paris.

This passage employs another favorite Hemingway technique for rendering a character's underlying emotional obsessions—indirection. The two-sentence paragraph, except for its first and final clauses, is devoted to the morning activities of the American lady, but it is really about the narrator's suppressed panic. We see this in the way the narrator unconsciously mimics the train's relentless progress in his run-on sentences. Hemingway understood that a stream-of-consciousness passage does not have to be free-associational, that it can focus on the speaker's observations of the external and need not limit itself to that character's direct expression of his or her inner feelings. It can also, as in this case, depict how a character's unconscious bursts into an otherwise organized pattern of conscious thought. He knew that the depth of a character's anxiety may be measured not only by how he dwells upon his fears (as in "A Way You'll Never Be"), or how those feelings influence his perceptions (as in Avignon station), but also by the character's efforts to repress troubling thoughts only to have them reappear in his consciousness (as in this passage or a story like "Now I Lay Me").

The bulk of the passage is devoted to the American lady, since she is the one the narrator chooses to focus upon (so much so, that he again uses a passive construction to omit any mention of the porter, who must have been the person who came in to make up the room). Unlike the narrator, she is a bustle of activity, and strikingly efficient. On the surface it seems an agreeable scene, pleasantly domestic and wholesome with the middle-aged American lady going off to breakfast, the beds converted into seats, the preening bird, and the sunlight (unlike the earlier breeze) "that came through the open window[.]" The passage heralds a new day—sunny, airy, and fresh. But it is the last new day that the narrator and his wife will greet together, and this is a portrait of the female domesticity that he is about to lose; he and his wife will never be middle-aged together. The sunlight through the window diverts his attention away from this, the only pleasant compartment scene in the story, and as he again looks out the window, grim reality smacks him in the face—"the train was much nearer Paris."

The American lady is, of course, unaware of the narrator's thoughts, and continues to be of cheer. In her second direct speech, she talks about her canary, how she is taking him home to her "little girl," and the bird, in the midst of preening, breaks into song. Although the canary in a cage is as obvious a device in this story as it is in, say, Rebecca Harding Davis's *Life in the Iron Mills* or Frank Norris's *McTeague*—a symbol of the entrapment of the American lady's daughter and/or of the narrator and his wife in the compartment—Steven Carter makes a fascinating ornithological observation that enriches its signification. Hemingway twice states that the bird "pecked into his feathers," which in caged birds can be an act self-mutilation caused by "acute distress." This symptom, caused by a sudden change that threatens the caged bird's sense of security, can also be accompanied by eating disorders.[16] Such an ecocritical context, which Hemingway might very well have known, adds another, subtler dimension to the symbolic function of the canary.

The narrator stares glumly out the window and watches, like a condemned man, as his fate unfolds:

> The train crossed a river and passed through a very carefully tended forest. The train passed through many outside of Paris towns. There were tram-cars in the towns and big advertisements for the Belle Jardinière and Dubonnet and Pernod on the walls toward the train. All that the train passed through looked as though it were before breakfast. For several minutes I had not listened to the American lady, who was talking to my wife.

This key transitional passage is the last narrative description before the train enters Paris; it is one of the passages most expressive of the narrator's feelings of helplessness; it concludes with the first mention of the narrator and his wife (so that we now know that this is a first-person narrative as well); and it introduces the first of two dialogues that provide us with our only reliable unmediated view of the three characters.

In this story of a journey from marriage to separation, the progress of the trip, as well as of the narrator's emotional responses, is grounded in the literal train ride from a location east of Marseilles to Paris. This progress has three components: visual/aural, spatial, and temporal. The visual/aural component consists of the sensory impressions recorded by the narrator during the trip, whether these be the sights he observes through the windows or the scenes he experiences in the compartment. The spatial aspect is denoted by the towns mentioned charting the train's physical movement toward Paris. And the temporal element, closely related to the spatial, is the *reader's sense* of the time elapsed and the time remaining before they will reach Paris. This temporal aspect is marked, as is the spatial, by the train's forward advance. The line that holds this story together, that forms the skeleton so to speak, consists of those sentences in which the train appears as the subject. This framework begins with "The train passed very quickly" and ends with "Then the train was in the dark of the Gare de Lyons, and then stopped"; in between, the train's progress is marked by phrases in which the train "slowed down," "followed," "stayed," "left," "passed," "was in," "went," "was near," "and crossed." In this five-page story, the train is mentioned 19 times. Indeed, it functions almost as a fourth, and hardly the least important, character.

In the above passage, the narrator mentions the train four times in four sentences; in three of these he shows the train moving. Because he has only just alerted us, with some alarm, that "the train was much nearer Paris[,]" these four mentions of the train, coming one after another like death knells, act to speed up our awareness of how quickly time is passing. This awareness is complemented by our knowledge that the train is now moving through "outside of Paris towns" (the towns need not be named; they are relevant only for their proximity to Paris). Time and space are also compressed by having the bulk of the journey, the roughly 360-mile stretch between Avignon and Paris, take place during the night and therefore go unrecorded (except for the narrator's displacement of his anxieties about his impending separation onto the American lady's anxieties about a possible train wreck). At the end of the fifth paragraph, we are in Avignon, in southern France. Two paragraphs later, we are approaching Paris. In the very next descriptive paragraph we see the train advancing relentlessly on Paris.

If unity of place is important to this story, so too is unity of time. Hemingway could have placed his unhappy husband and wife on a train that was not a *rapide,* or started the narrative earlier in the trip, or, since he did not have to make this fictional journey the same as the one he and Hadley took, he could have started the story in Rome, or Madrid, or Tibet for that matter. Instead, he *chose* to put them on the fastest practical vehicle that possessed the qualities he needed to tell the story, and he made the narrative begin in the late afternoon and conclude the following morning with most of the actual trip taking place during the night so that even though the story takes perhaps fourteen or so hours it would seem much shorter once morning came, a little less than halfway into the narrative.

From the moment we see the train going through the outside-of-Paris towns, the pace of the narrative slows down and more closely approximates the passage of time in the fabula (of course, in the dialogues, fabula time and narrative time are roughly equal). Yet, because so much time was lost in the night (one paragraph covering over 300 miles) and now Paris and the end are so near, the pace of the story actually *feels* faster to both the reader and the narrator. (This is abetted by the fact that, as a reader approaches the end of any story, he or she picks up the reading pace, a phenomenon caused by the reader's anticipation of the approaching end.)

At the same time, we are now aware of the first-person narrator, and his wife, and realize that it is through his eyes that we have been observing events transpire. What purpose is served by having the first half of the story disguised as a third-person narrative focalized through the American lady? Is this strategy, as one group of critics has called it, a "major flaw" in which "the purpose of this unexpected reorientation is by no means clear, nor the reason for the delay"[17]—or is there a sound reason for it? Normally, the main advantage of employing a first-person narrator is that it is more likely to evoke the reader's interest, to create sympathy for the narrator, and, as Wayne Booth observes, to decrease the emotional distance between the reader and the story.[18] When the narrator is a character in the story, we tend to forget that an author is also present and are therefore more willing to suspend our disbelief. One would suppose that in this story, whose entire purpose is to make the reader feel the emotional state of the husband, a first-person narrator would be in order.

And so it is, for even though the narrative is disguised during the first part of the story, it is no less a first-person narrative for that. But another quality of first-person narratives is that even though readers are more willing to suspend their disbelief in the activity of reading, they are conversely more apt to scrutinize *what* they are reading. One does not deeply ponder, in a narrative that is not self-reflexive, the reliability of a third-person narrator to the extent one does with that of a first-person narrator, no matter how honest, accurate, and altogether virtuous the latter might seem. For instance, had we known we were in the hands of a first-person narrator, we would have blinked when we read of the breeze that did not come in through the open window or the soldiers who were too tall to stare. Since the narrative was disguised, however, we passed quickly over such oddities and were affected by them emotionally without questioning them critically (we felt but did not understand them). This is precisely what Hemingway was trying to do, what he meant when he wrote that he was attempting to make a "story so real beyond any reality that it will become a part of the reader's experience and a part of his memory." In words that well apply to his method in "A Canary for One," he says: "There must be things that [the reader] did not notice when he read the story or the novel which without his knowing it, enter into his memory and experience so that they are a part of his life. This is not easy to do."[19] What we see here, then, is an innovative example of Hemingway's technique of omission in which the "thing left out" in the first half of the story is the existence of a first-person narrator. It is precisely this omission that causes readers to "feel something more than they under[stand]."[20]

Disguising the first-person narrative serves three other functions. First, it enables Hemingway to avoid making the narrator the subject of sentences, which focuses the narrative and the attention of the reader on those scenes that are affecting the narrator rather than on the narrator himself. This is what I defined in *Art Matters* as pure impressionism—what immediately affects the narrator affects the reader directly, not second hand through a narrator who has processed these impressions and reports them in retrospect.[21] For instance, when one reads that "the train passed quickly," one can imagine oneself on a train passing quickly, without any intervening reasoning. But if we were to read "we passed quickly," we would first have to put ourselves in the narrator's place and then feel what it would be like to experience the train's movement. Such activity would engage us in exactly the sorts of mental processes that Hemingway wishes us to avoid. On the other hand, although the narrator maintains the "train-verb" construction consistently throughout the story, he will abandon it when they pass the wrecked train cars: "We were passing three cars that had been in a wreck." Here Hemingway does not want the train to be the subject of the sentence because he wishes to make the analogy between the three wrecked cars and the three wrecked people, not between the wrecked train and the train they are on. Or take the sentence where the narrator looks back at Marseilles and sees the harbor and the "last of the sun on the water." As written, with the inert "there was . . . the town of Marseilles" construction, Marseilles is the subject and center of the sentence and the reader sees, thinks of, and is affected by nothing but what impinges on the narrator's consciousness. Had the sentence been "he saw the town of Marseilles," then "he" would have been the subject and we would have been aware not only of "him," but of whoever was telling us about "him." A first-person construction, "I saw the town of Marseilles," would work better, since we would be getting the image from the narrator himself, but the narrator's "I" would still stand between us and what Hemingway wants us to see and feel.

The second function of the disguised narrative is related to the previous one. With the inert constructions effacing the narrator, we assume we are reading a third-person narrative about the American lady, who seems to be the only character in the tale. Because of this, it heightens our sense of the narrator's passivity; not only is the train carrying him inexorably to his fate, but a third party is dominating the action of *his* story (of course we do not realize this until the shift into the first-person). Once this shift occurs, however, as it eventually had to or else the story really would have been about the American lady, the narrator stays passive by presenting dialogue in which he takes almost no part. The dramatic effect of this diminished first-person narrator is to convey his sense of disconnection and powerlessness, that is, his emotional state.

The last function of the disguised narrative has to do with the story's indirection and its hermeneutic code. As Julian Smith observes, "the sudden introduction of the two new characters in the middle of the story begins a pattern of refocusing that is completed with the last sentence; thus, we progress from interest in the American lady alone to interest in the American lady *and* the American couple to interest in the American couple alone."[22] This pattern of refocusing, like the similar indirection we saw in "Indian Camp" (and see in many so Hemingway stories), keeps the reader alert and actively engaged in the text as he or she adjusts readerly expectations as to what, and whom, the story is about. In this sense, the American lady and her subsequent encounter with the American couple are, to use Roland Barthes's terminology, "snares" that maintain the story's enigma as it unfolds, and the process of refocusing proceeds according to the story's "reticence" (Eudora Welty's term) in revealing itself.

This transitional paragraph introduces not only the narrator and his wife, but also, in the very next passage, the first piece of dialogue in which more than one person speaks (i.e., the first conversation). The narrator has been thoroughly absorbed looking out the window until this moment, staring at the scenes that "were before breakfast" and, by his own admission, not listening to the American lady who, he notes, "was talking to my wife." His preoccupation is broken when he hears the American lady ask, "Is your husband American too?"

Evidently, the American lady has been chattering away (the narrator singles her out as the one he has not been listening to, and he also notes that she has been talking "to" and not "with" his wife). Perhaps he has been staring out the window not only because he is fixated on the impending terminus of the journey, but also because the conversation inside the compartment has become painful for him to hear. What, then, draws his attention away from the window? First, he is aware that he has not eaten any breakfast, a fact that he characteristically announces by projecting it onto the passing landscape. Breakfast carries for him the connotation of domesticity, and its absence serves as a synecdoche for what he is about to lose. At that precise moment, he hears the American lady mention him, and this catches his attention. She refers to him as a husband, something he will no longer be, and as an American, which points to his being a stranger in a foreign land, a statement that is true both literally (he is an American in France) and figuratively (he is about to enter into the strange state of being an ex-husband).

In response to the American lady's question about her husband, his wife answers, "We're both Americans," explicitly and perhaps unconsciously linking herself to him. The American lady says that she had thought they were English and his wife replies "Oh, no." Then the narrator speaks, the first of only two sentences he utters in the story:

> "Perhaps that was because I wore braces," I said. I had started to say suspenders and changed it to braces in the mouth, to keep my English character. The American lady did not hear. She was really quite deaf; she read lips, and I had not looked toward her. I had looked out of the window. She went on talking to my wife.

The few critics who have written on "A Canary for One" have had much to say about the American lady: she is narcissistic, insensitive, opinionated, xenophobic, and domineering. She is, to be sure, all of this, but one thing she is not is the protagonist of the story. Especially as we explore the last half of the narrative, in which her unpleasantness becomes increasingly evident, we should remember that—like Uncle George in "Indian Camp" or Mrs. Krebs in "Soldier's Home"—she is in the story only because she serves several functions, not because she is important in herself. First, her presence in the first part of the tale enables the narrator to express his emotional state by observing her instead of by addressing his feelings directly. Second, she serves briefly as a symbol of domesticity, what he is about to lose. Third, she contributes mightily to making the compartment unbearable by her obliviousness to those around her. Fourth, to the degree that she dominates the surface of the story she contributes to our sense of the narrator's powerlessness and passivity. Last, if she were not present the narrator and his wife would be compelled to talk to each other, which would kill the dramatic effect of the story because it is essential that the reader *hear the silence* between the narrator and his wife. Unlike, say, the unhappy couples in "Out of Season," "Cat in the Rain," "Hills Like White Elephants," or "The Short Happy Life of Francis Macomber," these two are done talking. There is nothing left for them to say.

What makes the American lady important, then, is the narrator's response to her; he finds her distasteful and he resents her. Having had to endure her unwanted presence during the final night and morning that he will ever share with his wife, he must now endure her stupid banter during the momentous and emotionally wrought entrance into Paris. Worse, she is busy engaging his wife in a conversation about marriage, which is a conversation that he especially does not want to hear and yet one that he cannot resist listening to. It hardly helps that her opinions about marriage are both simplistic and obnoxious. Her deafness and her mistaken assumption that the narrator and his wife are English are also significant. Her physical disability figuratively mirrors her "inability" to hear others, and neither can she "see" them for what they are, an unhappy American couple. To the extent that she is cut off from "knowing" others, she exemplifies how no one in this story truly knows anyone else, which is another aspect of the three characters being strangers in a foreign land. Incidentally, that is why no one in the story has a name. They are "the American lady," "I," and "my wife." And the narrator refers to her as "the American lady" with an almost contemptuous insistence (23 times in a five-page story), emphasizing the atmosphere of human alienation and isolation.[23] Strangers sharing an overnight compartment, especially strangers of the same nationality in a foreign country, introduce themselves to each other. Here, either they have not, or else, and this is certainly much more likely, they have, and the narrator is purposely being petulant in refusing to refer to the two women by their names. In any event, we may safely assume that he knows his own wife's name but nevertheless keeps referring to her as "my wife," a common phenomenon among separating couples (it is a way of attempting to maintain as familiar and personal that which is becoming increasingly unfamiliar and formal as the ties of marital intimacy shatter).

The American lady does not hear what the narrator says to her, but what is more significant is that, although he knows she is hard of hearing, he does not turn to her when he speaks ("she read lips, and I had not looked toward her"). We picture him from now on staring out the window all the way into the Paris station, even when he is listening to their dialogue. The nature of what he says is as important as his physical positioning. His attempt at a joke ("braces") barely masks his hostility toward the American lady and toward the futility of his situation, as well as toward his wife who, he knows, is the only one who will hear and catch his sarcasm. Characteristically, his is a quiescent sort of anger: accepting the American lady's mistaken assumption that he is English (based on the superficial detail of his wearing suspenders) and playing along by referring to "braces." By now, he is so passive that it is not even worth his while to turn in her direction, even though he is angry enough to utter a small protest, disguised as humor, which actually displays a half-calculated rudeness.

The American lady and his wife continue their conversation as though he has not even spoken, and the narrator reports it directly since they are talking about things that matter to him: American husbands, marriage, and, for reasons we will later learn, Vevey:

> "I'm so glad you're Americans. American men make the best husbands," the American lady was saying. "That was why we left the Continent, you know. My daughter fell in love with a man in Vevey." She stopped. "They were simply madly in love." She stopped again. "I took her away, of course."
>
> "Did she ever get over it?" asked my wife.
>
> "I don't think so," said the American lady. "She wouldn't eat anything and she wouldn't sleep at all. I've tried so very hard, but she doesn't seem to take an interest in anything. She doesn't care about things. I couldn't have her marrying a foreigner." She paused. "Some one, a very good friend, told me once, 'No foreigner can make an American girl a good husband.'"
>
> "No," said my wife, "I suppose not."

What matters is not the story of the American lady and her daughter, though that reveals much about the former's character, but how the narrator and his wife respond to the story. The narrator, as we have seen, is behaving passively (or stoically, if we wish to give him some benefit of the doubt). He has distanced himself from his wife (except for consistently referring to her as "my wife"), from the American lady, and from the conversation in the compartment. Yet, when he hears the word "husband" or contemplates his "breakfast-less" state, he listens very carefully to the two women. As the narrator, he is the one who decides what dialogue to report and how much to report directly. We must remember that we are getting only a small piece of the conversation between these two women; the rest of it he either ignores or else summarizes. Thus the reported conversation is significant *to him*, and he reproduces it in excruciating detail, right down to the American lady's pauses between sentences that, as Scott Donaldson notes, Hemingway deliberately added in the story's final draft.[24]

Aside from the references to Vevey and to marriage, why is he paying such close attention to this particular conversation? Surely he sees the irony in the statement that "American men make the best husbands." But more striking to him must be the similarity between the American lady's daughter and himself. Both were in love in Vevey, and the course of that love went awry, even if the love itself never ceased.[25] The daughter reacted as we have seen him react; she did not eat, had trouble sleeping, and lost interest in things (thus, the symbolic significance of the canary's possible pecking disorder). The account of the daughter's reaction articulates the very feelings that the narrator has tried, throughout the story, to repress.

His wife also responds to the story in an understandably self-referential way. Just as he uses the words "my wife" in an effort to hold onto what he is losing, so she replies to the American lady's question ("Is your husband American too?") by gratuitously connecting herself to him ("We're both Americans"). When she hears the tale of the American lady's daughter, her immediate response is to ask a question that is really about herself ("Did she get over it?"). The answer is hardly comforting to the narrator's wife who, like the daughter, was also in love with a man in Vevey. When she resignedly agrees with the American lady's friend that no foreign man can make an "American girl" a good husband, it is with the sorrowful knowledge that, at least in her case, neither could an American man. Unlike her husband, however, she will react to this disquieting story by turning her attention to the once happy past. He, on the other hand, will continue to stare out the window at his imminent future.

In the passage that follows, the talk focuses on clothing and the

American lady. The narrator's interest consequently wanes so that he merely summarizes the conversation, but remains strong enough that he does not ignore it altogether:

> The American lady admired my wife's travelling-coat, and it turned out that the American lady had bought her own clothes for twenty years now from the same maison de coutoure in the Rue Saint Honoré. They had her measurements, and a vendeuse who knew her and her tastes picked the dresses out for her and they were sent to America. They came to the post-office near where she lived up-town in New York, and the duty was never exorbitant because they opened the dresses there in the post-office to appraise them and they were always very simple-looking and with no gold lace nor ornaments that would make the dresses look expensive. Before the present vendeuse, named Thérèse, there had been another vendeuse, Amélie. Altogether there had only been these two in the twenty years. It had always been the same couturier. Prices, however, had gone up. The exchange, though, equalized that. They had her daughter's measurements now too. She was grown up and there was not much chance of their changing now.

This paragraph obviously furthers our awareness of the American lady's narcissism (her admiration for the other woman's coat launches her into a boring monologue about her own clothes shopping), and it also hints at the destructive consequences of her self-centeredness (she has the "measure" of her daughter and there is not much chance now that the girl will ever escape). In addition, if we have mistaken her for a provincial, we now see that she lives in an expensive part of New York, and has a certain cosmopolitan authority and shrewd competence that make her, to the narrator, even more oppressive in that she is quite formidable.

But from the craft perspective that I have been pursuing, the passage serves several purposes that are more directly relevant to the narrator. The American lady's random chatter is so banal that it dampens the narrator's interest enough for him to stop reporting her speech directly. It also presents a world of women in which he does not belong, thus further alienating him from the scene. In relating this exclusively female paragraph, which is also the only non-dialogue passage that refers to events outside of the main story, he eschews the term "the American lady" for an extended period of time and instead uses the pronoun "her" (six times, four in one sentence) and "she" (twice) to express his own vague impression of pervasive femininity. The only characters in the passage are the American lady, her daughter, his wife, and the two saleswomen, both of whom he goes unnecessarily out of his way to name (we thus know the names of the two utterly irrelevant saleswomen but not of the narrator, his wife, the American lady, or her daughter).

The entire paragraph has to do with power and control. The narrator can only listen to this conversation between two women about this world of women while he gazes impotently out the window, excluded from that world and from any influence within it. The American lady, however, is fully in control. She admires his wife's coat and uses it to talk about herself and to dominate the conversation. She has each vendeuse internalize her preferences and send her dresses from across the ocean. She outwits the customs officers and displays real taste by ordering fashionable dresses that seem, to a layman, inexpensive. And she prevents her daughter from achieving independence. She even has luck; in twenty years she has only had to deal with two saleswomen, and the change in the exchange rate neutralizes the rise in prices. The American lady, in short, is not really the vulnerable character she appeared to be at Marseilles station or during the night. This paragraph, which serves as testimony to her genius in the art of manipulation, by contrast reminds the narrator, and us, of his inability to exercise control over anything in the story.

The passage also serves as a segue between the first dialogue and the subsequent final passage of narrative description of the moving train. The narrator, passively listening to the American lady's chatter that both repels and attracts him, is again suddenly struck by what he sees outside the window:

> [1] The train was now coming into Paris. [2] The fortifications were levelled but grass had not grown. [3] There were many cars standing on tracks—brown wooden restaurant-cars and brown wooden sleeping-cars that would go to Italy at five o'clock that night, if that train still left at five; the cars were marked Paris-Rome, and cars, with seats on the roofs, that went back and forth to the suburbs with, at certain hours, people in all the seats and on the roofs, if that were the way it were still done, and passing were the white walls and many windows of houses. [4] Nothing had eaten any breakfast.

With the train entering Paris, the narrator loses all semblance of objectivity and the external scene he describes becomes completely a projection of his own emotional turmoil. Just as he exists between two states of being (marriage and separation), Paris is a city in transition between wartime (the grass has not yet grown back) and peacetime (the fortifications are leveled). To analogize further, with the fortifications that are necessary in war (and marriage) down, will the grass (and his life) regenerate? If I may be allowed an extratextual observation, it is hardly comforting to note, in this context, that the war had been over for nearly eight years at the time the Hemingways made their real-life trip in August 1926.

This final depiction of an external scene before the train trip concludes brings to a climax those qualities that marked previous descriptions. We may assume from the "if" clauses, which Hemingway added in the final draft,[26] that the narrator once knew his way about Paris, yet the city now seems strange. His looming separation has defamiliarized what was once well known to him, and he is like a tourist trying to locate his position with a map that he senses may be obsolete. The manner in which he is experiencing the city, as the train hurtles him into it, is entirely due to the way he is experiencing his marital identity.

The third sentence, occupying exactly 80 percent of the four-sentence paragraph, is a run on, producing an effect that imitates the narrator's drifting consciousness as well as the unbroken movement of the train, or rather, of the passing scenes by which the reader is aware of the train's movement. Consistent with earlier descriptions, inert constructions pervade this sentence ("There were many cars standing"; "passing were the white walls"). The narrator focuses on details that signify domesticity and stand in contrast to his experience of impending domestic loss: restaurant-cars and sleeping-cars, trains that carry suburban husbands home from work and suburban wives home from shopping, the veiling walls and revealing windows of people's domiciles. The Paris-Rome cars stand ready to make a symbolically ironic journey that reverses the trip he and his wife have just made. And all of this seems so unfamiliar to him; he wonders "if that train still left at five" (do people still fall in love and travel to Rome?) and "if that were the way it were still done" (do people still return to their families in the suburbs?). There is, moreover, no sign of life, just empty trains, white walls, and blank windows. The question that hovers over the scene, as described, is this—does life still go on? The narrator, characteristically, projects this question onto the landscape.

The passage concludes with yet another odd declarative sentence

("Nothing had eaten any breakfast") that once again makes sense only as an expression of the narrator's sense of his lost domestic life. As in the first passage of conversation, this second passage commences with the narrator becoming aware of his "breakfast-less" state and then hearing the American lady speak the words "American" and "husband." These words engage his full attention, and he reports their dialogue directly and completely. In this passage, Hemingway employs his full array of innovative dialogue techniques, especially repetition, to construct one of the finest and most subtly complex pieces of dialogue that the premier writer of fictional dialogue in the twentieth century—indeed the writer who permanently transformed the theory and practice of dialogue by enabling it to perform a constructive rather than merely an illustrative function—would ever compose:[27]

> "Americans make the best husbands," the American lady said to my wife. I was getting down the bags. "American men are the only men in the world to marry."
>
> "How long ago did you leave *Vevey*?" asked my wife.
>
> "Two years ago this *fall*. It's her, you know, that I'm taking the canary to."
>
> "Was the man your daughter was in *love* with a Swiss?"
>
> "Yes," said the American lady. "He was from a very good family in *Vevey*. He was going to be an engineer. They met there in *Vevey*. They used to go on long walks together."
>
> "I know *Vevey*," said my wife. "We were there on our honeymoon."
>
> "Were you really? That must have been *lovely*. I had no idea, of course, that she'd *fall* in *love* with him."
>
> "It was a very *lovely* place," said my wife.
>
> "Yes," said the American lady. "Isn't it *lovely*? Where did you stop there?"
>
> "We stayed at the Trois Couronnes," said my wife.
>
> "It's such a *fine* old hotel," said the American lady.
>
> "Yes," said my wife. "We had a very *fine* room and in the *fall* the country was *lovely*."
>
> "Were you there in the *fall*?"
>
> "Yes," said my wife.
>
> We were passing three cars that had been in a wreck. They were splintered open and the roofs sagged in.

"Look," I said. "There's been a wreck."

The American lady looked and saw the last car. (all italics mine)

On the surface, this conversation seems superficial and repetitious—just what one might expect from strangers in such circumstances. It is also a perfect example of how to use indirection in dialogue. Two kinds of indirection take place. First, the conversation appears to be about Vevey and the American lady's daughter, but it is really about the conflicted emotions experienced by the separating couple. Second, the passage amply demonstrates the Joseph Conrad / Ford Madox Ford "unalterable rule" for rendering "genuine conversations": "no speech of one character should ever answer the speech that goes before it." As Ford stated, such "is almost invariably the case in real life where few people listen, because they are always preparing their own next speeches."[28] (Sheldon Norman Grebstein refers to this dialogue technique as "incremental repetition" or a "type of stichomythia.")[29] But beneath the verisimilar surface the dialogue is constructive rather than merely illustrative: there is conscious calculation and involuntary self-revelation, character is expressed, and plot is advanced (the passage provides the emotional climax to any reading or re-reading of the story). The repetition here is not only verisimilar; by repeating words in different contexts Hemingway changes their referents and meanings. New qualities accrue to the repeated words and gather force each time the word reappears.

The narrator and his wife face forward. He looks out the window toward Paris and the future; his wife looks at the American lady with whom she is speaking; and the American lady looks backward to the rear of the train and the past. The American lady makes her comment about the exclusive virtue of American husbands in conjunction with the narrator's apparently quotidian act of getting down the bags, an act that seems to correspond to her views on American husbands but that is given ironic relevance in juxtaposition with what must surely be the narrator's sense of it as a physical step toward the separation of the couple's possessions. When the American lady repeats her observation, the wife asks about Vevey, partly to change the painful course of the conversation. Yet, by choosing to divert it with talk of Vevey, she involuntarily betrays her desire to talk about the once happy past. The egocentric American lady predictably takes the question about Vevey as a cue to talk about her daughter, and the wife goes along on that tack. But instead of conversing about the canary that the

American lady has just mentioned, the wife is irresistibly drawn to asking about the nature of the broken love affair that resonates, for her, as relevant to her own forthcoming separation. When the American lady then tells of the Swiss with whom her daughter fell in love, she twice mentions Vevey, causing the narrator's wife, in a moment of weakness and out of a desire to turn from the symbol of her imminent unhappy future (the daughter) to the memory of her once happy past, to utter the enormously understated "I know Vevey" and to reveal that it was the site of her honeymoon. From that moment on, the narrator's wife will try to hold onto Vevey and the past. At the same time, the narrator experiences her attempts, by dwelling on Vevey, to ward off the painful emotions caused by their ever-nearing separation. He, in turn, tries unconsciously to hold onto their married status by using, in his wife's remaining five speeches, the identification tags "said my wife" although these are obviously unnecessary for the purpose of identifying the speaker.

The American lady, who doesn't really care about the couple's honeymoon, predictably shifts the conversation back to her daughter's love affair, and inadvertently reveals that she feels somewhat defensive, perhaps even guilty, about what she has done. As in their first conversation, she uses the phrase "of course" to justify her actions. But the narrator's wife is no longer interested in the unhappy daughter. She drops even the amenity of talking about the daughter and continues her spoken reverie on Vevey. Here an extraordinary event occurs. The American lady, who throughout the story has been completely oblivious to others, *realizes* that the narrator's wife wants to talk about Vevey. For the rest of the conversation she actually focuses on what the narrator's wife wants to talk about, and she responds with questions about the honeymoon and with statements that attempt to reply to what the wife says.

Part of the emotional impact of the conversation derives from the fact that if the narrator's wife makes an impression strong enough to pierce the self-absorption and alter the discourse of the American lady, then it must be quite a strong impression indeed. The wife also emerges from her near anonymity to become the center of the scene, a transformation heightened by the drum roll of "said my wife" tags supplied by the narrator. And when the wife's speeches are stitched together, they are emotionally compelling in and of themselves: "I know Vevey. We were there on our honeymoon. It was a very lovely place. We stayed at the Trois Couronnes. Yes. We had a very fine room and in the fall the country was lovely. Yes."

When the American lady finally replies to what the narrator's wife is saying, she slips subtly into the present tense: "Isn't it lovely?" But then, in asking about the honeymoon, she returns to the past tense: "Where did you stop there?" The wife unconsciously changes the verb to "stayed" (avoiding the primary meaning of "stopped") and gives the name of the hotel. Hemingway deliberately chose the "Trois Couronnes" for its literary allusiveness; it is the exact same hotel in which Henry James's "Daisy Miller" takes place. Both stories present American travelers who are robbed of their innocent illusions (although in "Canary" we are presented with the aftermath of the characters' initiation). "Trois Couronnes" means "three crowns," but both James and Hemingway, with their excellent command of French, likely knew that it is also an idiom for "three fool's caps." If the narrator, so closely modeled on Hemingway himself, also knows the double meaning of "Trois Couronnes," then perhaps he is aware of the irony of the name as a reflection on the three inhabitants of the compartment.

W. R. Martin and Warren U. Ober point out other fascinating similarities of motif in this "Daisy Miller" intertext. For instance, Daisy is "trapped and caged by an unforgiving American expatriate society," one that half a century later seems well represented in its puritanical intolerance by Hemingway's American lady. James's symbol of imprisonment, the Colosseum, is duplicated by Hemingway's symbols of the birdcage and the train compartment. Most intriguing, Martin and Ober note that "Vevey's fame . . . depended on its proximity to . . . Europe's most famous prison, the Castle of Chillon, with its dungeon." In Lord Byron's poem, "The Prisoner of Chillon," the narrator shares his imprisonment with a bird that entered through a crevice, and he laments, "to see such a bird in such a nest"—a statement figuratively applicable to the situation of Hemingway's canary and the American lady's daughter. Martin and Ober conclude that "Hemingway's extended allusion to 'Daisy Miller' gives his 'A Canary for One' a structural force and a pathos that many readers have missed, perhaps because they have underestimated the subtlety of Hemingway's art or had some difficulty in seeing his work as being . . . in the tradition of James's."[30] How many of these connections the narrator recognizes, or whether he's even read "Daisy Miller," we cannot know, but Hemingway's deliberate intertext nevertheless maintains the potential to deepen the reader's emotional response to the story's events.

As noted, the conversation between the women is manifestly repetitious, which invests it with verisimilitude as they repeat, in various contexts, each other's phrases. The American lady, who seems incapable of meaningful conversation, is only able to parrot what the narrator's wife says. And the wife, lost in her memories, latches onto phrases used by the American lady that she herself finds, in the grip of these memories, meaningful. But, as also noted, the repetition serves a dual purpose, without which the entire passage, however mimetic, would be vitiated, as beneath the banal surface the repeated words and phrases expand in meaning because of the changing contexts in which they appear.

For instance, the words "fall," "Vevey," and "lovely" are each used four times and the words "love" and "fine" twice. The American lady tells the narrator's wife that she and her daughter left Vevey two years ago "this *fall*." Moments later, responding to the information that the couple had been in Vevey on their honeymoon, she says "[t]hat must have been *lovely*" but follows by saying that she did not know that her daughter would "*fall* in *love* with" the Swiss, changing the original meaning of "fall." The wife agrees that "[i]t was a very *lovely* place," slightly changing the referent of "lovely" from honeymooning in Vevey to Vevey itself. A second implied meaning accrues to Vevey here: that it was a place where one could "fall in love." The American lady then agrees with the wife who has just agreed with her, but she puts her statement in the present tense—"Isn't it *lovely*?"—changing the referent from Vevey past to Vevey present, and calls the Trois Couronnes "a *fine* old hotel[.]" The wife then utters her own recapitulation with variation, gathering up the repeated words and phrases to sum up her sense of the conversation: "We had a very *fine* room and in the *fall* the country was *lovely*." In her sentence, the meaning of "fine" changes from "prestigious" (revealing the American lady's values) to "nice" or "lovely" (indicating the wife's values); "fall" once more refers to a season (although it still echoes with the previous sense of "to fall in love"); and "lovely" describes Vevey in the past tense (conflating lovely, fine, falling in love, the room, the countryside, and Vevey—but locating it all in the past). When the American lady then asks if the couple was "there in the *fall*" and the wife replies "Yes," the conversation that began with the wife asking when the American lady left Vevey is brought full circle. Its focus has, by subtle increments, shifted from the American lady and her daughter in the present ("this fall") to the American couple in Vevey in the past (all italics mine).

The narrator sits through this moving discussion, listening carefully, the bags at his feet, looking out the window. Perhaps he too is being lured back into the past by the circular, mesmerizing conversation (which lacks discordant elements because of the repetitive phrases and the manner in which each speech seems to agree with and flow from the one that precedes it). But his eyes are glued to the window and he sees the wrecked train cars. When the American lady asks if they *were* in Vevey in the fall, his wife says yes, but now they *are* passing three wrecked cars. The narrator, in his second and final speech, calls their attention to the present—"Look"—and announces, "There's been a wreck." Just as in his earlier speech about his "braces," his statement seems commonplace but actually reveals his resentment: toward the American lady, the dissolution of his marriage, and this painful reliving of the happy past. His statement works a comparable change in focus and tone as Jake Barnes's reply to Brett Ashley in the final line of *The Sun Also Rises.* When Brett exclaims that they could have had "such a damned good time together[,]" Jake, watching a traffic policeman raise his baton, replies, "Isn't it pretty to think so?"[31]

When the narrator points out the wreck in five syllables totaling a mere twenty letters, his statement serves six functions (a remarkable example of Hemingway's dialogue compression) that bring together several strands of the story in a complex, multi-leveled speech act. First, he indicates the literal wreck that has occurred. Second, the wreck is the physical realization of the fears about a train crash that the American lady has expressed throughout the story. Third, the couple's marriage, which the narrator's wife has been reliving, is a wreck. Fourth, the three people, like the three cars they are passing, are also wrecks (the wreck symbolizes the three characters as well as the couple's marriage). Fifth, the narrator, by his statement, wrecks the women's conversation. Sixth, since that conversation has been a reenactment, of sorts, of their previously happily married state, he has perhaps repeated in the present (especially since the story is based upon the real-life first marriage that Hemingway wrecked) what he had done in the past. Certainly, his speech seems to, in Elizabeth Bowen's words, "crystallize relationships."[32] What he has said is pretty much the equivalent of "Shut the hell up!"

The American lady looks out the window and, since she is facing backwards, sees only the last wrecked car. The wreck confirms her anxieties, and she launches into a speech about how she had feared such a thing and how she will never again travel on a *rapide.* After having listened to someone else for the first time in the story, she now retreats back into her self-centeredness. As Julian Smith points out, she sees only one of the wrecked cars, just as she sees only herself.[33]

With the emotional climax of the story now completed, it is time for the denouement. The train has served its purpose—*for* the characters and *to* the story—and is no longer needed:

> Then the train was in the dark of the Gare de Lyons, and then stopped and porters came up to the windows. I handed bags through the windows, and we were out on the dim longness of the platform, and the American lady put herself in charge of one of three men from Cook's who said: "Just a moment, madame, and I'll look for your name."
>
> The porter brought a truck and piled on the baggage, and my wife said good-by and I said good-by to the American lady, whose name had been found by the man from Cook's on a typewritten page in a sheaf of typewritten pages which he replaced in his pocket.

Characteristically, the American lady seizes control, taking charge of the man from Cook's (the fact that a representative of such a prestigious firm attends to her confirms our earlier sense of her cosmopolitan authority and social status). But the narrator and his wife remain passive. The train, in repose, no longer commands respect or fear, and the porters descend upon it like vultures. The travelers "were out" on the platform; they do not "go out" onto it. The phrase "we were out on the dim longness of the platform" is surreal, conveying the narrator's emotional state through its emphasis of "long" by transforming it into a noun.

The man from Cook's accomplishes something that no one else in the story has been able to—he finds someone's name. But the narrator will not reveal that name to the reader, and the man puts it back in his pocket. The narrator and his wife say goodbye separately to the American lady, which is appropriate since they have dealt with her separately. The narrator, lost in his thoughts, only remembers to say goodbye after his wife does. The sentence is deliberately ambiguous; it could also be read as the wife saying goodbye to the narrator and her husband saying goodbye to the American lady or to his wife (since she, too, is an American lady). This would not be the logical way to read it, but the narrative discourse of this story has a logic of its own and the possibility of this reading leaves its mark.

The narrator has thus far used the first-person plural pronoun only twice, when "We were passing three cars that had been in a wreck" and when "we were out on" the platform. Both times, "we" referred to all three characters. (His wife, by contrast, uses "we" four times, in each case referring to her husband and herself.) In the final two paragraphs, the narrator uses the first-person plural pronoun twice, and each time it refers to him and his wife. The story concludes:

> We followed the porter with the truck down the long cement platform beside the train. At the end was a gate and a man took the tickets.
>
> We were returning to Paris to set up separate residences.

The narrator and his wife remain passive to the end. As the train that carried them toward the end of their marriage stands beside them, inert and lifeless, they are still being led to their fate as they silently follow the porter and their belongings down the platform. The scene is Kafkaesque in the archetypal starkness of its details: the long platform, a gate, a faceless man taking tickets. The French custom of taking tickets at the end of a train journey instead of when the passengers board the train also serves the story, as the tickets seem linked to the new lives that the narrator and his wife are embarking upon rather than to the train ride they have just completed.

There is little to add to what I have already said about the final sentence. It provides the explanation for the consistently curious aspects of the narrative we have just read, what we have felt but not fully understood while reading it, and compels us immediately to re-read the story. But it is in no way at odds with our first reading. The tone of the sentence is particularly effective and completely in character for the narrator. His formal, deliberately understated prose smacks of stoicism but draws attention to itself in the way that it combines self-pity with an attempt to suppress that self-pity. Had he said, for instance, "We had returned to Paris to get a separation" or some other common expression, the sentence would have been less charged with emotion. By employing the past progressive tense ("were returning") instead of the past perfect ("had returned")—either of which would have been technically accurate since they are already in Paris—Hemingway only slightly de-emphasizes what I term the *disjunctive bump* (the way we are rudely ejected from a short story),[34] reminding us that what we have read is but an episode in a much larger story: the end of a marriage and the future separate paths the two characters will pursue. By using a tense that indicates an ongoing action in the past, rather than one that is completed, he links the story to all that will happen in the American couple's future. The final sentence thus sends us backwards, to re-reading what has happened, and floats us forward, toward what will occur. In this way we are, in Sean O'Faolain's words, "mesmeriz[ed] . . . into forgetfulness of the vastness of [the short story's] convention which makes tiny bits of life speak for the whole of life."[35]

As in our first chapter, I have once again written a great number of words about a very short story, but such a lengthy analysis was necessary, both for the purposes of this book and to a meaningful appreciation of an extremely rich and brilliantly crafted but neglected story. In March 1925, Hemingway had claimed that his stories were "written so tight and so hard that the alteration of a word can throw an entire story out of key."[36] "A Canary for One," written a year and a half after that statement, confirms his assertion. In my belief that a short story demands the same sort of close scrutiny as does a poem, I have tried to show, as completely as possible, what "A Canary for One" is. If I have used many more words than Hemingway, it is because the discourse of his story is so suggestive, so compressed, and so rich that one cannot do it full justice with a briefer analysis.

Nor would it have been possible to appreciate this story without abandoning the currently prevailing methods of critical analysis. How Hemingway transmuted the materials of his own life into fiction, what the story tells us of the break-up with Hadley, what contribution this story makes to our understanding of Hemingway's attitude toward marriage, separation, human isolation and suffering, or to our larger understanding of 1920s codes of gender, class, or expatriation—these matters are manifestly important and interesting, but they are not what the story *is.* If today's methods of cultural criticism cannot help us to appreciate so fine a story as "A Canary for One," then the fault lies with our methods, not with the work of art they fail to penetrate.

I began Part II with an epigraph from Flannery O'Connor, the patron saint of this book, and I should like to conclude by returning to her. In an essay titled "The Teaching of Literature," which could just as well have been titled "The Understanding of Literature," she declared:

> The student has to have tools to understand a story or a novel, and these are tools proper to the structure of the work, tools proper to the craft.

> They are tools that operate inside the work and not outside it; they are concerned with how this story is made and with what makes it work as a story.[37]

O'Connor, by any measure one of the giants of fiction writing in world literature, penned these words half a century ago. Perhaps it's time for critics to take her seriously.

III

Metacritical and Metafictional Hemingway

You know I was thinking about actual sharks when I wrote the book [*The Old Man and the Sea*] and had nothing to do with the theory that they represented critics. I don't know who thought that up. I have always hoped for sound, intelligent criticism all my life as writing is the loneliest of all trades. But I have had little of it except from Kashkin and from you. Some of yours I disagreed with very much and others were illuminating and helpful.

—Hemingway to Edmund Wilson (1952), *Selected Letters*

From things that have happened and from things as they exist and from all things that you know and all those you cannot know, you make something through your invention that is not a representation but a whole new thing truer than anything true and alive, and you make it alive, and if you make it well enough, you give it immortality. That is why you write and for no other reason that you know of. But what about all the reasons that no one knows?

—Hemingway, interview by George Plimpton

4

Hemingway on (Mis)Reading Stories

"GOD REST YOU MERRY, GENTLEMEN" AS METACRITICISM

> All criticism is shit anyway. Nobody knows anything about it except yourself. God knows people who are paid to have attitudes toward things, professional critics, make me sick; çamp following eunochs of literature. . . . They're all virtuous and sterile. And how well meaning and high minded. But they're all camp followers.
>
> —Hemingway to Sherwood Anderson (1925), *Selected Letters*

> But all these guys have theories and try to fit you into the theory.
>
> —Hemingway to Harvey Breit (1956), *Selected Letters*

In our first three chapters, we have seen that craft approaches to the short story need not inevitably lead, as many academics now cavalierly assume, to "mere" formalism, or worse, "empty" formalism. I have tried to show that an understanding of form, craft, art, and technique contributes to cultural studies approaches and provides a path to more accurate explorations of a story's unique qualities. In these readings, the author has been very much alive and conscious, making decisions and constructing texts. The readings are not at odds with critical relevance; rather, they come into conflict only with criticism that proceeds through generalization, paraphrase, selective analysis as a means to an ideologically determined critical end, and what, for lack of a better phrase, we might call "cookie cutter" criticism—what Hemingway above refers to as fitting a writer or a text to a theory. In this chapter, I would like to give Hemingway himself a chance to address this phenomenon—how readers interpret and misinterpret texts, and why.

I

Hemingway's "God Rest You Merry, Gentlemen," published in 1933, seems a slight, if disturbing, tale; consequently, until as late as 2005 it was the subject of only four brief scholarly pieces and an explication. Peter Hays reads the story as a modern revision of the Fisher King legend; Julian

Smith sees it as an analeptic (flashback) tale told by Jake Barnes of *The Sun Also Rises* with the narrator's identity withheld; George Monteiro believes that its main interest lies in the light it sheds on Hemingway's attitude toward Christianity and the medical profession but faults it for having an unnecessary and unsubstantial first-person narrator who is not meaningfully connected to the plot; and Rick Moss argues that the narrator's current, almost mea culpa, perspective is the central point of the story, although aside from delving into the motivation of the narrator for telling the story, he does not offer much analysis of the text.[1] The main problem with these readings is that they implicitly view the story as thin and are therefore compelled to read it through a speculative (in Julian Smith's case, a wildly speculative) intertext.

Recently, three essays have attempted to uncover the depths that critics have long sensed in the story, but through more plausible literary, historical, and manuscript-based research. In 2006, Horst H. Kruse explored and connected the narrative's many allusions to Shakespeare's *The Merchant of Venice* and the *King James Bible* to show that Hemingway's "controlling purpose" was "satirizing Middle America and its puritanical attitudes." In 2008, Nicole J. Camastra examined at length Hemingway's knowledge of music and the history of singing Church *castrati,* associated with both Constantinople and Rome, the last of whom, Alessandro Moreseschi, died in 1922 when Hemingway was in Genoa. Within this context, she makes a case for the story being a "profound and complex prose hymn" that "celebrates the individual's relation to God amidst sectarian fragmentation." And in 2010, Shannon Whitlock Levitzke analyzed how the changes in earlier drafts of the opening paragraphs—which depicted Kansas City in detail as a city of "beauty and humanity . . . where people engage one another"—was trimmed until that city was sparsely portrayed as a "cold and barren place," making it "more generic and representative of urban life in America as a whole." Upping the story's ante, she concludes that the "barren physical topography" of Kansas City in the final version and the initial but otherwise unexplained mention of the physically distant Constantinople "are symptomatic of a more universal despair" and that "the impoverishment of modernity's waste land" lies at the heart of the story.[2] These new essays add valuable contextual layers to the story, showing it to be anything but slight, but they still leave us with the questions Monteiro raised four decades ago: why tell the story through a nearly anonymous narrator, and what on earth can the point of the story be?[3] Is it a merely a critique of the puritanical values Hemingway so detested, a celebration of faith in the face of societal fragmentation, yet one more lament about the bleak modern world, or, as these are not mutually exclusive, all three?

The point of the story, however, is ironically illustrated by all of these readings, for Hemingway's odd tale is about the problems of reading a text and the consequences of misreading. Specifically, it is about what I term *semiotic confusion,* a confusion that is caused by the failure of signifiers to point to appropriate signifieds (not merely the subtle forms of slippage that concern poststructuralists, but the sorts of wholesale aberrations that would bother even normal folks), and about how characters (and people) employ the wrong intertexts or misapply sign systems in their efforts to interpret signifiers. In other words, the story is about, in a sense, critics—good ones like Doc Fischer, bad ones like Doctor Wilcox, and apprentices like the narrator—and how they attempt to read a text.

Hemingway's fiction is filled with characters who are themselves texts that other characters (and readers) try to understand, and it is also replete with characters who employ the wrong sign systems in attempting these interpretations, often with disastrous results. For instance, in "Soldier's Home" Mrs. Krebs inappropriately tries to read her son's experiences in World War I through the intertext of what she has heard about her own father's experiences in the Civil War, and this sign system prevents her from accurately "seeing" her flesh-and-blood son for who he actually is. Although "God Rest You Merry, Gentlemen" focuses specifically on this process of employing incorrect intertexts and misapplying sign systems, and thus provides a cautionary tale for critics, the presence of semiotic confusion throughout Hemingway's fiction should serve as an admonition by the author for critics to read his works carefully and closely, to see exactly what's in them and what words he uses, and to be leery of producing interpretations merely by running them through the abstract *a priori* theories and methodologies that now increasingly constitute the tools of the academy.

II

In "God Rest You Merry, Gentlemen," an older (and wiser?) narrator recalls a scene from his earlier days in Kansas City when he was, perhaps, a reporter, hospital worker, or ambulance driver (his occupation is never specified in the final version of the text).[4] The story engages the theme of semiotic confusion from the opening sentence in which Hemingway employs a narrative strategy of presenting a description that describes nothing: "In those days the distances were all very different, the dirt blew off the hills that have now been cut down, and Kansas City was very like Constantinople."[5] This opening sentence, an extreme example of what I have termed Hemingway's technique of the *present absence* in which he offers the reader a scene that has vanished or else one he proceeds to snatch away,[6] offers a non-map with which to locate the story: by informing readers that their current sense of spatial relations is unhelpful, that the one image in the sentence (the hills) no longer exists, and that Kansas City can best be imagined through an intertext, Constantinople, which even if they have seen it would be of no use since he does not say, aside from the dirt, how the two cities are alike. As if this were not frustrating enough, we are immediately told: "You may not believe this. No one believes this; but it is true."

Having struck a Hawthornian note in which the actual will blend with the fanciful, the mundane with the uncanny, the narrator proceeds to describe a "neutral territory"[7] of deserted city streets on Christmas Day that are covered with falling snow in the early dark. Through the dimness and snow, an incongruous, concrete image appears—a silver French racing car in a lighted show window with the words "Dans Argent" on the hood. The narrator recalls that he "believed" this to mean "the silver dance or the silver dancer" and was "pleased" by his "knowledge of a foreign language[.]" Implied in his verb tense ("believed") is that he now knows that it meant either "in money" or "in silver,"[8] but thematically what is more important is that in the very first paragraph a signifier has been misread because of a faulty mastery of a sign system (French), and the character who misread it assumed that he read it correctly. The paragraph concludes with the narrator walking to the city hospital on the high hill (which, given the opening sentence, may very well no longer exist) where he enters the reception room and sees the two ambulance surgeons, Doc Fischer and Doctor Wilcox.

Here, the theme of semiotic confusion is further advanced by the problematizing of cultural stereotypes. Fischer is Jewish, but has "sand-blond" hair and "gambler's hands"; Wilcox is gentile, dark, and carries a book. The book, a medical aid titled *The Young Doctor's Friend and Guide,* gives symptoms and treatment on any subject, and is also "cross-indexed so that being consulted on symptoms it gave diagnoses." The incompetent Wilcox is sensitive about the book but cannot get along without it. Fischer, who holds Wilcox in contempt, has mockingly suggested that future editions of the book "should be further cross-indexed so that if consulted as to the treatments being given, it would reveal ailments and symptoms." This would serve, he says, "As an aid to memory[.]" Wilcox's dependence on the book reveals his inability to read the physical symptoms of the body on his own. Memory (competence within the sign system) enables Fischer to read these physical symptoms, but what if the illness is emotional and cultural rather than physical? This takes us into the heart of the tale.

Fischer asks the narrator, whom he calls "Horace" (which, in the spirit of the text, may or may not be his real name) for "news along the rialto[,]" a jocular Shakespearean allusion that further defamiliarizes the Kansas City streets and also demonstrates his erudition without him calling attention to it. Endowing the narrator with the name of a famous Roman poet is typical of his gentle, almost paternally affectionate sarcasm toward the young man, and quoting a line spoken by Shylock, a character generally considered to be among the most complex antisemitic stereotypes in literature, is characteristic of Fischer's wry wit. Such references to a poet from the Augustan Age and a line from *The Merchant of Venice*—neither of which his two auditors would presumably catch—are consistent with Fischer's "amused eyes" and his ironic sense of humor throughout the story.[9]

Fischer tells "Horace" that they had an "extremely interesting case" that morning—a boy who had come in the previous day seeking "eunuchhood." The narrator, who had been present on that occasion, recalls the excited, frightened, but determined sixteen-year-old who demanded to be castrated because he suffered from "awful lust." When Fischer tried to explain that sexual desire is "a natural thing," the boy replied that it is "a sin against purity" and "against our Lord and Saviour." He also told Fischer "you don't understand[.]" Fischer was unable to get the boy to listen to him; Wilcox called the boy "a goddamned fool," used a vulgar vernacular expression to tell him to go masturbate, and threw him out.[10] Fischer now informs Horace that they received the boy that morning "self-mutilated with a razor" but not castrated because he "didn't know what castrate meant." The boy may die from loss of blood, in Fischer's opinion because, "The good physician here, Doctor Wilcox, my colleague, was on call and he was unable to find this emergency listed in his book."

In this event, the boy is a text that the boy and the doctors try to read but cannot because they employ intertexts inappropriately and/or misinterpret signifiers. The boy interprets himself as impure by applying a Biblical intertext that he has read too literally (perhaps 1st Corinthians 6:13—"The body is not meant for immorality, but for the Lord, and the Lord for the body"; or Matthew 5:28—"But I say to you that every one who looks at a woman lustfully has already committed adultery with her in his heart"). In saying that Fischer does not understand, the boy insists on interpreting his body according to his own fundamentalist notions of a New Testament sign system, rather than according to less literal Christian interpretations of the New Testament or according to the contemporary secular sign system with which Fischer reads these same signifiers (perhaps a popular version of psychoanalytic theory that has filtered into American culture). In choosing a course of action, the boy again inappropriately employs a Biblical intertext that he reads in a literal rather than figurative manner, most likely Matthew 18: 7–9, in which Jesus says: "woe to the man by whom the temptation comes! And if your hand or your foot causes you to sin, cut it off and throw it away; it is better for you to enter life maimed or lame than with two hands or two feet to be thrown into the eternal fire." Similar metaphorical references to removing sinful parts are found in Matthew 5: 29–30 and Mark 9: 43–48. The boy's final act of misreading demonstrates his ignorance not only of the way the body fits into liberal Christian and secular sign systems, but also of the body as a biological text. He misinterprets his erection to mean that his penis is the body part causing his "awful lust," and therefore cuts off his penis instead of castrating himself. Since his desire was to cast off desire, his inability to read his body as a biological text leads to failure.

Wilcox, too, falls victim to semiotic confusion, although with less dire consequences to himself. He misreads the boy/text because he cannot find the symptoms in his book, which interprets physical signifiers rather than psychological ones. In addition, when he tells the boy to masturbate, he employs an inappropriate medical/biological sign system in assuming that mere sexual release will solve the boy's dilemma. His cruelty to the boy also shows his inability to anticipate/interpret the possible alternatives the boy will take, and, once they are taken, his book does not cover the particular physical emergency. Moreover, although nominally a Christian, Wilcox fails to read the true spirit of Christianity, a fact made amply clear by his insensitivity to the boy's desperation during the first visit and by his later implication that the boy's act has somehow polluted Christmas.

Fischer's reading is the most complex of all. He correctly reads the boy's symptoms as signifying an emotional disturbance. However, as a Jew, either he does not fully understand the persuasive force that a literal fundamentalist reading of the Bible has for the boy, or else he is simply unable to convince the boy of a more liberal interpretation of the New Testament that will help him to read and act upon his physical desires in a responsible manner. At first he tells him: "There is nothing wrong with you. That's the way you're supposed to be. There's nothing wrong with that." When the boy insists that his desires are wrong, Fisher tries again: "It's a natural thing. It's the way you are supposed to be and later on you will think you are very fortunate." The boy replies: "No. I won't listen. You can't make me listen." He again begs to be castrated. Having failed to convince the boy of his secular sign system in which sexual desire is natural, Fischer tries to combine that secular system with his own outsider's sense of a Christian perspective: "No one will castrate you. There is nothing wrong with your body. You have a fine body and you must not think about that. If you are religious remember that what you complain of is no sinful state but the means of consummating a sacrament." But his efforts are in vain, as the boy insists that his desire is "a constant sin against purity." Having failed to un-demonize the boy's symptoms, all Fischer can do is to refuse the boy's request. And so, the one character who genuinely cares about the boy is prevented, by his own cultural "otherness," from helping him.

Hemingway's treatment of Fischer's otherness—which the author approaches in his characteristically indirect fashion—is explored in the final two pages of the story and points to the larger cultural issue in this bitter and ironically titled Christmas tale. After Fischer implies that the boy may die due to Wilcox's incompetence, and Wilcox responds by telling his colleague to go to hell, Fischer disingenuously relents while staring down at his "gambler's hands" that had, as the narrator silently observes, "with his willingness to oblige and his lack of respect for Federal statutes, made him his trouble." This cryptic observation by the narrator—later brought into the open when Fischer admits that he had been too "damned smart on the coast"—introduces into the narrative Fischer's "back story": why this manifestly able doctor finds himself buried in a relatively lowly position as an ambulance surgeon in Kansas City. The famous Hemingwayesque "thing left out"—omitted yet powerfully present—here as in "Hills Like White Elephants," most likely has to do with abortions. The only other possibility that suggests itself is euthanasia, but that would have fallen under the criminal code and not the federal statutes. Also, had euthanasia been

Fischer's crime, it is difficult to believe that he would have avoided jail and/ or the loss of his medical license. Although the ban against performing abortions would have fallen under state rather than federal statutes, it's possible that Hemingway (or his narrator) was unaware of this.

Fischer's "gambler's hands" have made him into a criminal in the jurisprudential system just as, analogously, his ethnicity and religion place him outside the social pale; and both his legal and cultural otherness have as their specific analogue his current professional marginalization. This indirectly glimpsed past event, which Hemingway has *both* the narrator and, later, Fischer allude to lest the reader miss its significance, illuminates Fischer's response to the boy's mutilation, which has clearly reminded him of how he tried to prevent another kind of self-mutilation on the coast (i.e., the sorts of mutilations that frequently occurred when women attempted to self-abort or else found themselves at the mercy of incompetent or unscrupulous lay abortionists). In other words, what has happened to the boy bothers Fischer for the same reasons as it would disturb any doctor, even Wilcox (who has been drinking when the narrator enters the hospital); he has been unable to help someone in need. But it bothers him for other reasons as well. Fischer identifies with the boy because both of them, in different ways, have fallen victim to a culture of fundamentalist Christianity. And all of this helps to explain Fischer's dislike of Wilcox, who exemplifies, for Fischer, the hostile cultural mainstream through whose eyes he is obliged continually to view himself as a result of the double-consciousness that he has developed for his own self-protection.

On a more abstract level, one is tempted to say that the boy's amputated penis is a telling symbol of Fischer's own situation. Just as the boy, if he lives, will continue to feel desire but possess no outlet for its release, so too will Fischer continue to desire to escape his cultural and professional marginalization, but with no chance of doing so. Nor will he have an outlet for helping many others, pregnant women in distress among them, in order to fulfill his sense of vocation. Metaphorically, Fischer is both the amputated penis and the amputee; he has been cut off from the larger social body, and he is a man who is unable to act on his desires. It is, of course, highly doubtful that Fischer himself (or Hemingway, for that matter) perceives the amputated penis in these sorts of symbolic terms, but it is also clear that this incident resonates for him in a way that it does not for the other characters.

Although Fischer is aware of his own precarious position, his resentment is such that he can only feign, not feel indifference. His anger manifests itself in his constant derision of Wilcox's medical abilities. (He is clearly the source of the narrator's information on Wilcox's sorry record in medical school, information that, again in the spirit of this text, may or may not be true.) He also cannot resist baiting Wilcox, but in the passive-aggressive manner of one who understands his own powerlessness. After blaming Wilcox's incompetence for the boy's critical condition (his comment about Wilcox not being able to find the emergency listed in his book), being told by Wilcox "[t]he hell with you talking that way," and disingenuously claiming that he meant no offense—"I only meant it in the friendliest way, Doctor"—Fischer's animus takes another tack:

[P1] "Well, I wish you wouldn't ride me about it [Wilcox's medical guide]," Wilcox said. "There isn't any need to ride me."

[P2] "Ride you, Doctor, on the day, the very anniversary, of our Saviour's birth?"

[P3] "*Our* Saviour? Ain't you a Jew?" Doctor Wilcox said.

[P4] "So I am. So I am. It always is slipping my mind. I've never given it its proper importance. So good of you to remind me. *Your* Saviour. That's right. *Your* Saviour, undoubtedly *your* Saviour—and the ride for Palm Sunday."

[P5] "You're too damned smart," Doctor Wilcox said.

[P6] "An excellent diagnosis, Doctor. I was always too damned smart. Too damned smart on the coast certainly. Avoid it, Horace. You haven't much tendency but sometimes I see a gleam. But what a diagnosis—and without the book."

[P7] "The hell with you," Doctor Wilcox said.

Fischer's initial witticism in paragraph 2 signifies on Wilcox's idiomatic use of "ride me" (i.e., "make fun of me") and is intended to equate Wilcox with an ass (i.e., Jesus riding the donkey into Jerusalem on Palm Sunday). But it backfires because he inadvertently reminds the butt of his joke that he, the Christian Wilcox, ultimately possesses the upper hand. Wilcox seizes the opportunity, in a typically blunt fashion, by calling Fischer a "Jew" in a manner that makes the word sound like an imprecation. Fischer is thus once again confronted by his marginalized state, which relegates him to a position inferior even to the incompetent Wilcox. (There is even a small hint that Fischer may literally be Wilcox's subordinate. Although Fischer is clearly concerned about the boy in their first meeting, when

Wilcox orders his colleague to "Get him out of here," and the boy replies, "Don't touch me. I'll get out[,]" Fischer remains uncharacteristically silent.) In paragraph 4, Fischer again retreats behind a mask of aggressive passivity in his exaggerated disingenuous claims that his ethnicity is so unimportant that it slips his mind. But he cannot resist repeating and making more explicit his joke ("*Your* Saviour. That's right. *Your* Saviour, undoubtedly *your* Saviour—and the ride for Palm Sunday"), three times emphasizing "your," especially since Wilcox failed to catch it the first time around.

Yet, by returning to his "ass" joke, Fischer fails to shift the verbal exchange to safer ground, however much he manages to infuriate the less than glib Wilcox, who replies that Fischer is too smart. Wilcox's two trademark responses ("The hell with you" and "You're too damned smart"), each uttered twice in the story, have particular import for Fischer as expressions of cultural hostility toward his ethnicity. The former implies that, as a Jew, he has been damned to hell by the mainstream religious culture. The latter appeals to the stereotype of the "smart Jew" or "smart-ass Jew" (especially, to the midwestern mind, the smart Jew from the coast). Although Wilcox's blunt response may lack conscious purpose other than to express anger, Fischer is aware of the socially constructed forces that lie behind it. Without realizing it, Wilcox has accidentally read Fischer's situation effectively. Fischer's "ass" joke may be clever, but what is the point of being witty in the wake of the boy's tragedy? And what is the point of being smart in a world in which people are judged by their ethnicity and religion, where intelligence itself can carry negative connotations? Fischer is still smarting from his unhappy past and diminished present, all because he was, in a sense, too smart.

Recognizing the ineffectiveness of his witticism, his smartness, in paragraph 6 Fischer abandons his "ass" joke and adopts a rhetorical strategy of acknowledging his own failings ("I was always too damned smart"), addressing Wilcox indirectly by speaking to the narrator, and once again assailing Wilcox on the grounds of professional competence in his sarcastic comment on diagnosing without the book. In referring to the events on the coast, Fischer shifts the referent of being "smart" from the hostile host culture's antisemitic stereotype to a specific event, which gives it less blanket condemnatory power. By addressing Wilcox indirectly, he excludes his adversary from the verbal exchange and forces him to overhear, thus robbing him of the prerogatives of replying to a direct address. And by bringing up Wilcox's medical guide, he again puts Wilcox on the defensive by foregrounding Wilcox's professional inadequacies rather than his own cultural marginalization.

When Wilcox repeats, "The hell with you," he gives Fischer the opportunity to replay their first exchange, the one in which Fischer had responded to this curse by pretending that he meant no offense, and then making the ineffective "ass" joke that gave Wilcox an opening to attack:

> "All in good time, Doctor," Doc Fischer said. "All in good time. If there is such a place I shall certainly visit it. I have even had a very small look into it. No more than a peek, really. I looked away almost at once. And do you know what the young man said, Horace, when the good Doctor here brought him in? He said, 'Oh, I asked you to do it. I asked you so many times to do it.'"

In this speech, Fischer does not retreat behind a mask of disingenuousness, but accepts Wilcox's curse with patient reasoning. His putative agnosticism ("If there is such a place") is both an implicit claim of ethnicity—as a Jew he rejects the Christian notion of an afterlife—and a calm assertion of superiority, since hell holds no particular terror for him as, ostensibly, it would for Wilcox. Hell, for Fischer, is what happens on earth and the misfortunes, of which the boy's tragedy is the most recent, that he has had to endure. By invoking the words of the boy, who has also been victimized by the culture of Wilcox (whom Fischer insists on calling "the good physician" and "the good doctor" in a parodic allusion to St. Luke), Fischer goes beyond the specifics of Wilcox's incompetence and correctly signifies communal responsibility for the boy's tragedy ("I looked away almost at once") and communal guilt.

All of this is lost on the witless Wilcox (in earlier drafts of the story, punningly named "Cox"), who can only express the cultural code of anti-semitism without really reading or understanding it. He follows Fischer's speech by adding, "On Christmas Day, too," again revealing his inability to read the true spirit of Christianity. Fischer's chastening response—"The significance of the particular day is not important"—is an admonition that the tragedy is communal and transcends such matters as specific faiths. But Wilcox can only seize the opportunity to invoke, once more, Fischer's otherness—"Maybe not to you"—rejecting both the democratic and the Christian notions of a larger community that shares responsibility and guilt. Fischer may be too smart, but Wilcox is too dumb; his incompetence at medicine extends to all of his attempts to comprehend signifiers and employ sign systems. He can only express a distorted, bigoted version of Christianity that defines itself through exclusivity, not through any transcendent message of love and redemption. The final verse of the actual Christmas carol, "God Rest You Merry, Gentlemen," goes: "And with true love and brotherhood / Each other now embrace; / This holy tide of Christmas / All other doth deface." By his lack of love and brotherhood, then, it is Wilcox and not the boy who has polluted/defaced Christmas.

When Fischer is finally able to read Wilcox correctly as a text and not just as an adversary, he realizes the impossibility of his situation—he is a Jew and cannot remove from the Wilcoxes of the world this defining social construction—and he gives up by way of mock commentary as the story concludes:

> "You hear him, Horace?" Doc Fischer said. "You hear him? Having discovered my vulnerable point, my achilles tendon so to speak, the doctor pursues his advantage."
>
> "You're too damned smart," Doctor Wilcox said.

Wilcox's repeated reply—"You're too damned smart"—inadvertently underscores Fischer's point; the false sign system of racial/ethnic chauvinism, of which antisemitism is a symptom, has the final word in the text, as it does in life. Once again, a Jew who has "ridden an ass" is sacrificed in order for society to cover up its own shortcomings.

There is, I should note, a relevant biographical context worth considering, as is usually the case in Hemingway's fiction. "God Rest You Merry, Gentlemen" may have been Hemingway's attempt to apologize for his shabby treatment of Harold Loeb—writer, founding editor of the literary magazine *Broom,* and former member of Hemingway's circle in early 1920s Paris—who was deeply hurt by Hemingway's nasty and antisemitic portrayal of him as the hapless Robert Cohn in *The Sun Also Rises.* Like Cohn, Loeb was a Jew who had misread the social codes of his circle and was subsequently excluded from the group. It is more than likely that Hemingway—who typically felt retrospective remorse about his truculent behavior, vicious comments, and violent feelings toward people close to him, and who often expressed this guilt in self-accusatory fiction (e.g., "Cat in the Rain," "Fathers and Sons")—was trying to atone for his insensitivity toward his former friend in his portrayal of Wilcox and Fischer. In a 1954 letter, he confessed, "If there is a hell I shall certainly go to it if the rules are applied like The Immigration Act."[11] Here, he oddly echoes Fischer's statement that if there is a hell, he "shall certainly visit it." In choosing as his metaphor the notorious 1924 immigration restriction acts, which limited the number of people coming into the United States from non-anglophone cultures—such as eastern European Jews, Italians, and Asians—he consciously and unconsciously identifies himself with Fischer to express contrition for having, in his treatment of Loeb, behaved like Wilcox. As Robert E. Gajdusek observes in an extremely insightful essay, there is an abundance of evidence demonstrating "Hemingway's compulsive necessity to face his own moral failures with extraordinary completeness and rigorous honesty, and the necessity to somehow gain absolution from or amendment of them. . . . Hemingway's writing was his mode of moral purgation" and "through it, in abstract projection, he did not exonerate but held his life morally accountable[.]"[12]

III

If "God Rest You Merry, Gentlemen," as I have attempted to show, is about semiotic confusion—the failure of signifiers to connect with proper signifieds, the faulty mastery of sign systems, the employment of inappropriate sign systems, and the triumph of a false sign system—then this answers the concerns of those critics who have seen the story as scant and/or pointless. But the question of the narrator remains. What function does "Horace" serve in the text and why is he nearly anonymous? Why did Hemingway, whose techniques of focalization and choices of perspective were invariably carefully selected and employed, choose to place this story in the hands of an "undeveloped" first-person narrator? Although Hemingway is clearly using one of his favorite story construction techniques, what I term the *Conradian splitting* of the reader's attention between the focalizer and the main character of the tale,[13] in fact creating a double split since the narrator views Fischer who himself views the tormented boy, why is the focalizer/narrator in this story so obscure?

First, the narrator is not, as some critics have complained, extraneous. His misreading of the French words on the racing car offers the first clue that the story is about semiotic confusion. Second, the friendship between Doc Fischer and the narrator (it is significant that he is "Doc" and Wilcox is "Doctor") immediately guides the reader's sympathies toward Fischer and alerts the reader to the fact that Fischer will be the protagonist of the story, the one who, in Henry James's aesthetics, is the most capable of comprehending the narrative's main action, and in Hemingway's story aesthetics the most capable of feeling it emotionally.[14] Third, the narrator serves to link the foreshadowing scenes outside with the events that take place in the hospital (much as does, say, the similarly naive narrator of "In Another Country"). Fourth, the narrator provides the story's central character, Fischer, with a receptive audience for his recounting of the mutilated boy's story and for his mockery of Wilcox (if Wilcox alone were present, it is doubtful that Fischer would bother with these sorts of verbal exchanges, lacking an appreciative audience). Fifth, although we know little of the narrator, we know only slightly more about the other characters in this parable, and to add details to the narrator would obscure the few but significant details we are given about Fischer, Wilcox, and the boy. Last, the narrator's confusion about how to read the story's final action (Wilcox's antisemitic assault on Fischer and Fischer's passive-aggressive strategies of response) as well as the entire story that has unfolded before him—a confusion evident in his (not the author's) lack of a concluding statement of comprehension or sense-making—ends the story on the same note with which it began.

Aside from the initial reference to Constantinople—which it is highly unlikely the narrator would have visited by the time of the story's fabula—there is nothing in the text indicating, on his part, a retrospective understanding of events. But although Hemingway keeps his focalizer firmly inside the narrative's time frame, he clearly expects the reader to intuit that the older narrator is aware now, as Fischer was then, of the difficulties of reading texts, of producing accurate interpretations from the signifiers he observes. This current awareness is not something the narrator draws attention to, just as he does not mention that he now understands what the French words on the car meant, but the reader is in a position to grasp that the narrator has learned something, even if it is merely a humbling sense of epistemological, as well as societal, limitations. Like the story in which it is dramatized, this lesson, I should hasten to add, is hardly a slight one. All critics who interpret texts, not just young men like "Horace," would do well to keep it in mind.

5

Hemingway on (Mis)Writing Stories

"BIG TWO-HEARTED RIVER" AS METAFICTION

> Painting, Henri, is damned difficult. . . . You always believe you've taken hold of it, but you never have. . . . There is a different craft for each object. You never know your whole craft. . . . I could paint for a hundred years, a thousand years without stopping, and it would still seem to me as if I knew nothing. . . . I consume myself, kill myself, to cover fifty centimeters of canvas. . . . It doesn't matter. . . . That's life. . . . I want to die painting. . . .
>
> —Paul Cézanne, quoted in Joachim Gasquet, *Cézanne* (translation mine)

> A life of action is much easier to me than writing. I have greater facility for action than for writing. In action I do not worry any more. Once it is bad enough you get a sort of elation because there is nothing you can do except what you are doing and you have no responsibility. But writing is something that you can never do as well as it can be done. It is a perpetual challenge and it is more difficult than anything else that I have ever done—so I do it. And it makes me happy when I do it well.
>
> —Hemingway to Ivan Kashkin (1935), *Selected Letters*

In this chapter we move from a story about mutilation and despair to one about healing and hope, from a callow narrator undergoing an initiation into the complexities of human society to an experienced protagonist immersing himself in the non-human world. We also move from a story about reading texts to one about writing them, from metacriticism to metafiction. Hemingway chose to conclude *In Our Time* with Nick's search for spiritual renewal in nature, but he also decided to close with a story about writing stories, the very process by which he himself sought emotional healing and regeneration. As a story about the writing of stories, including the writing of itself, "Big Two-Hearted River" is an equally appropriate choice to conclude my two-volume study of Hemingway's art of the short story. In effect, this dying critic will respectfully defer to his dead author and let him have the final word.

I

Hemingway began "Big Two-Hearted River" in Paris in mid-May 1924, and completed what would become the first part of the story when his work was interrupted by magazine editorial duties and a trip to Pamplona for the bullfights. In Spain, he enjoyed trout fishing on the Irati River with John Dos Passos and Robert McAlmon, but he was also burdened by financial needs, his responsibilities to his wife and small child, and fears that he would not be able to write. Nevertheless, he managed to finish the first version of the full story before returning to Paris in July, and sometime in late summer decided to divide it formally into two parts. In October, in response to Gertrude Stein's comment that "remarks are not literature," he deleted the final nine pages of the text, in which he had written directly about actual people and events from his life, and, after several attempts, eventually rewrote the ending to his satisfaction. The story was subsequently published in the first issue of *This Quarter* in May 1925, and republished as the last full story of *In Our Time* in October, formally divided into two parts with a chapter/vignette from *in our time* placed between them. Hemingway considered it by far the finest story he had written to that point.[1]

Others shared this assessment, and "Big Two-Hearted River" quickly assumed a central place in the Hemingway canon, a rank forever secured when Malcolm Cowley, in his introduction to *The Portable Hemingway* (1945), made it the key to his interpretation of Hemingway's writing. Cowley's essay—which stressed the repetition of themes in Hemingway's fiction, the haunted consciousnesses of his protagonists, and their attempts to escape from a world of danger and pain through "the faithful observance of customs they invent for themselves"—implicitly linked "Big Two-Hearted River" to Nick's experience of war.[2] Seven years later, in the first major, full-length study of Hemingway, Philip Young further developed this "war-wound" thesis. Young's two main arguments were that the Hemingway hero is "pretty close to being Hemingway himself" and that "one fact about this recurrent protagonist, as about the man who created him, is necessary to any real understanding of either figure, and that is the fact of the 'wound,' a severe injury suffered in World War I which left permanent scars, visible and otherwise." Deriving from Hemingway's own wounding by a mortar shell near Fossalta di Piave on July 8, 1918, less than two weeks shy of his nineteenth birthday, it is the "figure in the carpet" of his fiction, as the author, acting under a repetition compulsion, returned to it continually in his writing. Like his creator, Nick, too, is a shell-shocked veteran, a "sick man" seeking to escape from the experience that has "complicated and wounded" him. That, Young asserted, is "the whole 'point' of an otherwise pointless story[.]"[3]

For thirty years, from the Korean War through the fighting in Vietnam, Young's thesis went unchallenged and was endlessly reiterated and further developed by other critics. Then, first in a 1981 essay, and later in a lengthy 1987 biography, Kenneth S. Lynn disputed the nature of Hemingway's wound and its place in his work. Concurring with Young that the Hemingway protagonist was usually a thinly veiled fictional persona for the author himself, Lynn posited a different kind of wound as the figure in the carpet—a troubled childhood. According to Lynn, Hemingway's lesbian-leaning, emotionally conflicted mother dominated his youth and produced in him a lifelong confusion over his sexual identity and a fear of his own androgynous impulses. "Hemingway's hurt began in childhood," Lynn explained, and "he was compelled to write stories in which he endeavored to cope with the disorder of his inner world by creating fictional equivalents for it." In "Big Two-Hearted River," Lynn suggested, Nick is not escaping from war memories, but from "a need to please his mother"; his tent is a sort of alternative home (his mother had thrown him out of the family's Michigan summer home on Walloon Lake in July 1920); and "the activity of his mind that keeps threatening to overwhelm his contentment could be rage." For Lynn, the war was a surrogate issue, imposed upon Hemingway criticism first by Edmund Wilson,[4] then by Cowley, and finally fully elaborated by Young. Once this thesis had taken hold, Hemingway embraced it and lent it a retrospective credibility because it served as a sort of subterfuge, even more effective than the enormous ambiguity of his fiction, that hid the true nature of his emotional problems.[5]

"Big Two-Hearted River" thus became a focal point in one of the major debates raging in Hemingway scholarship, although, in the quarter-century since Lynn's biography appeared, the majority of critics have agreed that Nick is suffering from shell shock, whatever other take they might have on the story.[6] This debate, however, will only be resolved once critics in both camps adopt a "both/and" rather than an "either/or" attitude and come to see that what, in 1991, I labeled the "war-wound" and "childhood-wound" theses[7] are not mutually exclusive, that Hemingway's experience of the war was gendered and that his sexual identity was influenced by his military experiences. In other words, when critics heed Roland Barthes's judicious warning that a text "consists not of a line of words, releasing a single 'theological' meaning (the 'message' of the Author-God), but of a multi-dimensional space in which are married and contested several writings,"[8] we will all be better off. In fact, the Young and Lynn interpretations only *seem* incompatible, mainly due to the late Professor Lynn's legendary belligerence in arguing his point. More interesting are the similarities: both perceive in Hemingway a severe psychological disturbance; both believe that once this problem is recognized and the fiction read in light of it, then the meaning of the texts becomes clear; and both acknowledge that the fiction, especially this story, is difficult to decipher without searching outside of the narrative for extratextual evidence.

Meanwhile, the question remains—what is "Big Two-Hearted River" really about, or better still, what else can it be about? A good place to start might be with what actually happens in the story. The final version begins with Nick jumping off a train in a hilly country near a river. There has been a fire and the whole landscape is "burned-over" ("Big Two-Hearted River" 209).[9] Where Nick expected to find the town of Seney, Michigan, all that is left are the chipped foundations of the old hotel. Nick surveys the landscape, picks up his backpack and fishing rod case, and heads uphill parallel with the river. After an arduous trek, he reaches a place where the fire line has stopped but keeps on walking until, hot and tired, he lies down to rest. He then walks some more until he finds a good place to camp, sets up his tent, eats, reminisces, and falls asleep.

In the second part of the story, Nick awakes in the morning, catches some grasshoppers for bait, fixes breakfast, and tidies up his "Indian camp." He enters the river, catches a small trout, and throws it back. He continues downstream where he hooks an enormous trout, nearly the size of a salmon, but loses it. Overcome with excitement, he sits down and smokes a cigarette until he is calm. Then he catches one good trout, loses another when his line gets snagged, and catches a second good trout. He smokes, has lunch, and looks at the river where it narrows and goes into a swamp. There are many big trout in the swamp but because "the fishing would be tragic" ("BTHR" 231) he does not want to go in there. He cleans the two fish and heads back to camp. The story concludes: "There were plenty of days coming when he could fish the swamp" ("BTHR" 232).

The story is filled with resonances and depths, yet, as this summary shows, these are not inherent in the plot. Lacking the necessary exposition, there seems to be no way for a reader, without going outside of the text, to answer any of the several questions raised by the story, a narrative that, as Don Summerhayes demonstrates, "often ingeniously declines to assent to what it so often confidently asserts"[10] Where has Nick been? Why is he so easily unhinged? What is he escaping from? What causes him to alternate between feeling excited and growing anxious lest he become too excited? What are the "other needs" ("BTHR" 210) he feels he has left behind him? Why would fishing in the swamp be "tragic" as opposed to, say, merely difficult or unsuccessful? "Big Two-Hearted River" is indeed magnificent fiction, but it nevertheless seems to have proven textually indecipherable purely on its own. Thus critics, with one exception (a wonderful ecocritical article by Fredrik Chr. Brøgger),[11] have been forced to go outside of the text to figure it out, and the meaning they find in the story, as Young and Lynn have demonstrated, therefore depends upon what extratextual evidence they choose to employ.

There is, however, one such piece of material that is particularly illuminating—the original ending that Hemingway deleted. This material, which once *was* textual, seems to me at least as relevant and close to the narrative as considerations of the story's location in *In Our Time,* which fail to treat the story as the autonomous text it originally was; considerations of the story's place in the Nick Adams saga, which not only neglect the story's autonomy but also ignore the many inconsistencies in that saga (there are, after all, very good reasons why Nick successfully served an enabling function for Hemingway in his stories but never as a protagonist in a novel); and biographical and psychoanalytical considerations that, however valuable and intriguing, must remain speculative. Hemingway expressed his feelings about such psychological criticism in a 1952 letter to Philip Young (and, one may safely assume, he would have had something a good deal stronger to say to Kenneth Lynn): "[M]y opposition to public psycho-analyzing of living people and my conception of the damage this may do to the people is not merely personal. It is a matter of principle. I thought your paper [containing the gist of Young's thesis] . . . was very interesting; but fairly shocking in the way the three critics [whom Young cited] and their critic [Young] lightly used serious medical terms without . . . being medically qualified to pronounce such judgements even in private."[12]

Although Hemingway wisely removed the original ending, which he called "mental conversation" and "shit,"[13] from the story, just as he had earlier deleted the equally defecatory opening of "Indian Camp," the omitted material gives significant clues as to what the story, in the author's mind, was "about." Jorge Luis Borges is correct when he warns "that there is often a difference between what a writer means to do and what he actually does,"[14] but the deleted ending of "Big Two-Hearted River" clearly shows what Hemingway was trying to do.

II

The original ending begins after Nick has hooked and lost the giant trout and then hooked and caught his first decent-sized trout, placing it in his sack that hangs in the water. It is forenoon: "It was getting hot, the sun hot on the back of his neck." The river is "shallow and wide," and many large trout will later gather "in the cool shadows on the other side of the stream" ("On Writing" 233). Nick knows this because he and his old fishing buddy, Bill Smith, had discovered it years ago on the Black River. The fish are waiting for the sun to go down before they move back out into the current:

> Just when the sun made the water blinding in the glare before it went down you were liable to strike a big trout anywhere in the current. It was almost impossible to fish then, the surface of the water was blinding as a mirror in the sun. Of course you could fish upstream, but in a stream like the Black or this you had to wallow against the current and in a deep place the water piled up on you. It was no fun to fish upstream although all the books said it was the only way. ("OW" 233)

The rewritten ending of the final version, which finishes off the story with what Hemingway called "just the straight fishing,"[15] uses this exact passage but removes the references to Bill Smith and to books. Thus the passage in that final version concludes: "It was no fun to fish upstream with this much current" ("BTHR" 229). From there Nick hooks another trout, but the line gets caught on a branch and the fish is lost; he hooks and catches a second trout; he smokes, eats, and looks warily at the swamp; and finally he cleans the fish and leaves, glancing back and thinking about the swamp.

But in the original version there is no second trout; Nick lets go the first trout he has caught because it is too big to eat and decides he will catch a couple of little ones for supper later by the camp. Nor is there any "tragic" swamp that obsesses him (although there is a casual mention of a swamp). And the narrative, which until now has concerned the action of trout fishing, takes an abrupt turn into a rambling, free-associative meditation on the lost friendships and activities of his youth, his new life as a married expatriate, and the nature of writing and his vocation as a writer.

Fishing in the river after an extended absence, engaged in an activity that he has loved since he was a small child, and remembering the adolescent companions associated with that activity, Nick is struck with nostalgia for *le temps perdu.* Hemingway was never as autobiographical in fiction as he was in this fragment, in which he and Nick are nearly one. He remembers how he and Bill Smith, the former Hemingway friend who served as the model for Bill in "The End of Something" and "The Three-Day Blow" (and who would later appear as Bill Gorton in *The Sun Also Rises*), used to have "fun with the books in the old days" that always started "with a fake premise" like the one about fishing upstream ("OW" 233). But then his present life intrudes as he remembers a silly statement made by Bill Bird's Parisian dentist. Bird was the American expatriate who had just published Hemingway's collection of vignettes, *in our time;* Hemingway and Bill Smith had undergone a falling out two years earlier and were no longer in touch. Remembering Bill Bird's dentist, he interjects, "Bill Bird, that is" and adds wistfully: "Once Bill meant Bill Smith. Now it means Bill Bird. Bill Bird was in Paris now" ("OW" 234).[16]

The change in "Bills" symbolizes what he has lost and how it saddens him. His new friends, Europeans and expatriate Americans living in Europe, cannot understand his youthful pursuits, how much they have formed him and how much a part of him they remain. He recounts a sarcastic remark that his new friend, the poet Ezra Pound, made about fishing, and repeats three times in different contexts the sentence: "Ezra thought fishing was a joke." His own feelings on the matter are quite clear when he follows the first of these sentences with the rejoinder: "Lots of people think poetry is a joke." Before his marriage to Helen (Hemingway's fictional name in this story for his own wife, Hadley),[17] he had been married to fishing. "Really married to it." Ezra was wrong: "It wasn't any joke" ("OW" 234).

But it was not his new life in Europe that had cost him his boyhood pals; his marriage to Helen/Hadley had done that. "When he married he lost Bill Smith, Odgar, the Ghee, all the old gang" because "he admitted by marrying that something was more important than the fishing." Fishing had drawn him and Bill Smith together; the experience had provided the bond of male companionship. Before that, Bill had been, figuratively speaking, a virgin: "Bill had never fished before they met. Everyplace they had been together. The Black, the Sturgeon, the Pine Barrens, the Upper Minnie, all the little streams. Most about fishing he and Bill had discovered together." The homoerotic nature of this male bonding is made even more apparent in the next passage: "Bill forgave him the fishing he had done before they met. He forgave him all the rivers. He was really proud of them. It was like a girl about other girls. If they were before they did not matter. But after was different." Marrying Helen was after. "So he lost them all" ("OW" 234).

Helen always thought his friends had left because they did not like her, but to Nick the real reason was more complex. He implies that they did not dislike Helen personally, but what she represented—something new and paramount in Nick's life. Nick remembers how Odgar loved Kate but that she only wanted a friendship, and he recalls how the Ghee visited brothels in Cleveland but nevertheless remained an ascetic, and how he, Nick, had been one also.[18] He concludes: "It was all such a fake. You had this fake ideal planted in you and then you lived your life to it." But what he had really loved was fishing and the summer. "He had loved it more than anything" ("OW" 235).

To this point, the material of the deleted ending would seem to link "Big Two-Hearted River" neither to the war nor to an unhappy mother-son relationship, but to those stories from *In Our Time* that favorably contrast male-male relationships with male-female relationships ("The End of Something," "The Three-Day Blow," "Cross-Country Snow") and stories that depict dissatisfaction with marriage ("The Doctor and the Doctor's Wife," "Out of Season," "Cat in the Rain," "Mr. and Mrs. Elliot").

After the statement about loving fishing comes a page-long, disjointed, euphoric reminiscence about his long-gone youth: digging potatoes with Bill, car trips, fishing in the bay, playing baseball, swimming off the dock, the long summers, home cooking, the fields and lake, drinking with Bill's old man, fishing trips, and even "just lying around" ("OW" 235). The memories become increasingly specific and evocative until they erupt into a metaphor that describes his very act of remembering—a muddy stream that overflows in the rain—and he wonders: "Where were the trout when a stream was like that?" ("OW" 236). Here, the trout stand as metaphors for stories themselves. In effect, what he figuratively asks is this: how does a writer capture stories from the river of memory?

But his meditations are suddenly interrupted by a different memory that seems to come from out of nowhere: "That was where a bull chased him over the fence and he lost his pocketbook with all the hooks in it" ("OW" 236). Just as the Spanish bullfights have replaced American trout fishing, so too have the European experiences of his young manhood replaced the American experiences of his childhood and adolescence—the fishhooks lost to the charging bull symbolize this transition. He had just been wondering where the trout were, but now he wonders where the bullfighters Maera and Algabeño have gone. Maera, the renowned matador whom Hemingway had admired since watching him at work in Pamplona the previous summer, was actually alive and at the height of his fame, though Hemingway had earlier killed him off fictionally in the sixteenth vignette of *in our time*. Here, caught up in his sense of loss and the passage of time, he has Nick wonder what has become of him.[19]

At first Nick had clung to earlier memories of things he understood rather than embracing a "sport" that seemed so foreign; "phrases from bullfight papers kept coming into his head all the time until he had to quit reading them." But soon he came to love the bullfights, and he lends his brief relationship with them a false legitimacy of duration by wistfully noting: "Maera's kid brother was a bullfighter now. That was the way it went" ("OW" 236). As for Maera, he was "the greatest man he'd ever known." In a lengthy passage, he recounts exciting scenes from one of Maera's bullfights. He also recalls "the saddest thing he'd ever seen": an old, fat picador who badly wanted to be a *cabellero en plaza* (a matador who fights on a trained, blooded horse).[20] Nick remarks on how magnificently one of these, young Da Veiga, could ride, but that it "didn't show well in the movies" ("OW" 237).

The next two paragraphs of this free association are transitional:

> The movies ruined everything. Like talking about something good. That was what had made the war unreal. Too much talking.
>
> Talking about anything was bad. Writing about anything actual was bad. It always killed it. ("OW" 237)

Until these paragraphs, the original ending has been about Nick's (and Hemingway's) past: the precious memories of friends and experiences that have shaped him—memories that this fictional return to the river has rekindled in his consciousness. But Nick and Hemingway are writers. For them, memories are more than nostalgic; they are vital to the process of creating fiction. Memories enable writing by producing the need to tell and by providing the material of fiction. That is precisely what these memories have done, leading Hemingway to the real subject of the deleted ending, as well as of the final version of the story from which it was removed—the nature of writing and the writer's vocation.

There are two reasons why the fragment now wends its way into a discussion of writing. First, the reminiscences of his youth were produced by, and further produced, his own pressing desire to tell about the past, to save it from the swift, effacing current of time and fading memory, to catch these trout of his past (the metaphor is inescapable) before they swim too far downstream to be hooked and reeled into the present. Like Mark Twain fictionally returning to the Mississippi in 1875 to rediscover and be inspired by the rich mine of memory from his own youth, Hemingway and Nick have returned to the river to rediscover theirs. Second, the example of Maera's competence at his craft, that which makes him in Nick's eyes the greatest man he has ever known, as well as Da Veiga's impressive riding skills, remind him of his own calling. It was Maera who caused Nick "suddenly" to know that he was "going to love bullfighting" ("OW" 237). He would love it because it was not a sport but an art, like writing, and Hemingway would later equate the two in his classic treatise *Death in the Afternoon*. But Maera was famous, a Joyce or Eliot, the embodiment of what Nick/Hemingway hope someday to become; for now, the analogy to young Da Veiga is much more appropriate.

There is time for Nick to follow his calling and become a Maera, and so the descriptions of the matador and the *cabellero en plaza* hold out the promise of a bright future. But equally motivating is the sobering sight of the old fat picador who "threw his hat into the ring hanging on over the *barrera* watching young Da Veiga" ("OW" 237). If Maera represents what Nick wishes to become, then the pic is a presentiment of what he hopes never to be—an old man who abandoned his true calling for a lesser vocation, who now watches with envy someone who is following the path he wishes he himself had pursued. "A country," Hemingway would later write, "erodes, and the dust blows away, the people all die and none of them were of any importance permanently, except those who practised the arts. . . . a work of art endures forever[.]"[21] Again, time is fleeting and threatening—writing is in so many ways a race against time, an effort to snatch immortality from the inevitable fact of human finitude.

Here I wish to segue briefly to a third major interpretation of "Big Two-Hearted River," one that also views it from the perspective of Hemingway's new vocation, but within the complex context of expatriation. J. Gerald Kennedy says of the Michigan stories that Hemingway was writing in Paris in 1924: "If the landscape of these stories bears a legible inscription, it is that of Hemingway's nostalgia for simplicity, which must be read against the emerging complications of his life in Paris." Also using the deleted ending as a key to the story, Kennedy shrewdly observes, "the problem that oppresses Nick as he fishes the Big Two-Hearted River is not postcombat trauma so much as an agonizing consciousness that in getting married, becoming a writer, and moving to Paris, he has forfeited the halcyon world of northern Michigan." Hemingway, in other words, is experiencing a "crisis of exile" as he realizes "the country that he had loved existed for him now only in memory and imagination." The deleted ending therefore

> permits us to gauge, as no other Nick Adams material does, the intensity of Hemingway's psychic attraction to the Michigan country and the nature of his alienation from the Parisian milieu. Through a series of imaginative displacements, Hemingway (working in Paris) portrays Nick Adams in Michigan, thinking back to his life in Paris and—from that exilic perspective—remembering the Michigan that he has already lost. The suppressed fragment thus represents Nick as a jaded expatriate, already estranged from the familiar terrain to which he has returned.[22]

Although I am deliberately pursuing the consciously metafictional aspects of the deleted ending, as well as their implications for the final version of the text, Kennedy's subtly persuasive reading of the story as enacting Hemingway's unconscious ambivalences about his new vocation, his marriage, and his life as an expatriate strikes me as getting to the heart of "Big Two-Hearted River" in a way that both the war-wound thesis and the childhood-wound thesis never have. The latter interpretations are based on unresolved trauma from Hemingway's past, but Kennedy's perspective filters these through the author's situatedness in the present, that is, at the moment of narration. Crucial to that situatedness are his vocation as a writer and his attempts to work out for himself the relation of this vocation to a past that increasingly exists only in memory. The war and his unhappy filial experiences are, of course, important elements of that past, but they are only a part of the story, and not necessarily the determining part of this particular story. Thus Kennedy's reading brings to light a deeper layer of meaning in this rich but cryptic narrative and leads me to conclude that, rather than "either/or" or even "both/and" interpretations, the story's richness demands a multitude of "many/and" readings.

To return, though, to my own analysis of "Big Two-Hearted River" as consciously self-reflexive, how can the fish be caught? How can the past be saved? How can the writer achieve his own apotheosis? Consideration of these questions has led to the transitional paragraphs above. Talking too much about something good ruins it; the representation of a powerful event, verbally or in a movie, makes the event feel increasingly distant as the simulacrum (anecdote or film) begins to replace the original experience that it attempts to copy. That was what had happened with the war, which was good for a writer because it provided so much fictional material. This is the only significant reference to the war in either version of the story, and perhaps it was the above realization that caused Hemingway to omit it in the final version. Certainly, Hemingway is beginning to understand that talking too much is exactly what he has been doing in this fragment of "mental conversation," and that recognition will eventually lead him to discard it and get back to the "straight fishing."

But he has not only been talking too much, he has been writing about something "actual." This also can kill the past. To capture the *truth* of the past, to create a reality that surpasses mere representational *accuracy,* the writer has to transmute it into fiction, which Hemingway had been successfully doing until he got to the original ending. The material of the story was based on an actual fishing expedition Hemingway made in September 1919 on the Big Fox and Little Fox rivers, accompanied by John Pentecost (nicknamed "The Ghee") and Al Walker, in which he really did hook "the biggest trout [he had] ever seen" but lost it when the hook broke at the shank. In an earlier version of the story, he included his two companions and employed a first-person narration. But in the final version he eliminated his two real-life friends and switched to fixed internal third-person focalization. He also changed the name of the Fox River, on the southern part of the Michigan peninsula, to a river on the northern part of the peninsula that he had never before fished; made Seney into a recently burned and now abandoned town (it had actually burned down nearly thirty years earlier and was not completely abandoned); altered the flat landscape around Seney so that Nick would have to walk uphill; and created grasshoppers that had been blackened by the fire (according to orthopterists, Sheridan Baker comments, "a highly unlikely phenomenon"). As Frederic J. Svoboda concludes in an extremely valuable article that details the history of the real-life Seney (nicknamed "Hell" back in its logging camp heyday), and which also reconstructs the Seney that Hemingway must have encountered on his actual 1919 trip—in the town and landscape of "Big Two-Hearted River" we find ourselves "in a Michigan selected by Hemingway to parallel Nick's states of mind as he looks for control."[23]

To save the past, the writer must maintain a considered distance, and he must shape it through art. That is why the remove provided by his new life in Paris served such a powerful enabling function in the Michigan stories he wrote there, forcing him to draw upon the memories of events rather than relying too much on the actual events themselves. In the original ending, however, Nick has been "talking" too much (through free indirect and immediate speech), and Hemingway has been writing about something "actual." Recognizing this, he tries to disengage himself, but doing so only causes him to continue talking too much about the actual. He defends himself from this implicit self-accusation by stating that the "only writing that was any good was what you made up, what you imagined" ("OW" 237). His defense is two-pronged; he accuses other writers of standing too close to real life, and he asserts that the stories he has written were made up. "Mac [Robert McAlmon] had stuff" but he failed to "digest life" and "then create [his] own people." In *Ulysses,* Stephen Dedalus "was Joyce himself, so he was terrible" but Bloom and Mrs. Bloom were made up; the former was "wonderful" and the latter was "the greatest in the world." Oddly and tellingly attributing his own stories to his fictional persona, Hemingway says that Nick had never seen a jockey killed before he wrote "My Old Man," and he insists: "Nick in the stories was never himself. He made him up. Of course he'd never seen an Indian woman having a baby. That was what made it good. Nobody knew that. He'd seen a woman have a baby on the road to Karagatch and tried to help her. That was the way it was." This is what his family did not understand. "They thought it was all experience" ("OW" 238).[24]

Now reflecting on "Indian Camp" and unable to extricate himself from this self-absorption, Hemingway gives up the struggle and pours out his innermost thoughts and feelings in a passage that may very well be the most touchingly honest, direct statement he would ever make about what writing meant to him:

> He wished he could always write like that. He would sometime. He wanted to be a great writer. He was pretty sure he would be. He knew it in lots of ways. He would be in spite of everything. It was hard, though.
>
> It was hard to be a great writer if you loved the world and living in it and special people. It was hard when you loved so many places. Then you were healthy and felt good and were having a good time and what the hell.
>
> He always worked best when Helen was unwell. Just that much discontent and friction. Then there were times when you had to write. Not conscience. Just peristaltic action. Then you felt sometimes like you never could write but after a while you knew sooner or later you would write another good story.
>
> It was really more fun than anything. That was really why you did it. He had never realized that before. It wasn't conscience. It was simply that it was the greatest pleasure. It had more bite to it than anything else. It was so damn hard to write well, too. ("OW" 238)

This remarkable affirmation of vocation almost completely abandons any pretense to being fiction. The use of a third-person pronoun and the fictional name for Hadley are but trappings; more indicative of the confessional tone of this passage is the way Hemingway uses the second-person pronoun to affect the reader with persuasive force. This is akin to a slip into immediate speech and the first-person pronoun earlier in "Big Two-Hearted River" when describing the enormous trout that got away: "By God, he was the biggest one I ever heard of" ("BTHR" 227).[25]

Just as Nick has faith that the country "could not all be burned" ("BTHR" 211), so Hemingway has faith that he will someday be able to write stories like "Indian Camp" at will. Just as Nick puts behind him "other needs" to go fishing, Hemingway sets aside his need to explain his writing to his uncomprehending family and his need to be a responsible husband to attend to his calling. The exhilaration that Nick feels in setting up camp is the joy a writer feels in sitting down to write, on his own, attentive to nothing but the appointed task, free from all social obligation and conflicting demands on his time and consciousness, responsible only to himself and his art. Nick in his fishing and Hemingway in his writing will succeed "in spite of everything." This steady faith is what earlier enables Nick to "choke" ("BTHR" 218) back anxious thoughts when his mind starts to work, and to go to sleep, knowing that he is "in the good place" ("BTHR" 215) where he belongs. Hemingway, too, can set his mind at ease when he is writing, knowing that his faith in his vocation will transcend his doubts. The image of Nick "awkward and professionally happy with all his equipment hanging from him" ("BTHR" 223) as he steps into the stream is a figurative description of young Ernest sitting down to write.

A writer is selfish; Hemingway makes no apologies for this fact. It has nothing to do with conscience and he will not justify it by invoking some notion of the sublimity of art. Writing is simply "more fun than anything." His first love, fishing with his male friends, had been replaced by a "fake ideal," marriage, which in turn has yielded to a greater love, writing, which feeds off of his earlier loves, both real and fake. This new love is truer than all the others. It is involuntary, something almost biological—"peristaltic action"—and Hemingway needs and enjoys it in the same way that Nick relishes cooking and eating his food. "Geezus Chrise" ("BTHR" 216) is the ecstatic reaction of both.

But writing is hard. A writer must live well and "digest life," yet not become so absorbed in that life that he settles for its many tangible comforts and neglects his calling. That is why a certain amount of "discontent and friction" can be helpful, by turning him away from the world as, paradoxically, he searches for fictional ways of representing that world. The joys of setting up camp and fishing for trout compel Nick onward in his arduous walk uphill to his campsite, and the same is true, metaphorically, for Hemingway, who looks forward to the "bite" of writing even when, as he says at the end of the first paragraph of the passage: "It was hard, though." This is an important enough statement to repeat at the end of the passage: "It was so damn hard to write well, too."

A writer must avoid the temptation to neglect his difficult work for mere worldly delights. He must also avoid false writing: "There were so many tricks." It would have been easy for Nick to have set up camp near Seney, or after he had gotten clear of the fire line, yet he struggled uphill until he reached the place where he knew he should be. When he fishes, he employs real bait instead of the manufactured lures that are easier to use and that guarantee a higher rate of success.[26] The lures are tricks, and neither Nick nor Hemingway will countenance tricks: "It was easy to write if you used the tricks. Everybody used them. Joyce had invented hundreds of new ones. Just because they were new didn't make them any better. They would all turn into clichés" ("OW" 239).

Almost a decade later, Hemingway returned to this matter of "true" writing and "trick" writing, first in *Death in the Afternoon* and then in *Green Hills of Africa.* In the latter, as he converses with a hunting companion about the difficulty of the kind of writing he is trying to do, he defines it as "a fourth and fifth dimension that can be gotten":

> "But that is poetry you are talking about."
>
> "No. It is much more difficult than poetry. It is a prose that has never been written. But it can be written, without tricks and without cheating. With nothing that will go bad afterwards."
>
> "And why has it not been written?"
>
> "Because there are too many factors. First, there must be talent, much talent. Talent such as Kipling had. Then there must be discipline. The discipline of Flaubert. Then there must be the conception of what it can be and an absolute conscience as unchanging as the standard meter in Paris, to prevent faking. Then the writer must be intelligent and disinterested and above all he must survive. Try to get all these in one person and have him come through all the influences that press on a writer. The hardest thing, because time is so short, is for him to survive and get his work done."[27]

The "prose that has never been written"—like the giant trout that Nick could hook but not catch, is still out there—the latter in the actual river and the former in a metaphorical river: the stream of memory. Neither can be captured with tricks, which only lead to competent fiction or average-sized fish. To get perfect prose or a giant trout, you need luck, talent, and discipline, and you must survive. The need for luck is manifest; both the writer and the fisherman must be in the right place at the right time. Moreover, if he is to succeed, there must necessarily be things he does of which he is not fully conscious—the mystery of great art that Hemingway said "does not dis-sect out."[28] He must also possess talent and discipline; talent without discipline leads to dissipation, what Hemingway later believed had happened to Scott Fitzgerald, discipline without talent to futility. It is talent that led Hemingway back to the scenes of his youth; it is discipline that leads Nick to put behind him "other needs." The greater the talent and discipline, the greater the competence. If both reach a high enough level, the fisherman or writer can achieve mastery and, with luck, something beyond even that.

III

For Hemingway, the *beau ideal* of the artist was Paul Cézanne; Nick and he "wanted to write like Cezanne painted":

> Cezanne started out with all the tricks. Then he broke the whole thing down and built the real thing. It was hell to do. He was the greatest. The greatest for always. It wasn't a cult. He, Nick, wanted to write about country so it would be there like Cezanne had done it in painting. You had to do it from inside yourself. There wasn't any trick. Nobody had ever written about country like that. He felt almost holy about it. It was deadly serious. You could do it if you would fight it out. If you'd lived right with your eyes. ("OW" 239)

Cézanne—so temperamentally similar to Hemingway with his dedication above all else to art; his attempts to convey emotion through a technique of simple, carefully selected images rather than through the piling up of realistic details or other sorts of elaboration; his distrust of intellectual abstractions; and even his occasionally boorish manners, emotional outbursts, and subject matter that was so often, to use Stein's expression, *inaccrochable*—had early on learned the techniques of his craft from the works of past masters in the Louvre and from his Impressionist companions, especially Camille Pissarro.[29] But then he had moved beyond them into an aesthetic of his own, a sort of proto-cubism that Hemingway would later emulate. Referring to his paintings as "constructions [from nature] based on the means, feelings and approaches suggested by [nature]," Cézanne sought to discover the actual form that existed within the subject rather than imposing one upon it from the outside. To do that meant, as Hemingway put it, "liv[ing] right with your eyes"—neither ordering details nor merely replicating them, but seeing their underlying form and expressing it. The landscape's natural order impresses itself upon the artist's eye and he, ignoring social conventions and the distortions of his own subjectivity, works "from inside [him]self" to depict exactly what he sees with no sentimental or intertextual associations. "[T]he thesis to be expounded," Cézanne told a fellow painter, "is to render the image of what we see"; that, for the painter, is the hardest task of all. And the same, Hemingway believed, holds true for the writer. Eight years after writing "Big Two-Hearted River," he would echo Cézanne's thoughts on painting in a recollection of his own early attempts at depiction in fiction, a statement that also articulates his method of literary impressionism: "I was trying to write then and I found the greatest difficulty, aside from knowing truly what you really felt, rather than what you were supposed to feel, and had been taught to feel, was to put down what really happened in action; what the actual things were that produced the emotion that you experienced." This would be "the real thing" that "if you stated it purely enough" would be valid "always[.]"[30]

Cézanne's forms, like Hemingway's sentences, are deliberately simple. As Hemingway would later say, "Prose is architecture, not interior decoration, and the Baroque is over."[31] Both use basic, striking colors. Both move the reader's eye in a specific direction over particular objects; as Sheldon Norman Grebstein observes, they often alternate "different components of the landscape (earth, trees, houses, mountains) in such a way that each is distinct as the eye focuses on it separately, yet tends to blend into the next as the whole composition is viewed." Even Hemingway's search for the critical detail that will convey a scene's emotional essence is, as Grebstein further speculates, "perhaps the literary equivalent to Cézanne's search for the point of most striking light as the axis of the object or mass to be painted."[32]

There is, it should be noted, some debate on this matter of a "central" or "culminating" point in the artist's paintings. Although Cézanne explicitly stated the theory near the end of his life,[33] several art historians have observed a significant divergence between his theory and his actual practice. Erle Loran, for instance, notes that "Cézanne's space is compensated, balanced, related to the picture plane; and thus often rotates *around,* not toward, a central point."[34] But if this weakens Grebstein's analogy between Cézanne's central point and Hemingway's critical detail, it also opens up possible analogies to Hemingway's method of indirection and, more important, to his theory and practice of omission. As Theodore L. Gaillard Jr. points out in this regard, "in several of his later paintings, Cézanne would intentionally leave small areas of canvas blank in the midst of a sea of roofs or on the side of a hill, causing viewers to fill spaces with preconscious constructs of complementary line and color, subtly moving toward the substitution of impression and feeling for cognition."[35] Or, as Hemingway might have put it, Cézanne used omission to make them *feel* something more than they *understood.*

In 1950, Hemingway would recall, "I learned how to make a landscape from Mr. Paul Cézanne by walking through the Luxembourg Museum a thousand times with an empty gut, and I am pretty sure that if Mr. Paul was around, he would like the way I make them and be happy that I learned it from him."[36] Years earlier, while working on "Big Two-Hearted River," he wrote to Gertrude Stein and Alice B. Toklas that he was "trying to do the country like Cezanne . . . and sometimes getting it a little bit."[37] One of the best of these Cézanne passages occurs as Nick starts up the burned landscape:

> The road ran on, dipping occasionally, but always climbing. Nick went on up. Finally the road after going parallel to the burnt hillside reached the top. Nick leaned back against a stump and slipped out of the pack harness. Ahead of him, as far as he could see, was the pine plain. The burned country stopped off at the left with the range of hills. On ahead islands of dark pine trees rose out of the plain. Far off to the left was the line of the river. Nick followed it with his eye and caught glints of the water in the sun.
>
> There was nothing but the pine plain ahead of him, until the far blue hills that marked the Lake Superior height of land. He could hardly see them, faint and far away in the heat-light over the plain. If he looked too steadily they were gone. But if he only half-looked they were there, the far-off hills of the height of land. ("BTHR" 211)

The scene is composed like a painting, with Nick standing at mid-height (typical for the viewer in many of Cézanne's paintings): above the pine plain and below the distant hills. The winding road, or *route tournante,* takes us into the scene, as it does in both Cézanne's late landscapes and their literary equivalents in Hemingway's fiction.[38] The picture is framed on the left by the range of hills and the line of the river, and on the top by the far blue hills. Nick's view spans to the left, suggesting that his perspective is from the right side of the canvas. Each of the three main areas of the painting is distinguished by a particular quality of light: on the left the glints of sunlight reflecting off of the river (which contrast with the darkened burned country and the range of hills), at the top the faint blue hills in the heat-light, and in the center the pine plain that is lighter than the burned country but darker than the blue hills. Each element of the scene is distinct, but they work together to establish an overall effect. What Hemingway says of the far blue hills at the end of the passage is also true of each of the other components of the scene; if you look too closely at any one of them it disappears (as in an Impressionist painting, none has enough specificity of detail to sustain it in isolation), but if you only half-look, it is there. In other words, the particular shapes and planes matter only insofar as they contribute to the totality of the painting, and each of them is essential to that larger effect.

Ron Berman observes that viewers in the 1920s understood Cézanne through the ideas of Roger Fry, his foremost critic and leading champion. Four elements of Cézanne's late landscapes that Fry emphasized were "[1] the motif of the road, [2] the organization of detail into harmony, [3] the warning that there are elements in his work that outrange our 'pictorial apprehension'" and "[4] the conception of landscape as a dominant idea." Berman also explains that, in Hemingway, "the winding road is by no means a still, formal part of a described scene. It is an entry into a divided realm." In Cézanne, the *route tournante* provides only limited access to the natural world. "The roads," Berman notes, "are everywhere, yet there are in all these canvases areas that cannot be fully explained. On this, the painter was adamant, even stating that a blank space would be preferable to inserting something that would fake comprehension" (this is what Fry meant when he spoke of elements beyond our "pictorial apprehension").[39] Berman insightfully concludes that Cézanne's notion of limited access (and thus epistemological roadblocks) is one of the major lessons Hemingway learned from the painter and incorporated into his own landscape depictions:

> The premise of roads and also of inquiries is that they go somewhere. *Routes tournantes* invariably fail to reach certain symbolic objects on their horizon. . . . We move from perspective to a point beyond viewing, and from technique to meaning—we now know the tendency of the story, from known to unknown. It is characteristic in Hemingway to begin on a straight road or roadway, then to experience an entirely different kind of locus of movement—and also of the mind.[40]

When the *route tournante* in the above quoted passage from "Big Two-Hearted River" comes to its terminus, it leaves Nick with his view of the pine plain and the far blue hills. But it has led him only to a vista, not to a destination; the symbolic blue hills remain on the distant horizon. In addition, his knowledge of their physical reality, his access to them, is limited to what he makes of them solely through his sense of sight, an epistemological conduit that is further undercut by their faintness and by the fact that he can perceive them only by not focusing on them, that is to say, only by viewing them within the entire scene.

Here is where we see a different kind of movement "from technique to meaning," from the external landscape to the internal terrain of the mind. The passage is one of Hemingway's most complex objective correlatives, a good deal more intricate than the bacon fat hardening on Harold Krebs's plate. Employing external focalization, Hemingway expresses the emotion of the scene purely through the depiction of the landscape, without any mention of what Nick is thinking or feeling. The burned country, signifying Nick's past, is behind him. He has reached a certain elevation, or realization of his writing abilities. In the distance he can barely make out the Lake Superior height of land, which resonates symbolically as the sort of true writing he wishes to achieve but, at this point, can only glimpse. Between those hills and where he now stands is the vast pine plain with its islands of dark pine trees like so many steps along the way. The road he has traveled to this point has risen and dipped but has steadily climbed. Now, however, it has ended, and he is on his own. He will have to keep "his direction by the sun" ("BTHR" 212). Cézanne had continually urged his fellow painters not to "be content with the fine formulas of . . . illustrious forebears" and to "free [their] minds" through "contact with nature, and with the instincts and with the artistic sensations within."[41] Like Cézanne before him, Nick has learned all that can be learned from others; from now on he will have to teach himself. As both he and his author have come to realize, if you want to do in writing what Cézanne had done in painting, "You had to do it from inside yourself" ("OW" 239).

Hemingway's first artistic achievement had been to create individual true sentences, but, as he later recalled, what he learned from Cézanne "made writing simple true sentences far from enough to make the stories have the dimensions that I was trying to put in them. I was learning very much from him but I was not articulate enough to explain it to anyone."[42] We may speculate, as I have here, as to exactly what he did learn from the French master; yet, as the passage about Cézanne shows, Hemingway was never able to communicate it clearly. After unsuccessfully trying to say what he learned, he cuts short the attempt: "It was a thing you couldn't talk about." But inspired by the great painter, frustrated by his inability to articulate that inspiration, and determined "to write like Cezanne painted," he re-affirms his sense of vocation, voicing a determination that survives in the face of doubt: "He was going to work on it until he got it. Maybe never, but he would know as he got near it. It was a job. Maybe for all his life" ("OW" 239).

With this, the deleted ending, and the story to which it was originally attached, reaches its climactic moment of recognition. Yet Hemingway, unable to convey clearly the nature of the prose he wishes someday to write, continues in vain in a rambling attempt to define it. He talks about how "[p]eople were easy to do" and how "[a]ll this smart stuff was easy"; he contrasts e. e. cummings's smart "automatic writing" with the hard-earned prose of cummings's *The Enormous Room;* and he surveys the literary landscape but finds it, on the whole, wanting. Whatever the accomplishments of his fellow writers, he concludes, "They weren't after what he was after" ("OW" 239).

This statement turns his attention, once again, to Cézanne, and he remembers a number of Cézanne portraits he has viewed, including the one at Gertrude Stein's home. Stein becomes the vessel through which the deceased painter will acknowledge him if he ever achieves his ideal: "She'd know it if he ever got things right" ("OW" 239). He again speaks about how people are easy to do and takes one last cheap shot at his friend Joyce, who by now has become the polar opposite of Cézanne, the writer who has luck and talent but not discipline.[43] He imagines how "Cezanne would paint this stretch of river" and exclaims: "God, if he were only here to do it. They died and that was the hell of it. They worked all their lives and then got old and died" ("OW" 240). Cézanne had luck, talent, and discipline, but he had failed to survive.[44]

These considerations of Cézanne's finitude cause Nick to feel the press of time and finally to cut short his desultory musings. He turns his attention to his surroundings, which, in his present state of mind, he views as a painting: "Nick, seeing how Cezanne would do the stretch of river and the swamp, stood up and stepped down into the stream. The water was cold and actual. He waded across the stream, moving in the picture." The water is cold and actual, but Nick's task now is to turn it into art. He needs to write. He releases the big trout he has caught ("He was too big to eat") and decides to "get a couple of little ones in front of camp for supper." He hurries up the bank and starts through the brush. "He was in a hurry and the rod bothered him. He was not thinking. He was holding something in his head. He wanted to get back to camp and get to work" ("OW" 240). In his haste, the line catches on a branch, but he cuts the leader and reels in so he can get back. Nothing must interfere with his immediate return to camp so he can write the picture he is holding in his head. Less than a year before, Hemingway had described himself as "constipated" with stories that needed to get written,[45] and earlier in the deleted ending he spoke of "peristaltic action." Now the metaphor has shifted from his digestive tract to his head, reflecting his growing understanding of, and control over, his craft.

Along the trail he sees a rabbit who has been paralyzed by two large ticks. He stops grudgingly and removes the parasites. He lays the rabbit under a sweet fern bush and wonders whether it will revive. "Probably the ticks had attached themselves to it as it crouched in the grass. Maybe after it had been dancing in the open." In this allegory about writing, even the rabbit becomes a metaphor of the writer. Was he stopped while in the grass in contemplation, or as he danced in the open in the practice of his own craft? Nick "did not know." But he has no time to think about it. There is work to do. "He went on up the trail to the camp. He was holding something in his head" ("OW" 241).

IV

The original version of "Big Two-Hearted River" ends at this point, with Nick, having affirmed his vocation, hurrying back to camp to write. In both the original and final versions, fishing is used as a metaphor for writing. The rushing river is the writer's life; downstream it is his memory of the past, upstream the future, and where he stands the present. The trout are stories that he fishes for in his memory, and the success of both the fisherman and the writer depends upon luck, talent, and discipline. The giant trout that gets away in both versions represents the kind of ideal fiction he is trying to achieve, something he can but glimpse since he does not yet possess the artistic ability to catch it. In both versions, writing has its difficulties and risks, but always its potential rewards. Thus, when the sun is nearly down the water is blinding and it is almost impossible to fish, but "you were liable to strike a big trout anywhere in the current" ("OW" 233; "BTHR" 229). You can avoid the sun's glare by fishing upstream, figuratively avoiding the difficulties of the task by turning away from the material of the past and memory, but this is unsatisfactory. And so you fish in the dark, blinded by the sun's glare, and make do as best you can. "The rest," to complete Hemingway's echo of Henry James, "is the madness of art."[46]

In both versions, the story was titled "Big Two-Hearted River" and divided decisively into two linked parts; in *In Our Time*, "Chapter XV" is placed between them. In the original version, Nick decides to release the big trout he caught and get two smaller ones later by the camp. This decision takes place right after he has unsuccessfully tried to explain the kind of prose he is after. He could hook but not catch the giant trout, an incident that literally takes his breath away. The trout he catches, although not nearly as big as the first, is still too large to eat, so he will settle for the two smaller ones by the camp. Figuratively, the little trout he initially caught and threw back is a story too unambitious for him to keep, like writing one true sentence; the giant trout that gets away is the kind of story that he aspires to write, but which is, for now, beyond his reach; and even the large trout he catches is too much, like explaining the influence of Cézanne, for his ability to digest and communicate. The two smaller trout he will catch back at camp represent the two parts of the story he will write, less ambitious in his eyes than the trout/story he releases, but within the range of his art.

I do not intend, in making this assessment, to demean the remarkable achievement of "Big Two-Hearted River," a story rich enough to inspire such a wide and plentiful range of excellent scholarship: not just from war-wound and childhood-wound critics, but also from myth critics, ecocritics, feminist critics, historicist critics, and virtually every other kind of critic. My comment on what Hemingway wanted to do, as opposed to what he was able to do, is strictly limited to his inability to combine his ideas about writing in the deleted ending with the main plotline of the fishing story, even though, to me, more than enough self-reflexive elements remain for the final version to be read as metafictional. As James R. Mellow observes:

> Had Hemingway been capable at this stage of his career of bringing together the two streams of narrative, the objective account of the experience on the river and Nick Adams's subjective ruminations on writing (as, say, Proust had done in the final pages of *Remembrance of Things Past*), he would have accomplished a tour de force in modern writing. As it was, he had lacked the talent to bring it off, lacked the style to accomplish the tricky merger of fact and fiction. It would be twelve years

before he was to accomplish that peculiar narrative feat with a masterpiece, “The Snows of Kilimanjaro.”[47]

When Hemingway wisely decided to revise the ending of the story, he retained the bipartite structure and symbols; the Big Two-Hearted remained two-parted. In the final version, having caught “one good trout” (“BTHR” 228), the first part of the story, he describes his successful but difficult efforts to catch another, the second part. The trout he hooks feels heavy as a log, and Hemingway depicts in great detail how hard it is to capture this trout that Nick fights “against the current” (“BTHR” 230). This struggle, of course, figuratively represents the efforts of the author to finish the second part of the story. With both trout in his sack, Nick then sits down to smoke and eat and watch the river.[48]

Difficult as it was to write the second half of the story, Hemingway’s eventual success lent it a certain liveliness that makes it qualitatively different from the first part. Throughout the deleted ending, he has emphasized two aspects of writing: its difficulty and its potential for joy. These two aspects are mimetically reinforced by the two parts of the final version. The first part, with its short, methodical sentences, its disciplined prose, the images of Nick’s uphill journey, and his careful preparations for fishing, imitates the laboriousness of writing. The second part, with its long, graceful sentences, its lively prose, and its incidents of various accomplishments, from catching the two big trout to hooking the giant trout, produces something of a sense of the euphoria that can come from writing—the reward for the hard work of the first part.

In this final version, aside from the capture of the second trout and the symbolism this entails (he has at last “caught” the second part of the story), the material about the past and about the nature of writing has been replaced by another fictional representation—the swamp. In the swamp the river narrows, the sun does not shine, and the current is fast and deep. The trout there are large, but whether they represent the trauma of Nick’s (and Hemingway’s) war wound at Fossalta where the Piave River similarly narrowed, or of his unhappy childhood, he is not eager to go after them. They are “impossible to land” (“BTHR” 231) because he does not yet possess the art to capture them. When viewed as a metafictional story, this is what matters most. As Glen A. Love wisely observes, by the end of the narrative we realize that “Nick *does* want to fish the swamp, and that Hemingway wants it for him.”[49] But for now it’s important that Nick and Hemingway not reach for something that too far exceeds their grasp. It would be a "tragic adventure" and "Nick did not want it. He did not want to go down the stream any further today" ("BTHR" 231). He takes the two fish/stories he's caught and lays them "side by side" on a log. "They were fine" ("BTHR" 231). He cleans them, rolls them up in his sack, and heads back to camp.

Near the end of his life, Hemingway confessed: "I love to write. But it has never gotten any easier to do and you can't expect it to if you keep trying for something better than you can do."[50] A writer's craft is achieved in increments, his development a daily battle. Along the way, he must stop by many islands of dark pine trees. Throughout his career, Hemingway would keep "trying for something better," setting new challenges for himself in the story, the novel, and non-fictional prose. But as he cast a backward glance and recalled those early days when he was writing "Big Two-Hearted River," it's apparent that he had always known what he needed to do to reach those far-off hills: "[I]n the morning the river would be there and I must make it and the country and all that would happen. There were days ahead to be doing that each day. No other thing mattered. . . . All I must do . . . was stay sound and good in my head until morning when I would start to work again."[51] As Nick and Hemingway look back over their shoulders, the river is still showing through the trees, and they have faith. There would be time enough to return and fish the swamp.

Acknowledgments

Warner Berthoff, Marc Dolan, and Philip Fisher read the initial version of this manuscript, and their many insightful comments contributed to making it into a much better book. I am deeply grateful to LSU Press's external reader and Hemingway scholar extraordinaire, Joseph M. Flora, for his meticulous reading of my work and his excellent comments and suggestions. Daniel Aaron, Jeff Baxter, Susan F. Beegel, the late David Herbert Donald, Wendy Stallard Flory, Leonard Neufeldt, the late Joel Porte, the late Michael Reynolds, S. K. Robisch, the late William Stuckey, G. R. Thompson, and Kermit Vanderbilt also commented on earlier parts of the manuscript, greatly to its benefit. I am genuinely thankful to all of these good people for the time, thought, and advice they generously gave me.

I would like to thank my extended family, those whom I love and whose love has always brought out the best in me: Dorrie Armstrong and Ryan Schneider, Mally and Emmy Armstrong-Schneider, Ellen Bayer and Alexander Lesher, Dexter, Max, and Sparkimus Bayer-Lesher, Jenny (Wright), Brad, and Joe Buchheit, Wendy and David Flory, Sarah and Riley Hagelin, Patricia Henley, Alice, Cricket, and Jack Henley-Robisch, the late Annie Henley-Robisch, Kate Jordan and Mike Mansfield, Travis, Oliver, and Patches Jordan-Mansfield, Elizabeth Boyd Lamb, Simone Nicole Lamb, the late Nicky, Wendy, Tiger, Percy, Emily, Toby, Big Syd, and Homer Wells Lamb, Stephanie LaTour and Marc Dolan, Robert LaTour Dolan and Stephen LaTour Dolan, Laura, Brian, Buddy, and Tippy McCammack, the late Esther and Charlie Mushaw, MaryAnn, Kevin, Connor, Maisie, Whitman, Dante, and Peanut Scott, the late Truman and Daisy Scott, the late Adele and Jack Stotter, Elizabeth Boyd, Dick, Edgar Allan, Emma Claire, and Lili Marlene Thompson, the late Cassandra and Buck Thompson, Maria Windell and Jason Gladstone, Trina and Yuki Windell-Gladstone, and my late parents, Lena and David Lamb, who taught me, through their words and actions, the best values to live by and always to treat others with kindness, sympathy, and decency.

I would also like to thank, for their friendship and/or encouragement along the way, Mike Anesko, the late Saul Bellow, Bert Bender, Brandi Bennett, Margie Berns and Tony Silva, Kitty Berns-Silva, Mark and Darwin Bousquet, Robert Olen Butler, Mark Cirino, Deb Cunningham and John Stauffer, Kirk Curnutt, Susan Curtis, Donald Daiker, Linda and Rob Davidson, Morris Dickstein, Clare Virginia Eby, Grace Farrell, Shelley Fisher Fishkin, Dr. Joseph Fruland, Nancy Glazener, the late Andy Goodman, Lisa, Gracie, Janie, and Toby Hartman, Seamus Heaney, Tom Hertweck, Jay Hopler, J. Gerald Kennedy, John King, Mark Leahy, Clayton Lein, Lois Leveen, Dr. Alan Leventhal, Al Lopez, Robin and Joe Mallory, John Matteson, Michael J. McDonough, Dr. Richard McPherson, Bill Miller, Joe Palmer, Nancy Peterson, Nush Powell and Derek Pacheco, Henry and Pickles Powell-Pacheco, Larry Prusak, Marilynn Richtarik, John Carlos Rowe, Aparajita Sagar, Rebecca Saulsbury, Kathy Schroth and John N. Duvall, Patrick, Margaret, and John S. Duvall (#70 for the West Lafayette Red Devils and a future top 10 pick in the NFL draft), Arthur Shippee, the late Judith Shklar, Amanda Siegfried and Derek Royal, Donna Smith, June and the late Bill Stuckey, Patricia Sullivan, Frederic Svoboda, the late Eugene Sweeney, Gwen Athene Tarbox, Gerald Vizenor, Jeane and the late Big Syd Weinstein, Jon Weinstein, the late Peter Weinstein, Bud Weiser, Mike and Marissa Windell, and Patsy Yaeger.

Much earlier versions of parts of this book were previously published in *The Hemingway Review, Modern Fiction Studies,* and *Studies in Short Fiction,* as well as a few pages in an article in *Twentieth-Century Literature.* I am grateful to the editors of these journals for permission to use revised and extended versions of material they originally published. There are also four brief passages that first appeared in my earlier book, *Art Matters,* which I needed to put back into the full readings of the stories from which they came. I am grateful to LSU Press and, I suppose, myself for allowing me to do so.

Once again, it is a pleasure to express my heartfelt appreciation to my friends at Louisiana State University Press, whose professionalism, thoughtfulness, humanity, and common sense have made me the envy of my colleagues. I would especially like to thank my wonderful acquisitions editor Margaret Lovecraft, whose encouragement and kindness carried this project through to production, managing editor Lee Campbell Sioles, who brilliantly oversaw the book's production, marketing manager Erin Rolfs, financial operations manager Becky Brown, marketing coordinator Lauren Tussing-White, and the immensely talented Laura Gleason, whose cover and book designs are simply unexcelled in academic publishing. I am also grateful to the press's director MaryKatherine Callaway and former publications manager Jeddie Smith for their support, acquisitions editor emeritus John Easterly for originally suggesting that I write a sequel to *Art Matters*, and Stan Ivester for his expert copyediting of the manuscript. Last, my gratitude to Roxie Livingston, the daughter of Earl Theisen, for her gracious permission to use her father's photograph of Ernest Hemingway at work, which was taken for *Look* magazine in 1953 during a safari in Kenya.

S. K. Robisch was an assistant professor at Purdue University from 2001 to 2007, where he published a 500-page book lavishly praised by leading scholars, received an English department excellence in teaching award every year, and single-handedly developed a nine-course ecocritical curriculum that was always overenrolled. He also bridged the gap between the arts and sciences, gaining the admiration of faculty in Purdue's renowned engineering and science communities. The *beau ideal* of a colleague and an innovative, remarkably interdisciplinary scholar, Kip was also the best classroom teacher I've ever seen in action, going well above and beyond the call in encouraging and empowering all of his many students to fulfill their potential. It was a privilege to work with him, and it's an honor to call him my friend and brother. I'm proud to dedicate this book to Kip—and I do so with love and the greatest imaginable respect.

Notes

PREFACE

1. *Art Matters,* 21–22.

2. Barthes, "The Death of the Author," 50, 53–54.

3. For an insightful historical study of how Hemingway achieved this preeminence in creative writing programs, see Eric Bennett, "Ernest Hemingway and the Discipline of Creative Writing." Bennett observes that in "the union of his persona and his writing, Hemingway reconciled competing emphases in literary study [between the New Humanists and the New Critics], and the reconciliation contributed to the rise of a coherent, collegiate pedagogy for creative writing" (545).

4. Frank O'Connor, interview by Anthony Whittier, 165; Wallace Stevens to Henry Church, 2 July 1942, *Letters of Wallace Stevens,* 411–12; Ernest Hemingway quoted in Mary Welsh Hemingway, *How It Was,* 352.

5. Nick, of course, was first introduced in a sketch in 1924's *in our time,* but "Indian Camp" is the first formal story in which he appears.

6. Flannery O'Connor, "The Teaching of Literature," 128.

7. Frye, *Anatomy of Criticism,* 25.

CHAPTER ONE

1. The stories were, in rough order of composition, "Indian Camp," "Cat in the Rain," "The End of Something," "The Three-Day Blow," "The Doctor and the Doctor's Wife," "Soldier's Home," "Mr. and Mrs. Elliot," and "Cross-Country Snow." The following month, May 1924, he began writing "Big Two-Hearted River." For the individual compositional histories of these stories, see Paul Smith, *A Reader's Guide.*

2. The most comprehensive and insightful study of Nick Adams, and of Hemingway's autobiographical connections to him, is Joseph M. Flora's *Hemingway's Nick Adams.*

3. All quotations of the final version of "Indian Camp" in this chapter are from Ernest Hemingway, *The Short Stories of Ernest Hemingway,* 91–95, and all quotations of the original and subsequently deleted opening, entitled "Three Shots" by Philip Young, are from the posthumous Hemingway collection edited by Young, *The Nick Adams Stories,* 13–15.

4. Ernest Hemingway, interview by George Plimpton, 233.

5. Carlos Baker, *Hemingway,* 109–14; Reynolds, *Hemingway: The Paris Years,* 125–44.

6. Fenton, *The Apprenticeship,* 242–57; Carlos Baker, *Hemingway,* 115–17; Reynolds, *Hemingway: The Paris Years,* 144–50; Ernest Hemingway to Ezra Pound, 13 October 1923, *Ernest Hemingway: Selected Letters,* 93.

7. Carlos Baker, *Hemingway,* 117; Ernest Hemingway to Ezra Pound, 13 October 1923, *Ernest Hemingway: Selected Letters,* 96; Ernest Hemingway to Gertrude Stein and Alice B. Toklas, 11 October 1923, *Ernest Hemingway: Selected Letters,* 93–95.

8. Ernest Hemingway to Edward J. O'Brien, 20 November 1923, *Ernest Hemingway: Selected Letters,* 104.

9. Lynn, *Hemingway,* 224–25; Reynolds, *Hemingway: The Paris Years,* 157; Ernest Hemingway to Dr. Clarence E. Hemingway, 7 November 1923, *Ernest Hemingway: Selected Letters,* 99–100; Sanford, *At the Hemingways,* 218–19.

10. Lynn, *Hemingway,* 226–27; Reynolds, *Hemingway: The Paris Years,* 162; Ernest Hemingway, *A Moveable Feast,* 82; Ernest Hemingway to Ezra Pound, 10 February 1924, *Ernest Hemingway: Selected Letters,* 110; Ernest Hemingway to Ezra Pound, 17 March 1924, *Ernest Hemingway: Selected Letters,* 112.

11. Quoted in Hotchner, *Papa Hemingway,* 57.

12. Carver, interview by Simpson and Buzbee, 313, 308; Welty, "Writing and Analyzing a Story," 109; Ernest Hemingway, "[On Writing]," *The Nick Adams Stories,* 238.

13. Sanford, *At the Hemingways,* 28–30.

14. Helstern, "Indians, Woodcraft," 62–64.

15. Carlos Baker, *Hemingway,* 125–26.

16. Lynn, *Hemingway,* 228.

17. Chekhov to E. M. Sh——, 17 November 1895, *Letters on the Short Story,* 82–83.

18. Quoted in Carlos Baker, *Hemingway,* 5.

19. Tillich, *Systematic Theology* 1: 191. My notion of *ontological shock* derives from Tillich, most especially from the third chapter of *The Courage to Be* and the three volumes of *Systematic Theology.*

20. Chekhov to A. S. Suvorin, 27 October 1888, *Anton Chekhov's Short Stories,* 272.

21. Ernest Hemingway, *Death in the Afternoon,* 17.

22. "The Revolutionist," which begins with the past progressive, was originally one of the vignettes from *in our time.* "The Short Happy Life of Francis Macomber" also begins with the past progressive. There it is not particularly effective, but the length of the story prevents it from causing any damage.

23. Welty, "Looking at Short Stories," 88.

24. Wharton, *The Writing of Fiction,* 51–52.

25. Gardner, *The Art of Fiction,* 98.

26. Anton Chekhov to Alexander P. Chekhov, 10 May 1886, *Letters on the Short Story,* 71; Chekhov to Maxim Gorky, 3 September 1899, *Anton Chekhov's Short Stories,* 275.

27. Frank O'Connor, interview by Anthony Whittier, 169; Flaubert to Mlle. Leroyer de Chantpie, 8 March 1857, *Letters of Gustave Flaubert,* 230; Anton Chekhov to Alexander P. Chekhov, April 1883, *Letters on the Short Story,* 69.

28. Gardner, *The Art of Fiction,* 30–32.

29. O'Faolain, *The Short Story,* 161.

30. Bowen, "Notes on Writing a Novel," 255. On the uses of dialogue, see *Art Matters,* chapter 8, especially 175–79.

31. O'Faolain, *The Short Story,* 120.

32. On the terms *focalizer* and *focalization,* and on the evolution of Hemingway's use of point-of-view during the 1920s and 30s, see *Art Matters,* chapter 4.

33. Anton Chekhov to Maxim Gorky, 3 September 1899, *Anton Chekhov's Short Stories,* 275; Frank O'Connor, interview by Whittier, 181, 169.

34. Chatman, *Story and Discourse,* 27–31.

35. Barthes, *S/Z,* 82.

36. On *implication omissions,* see *Art Matters,* 45–46.

37. The most valuable analysis of the relationship between fabula time and narrative time is in Gérard Genette, *Narrative Discourse,* 86–112.

38. Sean O'Faolain notes that in a good story "we do not notice how the mental camera moves, withdraws to a distance to enclose a larger view, slips deftly from one character to another, while all the time holding one main direction of which these are only variations" (*The Short Story,* 204). However a writer handles camera angle and distance, if he or she is effective the fictional dream proceeds undisturbed.

39. Barthes, *S/Z,* 19, 84.

40. Welty, "Looking at Short Stories," 105.

41. Barthes, "Textual Analysis of a Tale by Edgar Allan Poe," 291.

42. Barthes *S/Z,* 75.

43. Barthes, *S/Z,* 75–76.

44. Welty, "Looking at Short Stories," 88.

45. Anton Chekhov to Alexander P. Chekhov, 10 May 1886, *Letters on the Short Story,* 71.

46. Barthes, "Textual Analysis of a Tale by Edgar Allan Poe," 288–89; *S/Z passim.*

47. Speaking of the cultural code, Barthes states: "We must not be troubled by the fact that we can constitute as a code some extremely commonplace notations: on the contrary it is their banality, their apparent insignificance which predispose them to being a code, as we have defined it: a body of rules so worn down that we take them for natural features" ("Textual Analysis of a Tale by Edgar Allan Poe," 289). The enormous work being quietly done by the cultural codes of a text is most apparent when examining literature in translation. How, for example, can a translator possibly convey to a reader the cultural resonance and connotations of a simple word like the French "*pain*" by translating it as "bread"? Or, to recross the Atlantic, what sense can a reader in a racially homogenous European country possibly make of the ubiquity of race in Faulkner without having annotations that quadruple the size of the text? It has always seemed to me that European critics' valuation of *The Sound and the Fury* over Faulkner's greatest novel, *Absalom, Absalom!* is purely a function of their inability to grasp fully (a limitation shared by the Canadian Shreve McCannon in the text) the cultural codes of race that so saturate the latter novel.

48. Flora, *Hemingway's Nick Adams,* 24.

49. Strychacz, *Hemingway's Theaters of Masculinity,* 55. For an excellent study of the sorts of stereotypes Hemingway and his readers might be expected to have drawn upon, see Robert F. Berkhofer Jr., *The White Man's Indian.*

50. Because a narrative that uses simple past tenses to denote the narrative present is read by the reader in the reader's present (and the events narrated are correspondingly ex-

perienced by the characters in their present), if the reader is truly engaged in the story he or she unconsciously shifts tenses so that simple past tenses read like present tenses and the past perfect tenses read like simple past tenses. Therefore, past perfect tenses seem less distant than, in normal discourse, they usually are.

51. Thomas Strychacz views the Indian father's "futile attempt" to join the Indian men symbolically through smoking as part of his larger study of how masculinity is performed throughout "Indian Camp" and in other Hemingway texts (*Hemingway's Theaters of Masculinity,* 56).

52. This point may be illustrated by way of a personal example. Growing up in the heyday of westerns, both in cinema and on television, as a boy I devoured them uncritically, drawing upon the cultural codes about specific Indian nations and Native American culture in general that these films and television shows both expected me to access and were themselves in the process of constructing and maintaining. Later in life, whenever I tried to watch one of these fondly remembered movies I was surprised to find that I couldn't because of their historical inaccuracy and racist stereotypes. Even so noble project as John Ford's final western, the elegiac *Cheyenne Autumn,* in which he tried to atone for his portrayals of Native Americans in his earlier films and to expose the U.S. government's atrocities, left me overly critical of the movie's flaws. In trying to watch these films, I could only do so as a critic of ethnic representations and could not take any sort of viewing pleasure in the narrative.

Perhaps the most notorious example of this sort of experience is D. W. Griffith's *The Birth of a Nation,* a film that defined for generations the actual history of Reconstruction, and one that a putative historical scholar like President Woodrow Wilson could actually claim to be perfectly historically accurate. Today, despite the fact that, in terms of cinematic techniques, *The Birth of a Nation* is one of the most important films ever made, it is so disgustingly racist, historically false, and morally pernicious that I, along with many others, simply cannot watch it. To put it in the terms I've been employing, the cultural code regarding race that Griffith drew upon, and that Wilson and so many other contemporary racist viewers shared, has nothing remotely in common with the historically informed cultural codes that I and most viewers today draw upon. In fact, the codes do not merely fail to overlap, but are completely at odds.

53. Flannery O'Connor, "The Nature and Aim of Fiction," 76.

54. For an illuminating historical account of this controversy, see Ken Ryan, "The Contentious Emendation."

55. Anton Chekhov made a number of statements about what has come to be known as "Chekhov's gun." In 1889, he was reported by Ilia Gurliand as saying: "If in Act I you have a pistol hanging on the wall, then it must fire in the last act" (quoted in Rayfield, *Anton Chekhov,* 203).

56. Ernest Hemingway, interview by George Plimpton, 229.

57. Roland Barthes refers to these details as contributing to verisimilitude by their very insignificance. See "The Reality Effect," 141–48. In many of Hemingway's stories there is some such purposefully gratuitous detail, for instance, one that critics have commented on in "The Killers": when Nick addresses the woman in Ole Andreson's rooming house as Mrs. Hirsch and she replies that she is Mrs. Bell.

58. Helstern, "Indians, Woodcraft," 68.

59. Ernest Hemingway to Bernard Berenson, 20–22 March 1953, *Ernest Hemingway: Selected Letters,* 809.

60. Strychacz, *Hemingway's Theaters,* 8, also see 55–58. Although Professor Strychacz and I pursue different paths through this story, I find his analysis thoroughly persuasive and I consider *Hemingway's Theaters* to be one of the finest books on Hemingway, as well as one of the best examples of masculinity studies, extant. It's a shame that it hasn't put an end, once and for all, to the general misunderstandings that pervade the academy regarding Hemingway's hyper-masculine image. Strychacz is absolutely correct: Hemingway was consciously aware of how manhood is performed; this awareness pervades his works and is represented in his characters; and he was deeply sensitive to the nuances of both masculinity and gender as theatrical cultural phenomena.

61. On Gertrude Stein's aesthetics, how these differed from Hemingway's, and what he learned from her, see *Art Matters,* chapter 5.

62. Ernest Hemingway, *Death in the Afternoon,* 2.

63. On the technique of *sequence displacement,* see *Art Matters,* 32.

64. Flora, *Hemingway's Nick Adams,* 23.

65. Young, "'Big World Out There,'" 32; Waldhorn, *A Reader's Guide,* 55.

66. On *recapitulation with variation,* see *Art Matters,* 123.

67. Ernest Hemingway to Owen Wister, 25 July 1929, *Hemingway: Selected Letters,* 301.

68. On the relation between Hemingway's impressionism (combining the depiction of concrete details with external focalization) and what T. S. Eliot termed the "objective correlative," see *Art Matters,* 70–72.

69. On the *float-off* and other types of endings, see *Art Matters,* 144–53.

70. Susan F. Beegel identifies such ironic disjunctions as one of five categories of omission in Hemingway's fiction (*Hemingway's Craft of Omission,* 91).

71. Nabokov, *Lectures on Literature,* 251.

72. Flannery O'Connor, "The Teaching of Literature," 125.

73. Flannery O'Connor, "On Her Own Work," 111.

74. Linda Lizut Helstern observes, "No definitive reason for the Indian husband's suicide can be determined from the facts provided by Hemingway, who allows the motives of this subaltern . . . to remain opaque" ("Indians, Woodcraft," 67). Except in Helstern's article and my 1988 doctoral dissertation, however, the suicide has been universally misread. A very partial list of those who state that he either kills himself because of his wife's screams or the operation are such major Hemingway scholars as Carlos Baker, *Ernest Hemingway,* 125; Philip Young, *Ernest Hemingway: A Reconsideration,* 32; Scott Donaldson, *By Force of Will,* 296–97; Joseph M. Flora, *Hemingway's Nick Adams,* 31; and Wirt Williams, *The Tragic Art of Ernest Hemingway,* 31–32. Others include Malcolm Cowley, "Introduction," 49; Edmund Wilson, "Hemingway: Gauge of Morale," 175; Walter Allen, *The Short Story in English,* 149; Nicholas Joost, *Ernest Hemingway and the Little Magazines,* 85; Kenneth G. Johnston, *The Tip of the Iceberg,* 54; Leo Gurko, who for reasons that elude me seems to think that the incident actually happened, *Ernest Hemingway and the Pursuit of Heroism,* 9; Alan Holder, "The Other Hemingway," 104; Joseph DeFalco, *The Hero in Hemingway's Short Stories,* 28–30; and Nancy R. Comley and Robert Scholes, *Heming-*

way's Genders, 27. Two writers who have made this error are no less than Sean O'Faolain, *The Vanishing Hero,* 145; and Eudora Welty, "Looking at Short Stories," 89. A few sentences earlier, Welty issues a perceptive caution she should have heeded: "Action can indeed be inscrutable, more so than sensation can. It can be . . . much more desperately concealing." Somewhat blushingly I must confess that I, too, belong on this list of errant readers ("Eternity's Artifice," 43). This was my first publication, written in graduate school, and I would like to seize this opportunity to disown it.

75. Flannery O'Connor, "The Teaching of Literature," 125.

76. Ernest Hemingway to Harvey Breit, 27 June 1952, in *Ernest Hemingway: Selected Letters,* 770.

77. See William Faulkner, *Absalom, Absalom!* 80 (the acknowledgment by Mr. Compson that his lengthy explanation of why Henry Sutpen killed Charles Bon is inadequate) and 75–77, 94 (his insistence on that very explanation).

78. Herman Melville, *The Confidence-Man,* 1037.

79. Ernest Hemingway, *Death in the Afternoon,* 122.

80. Reynolds, *Hemingway's First War,* 238–59.

81. Barthes, "Introduction to the Structural Analysis of Narratives," 104.

82. Ernest Hemingway to Horace Liveright, 31 March 1925, *Ernest Hemingway: Selected Letters,* 154.

83. Genette, *Narrative Discourse,* 73–77.

84. Genette's term for the advance notice that points to an event taking place after the conclusion of the narrative is an "external prolepsis." His term for what I have called a "retrospective notice" is a "paralipsis" (*Narrative Discourse,* 68–70, 52–53).

85. Genette, *Narrative Discourse,* 75–77.

86. For a fuller definition the *illustrative stamp,* see *Art Matters,* 157–60.

87. All citations of "Fathers and Sons" are from *The Short Stories of Ernest Hemingway,* 488–99.

CHAPTER TWO

1. For a historical summary of this debate, see the beginning of chapter 5 below.

2. Hoffman, *The Twenties,* 98.

3. Warren, "Ernest Hemingway," 76; Sheridan Baker, *Ernest Hemingway,* 27; Hasbany, "The Shock of Vision," 237; Gurko, *Ernest Hemingway and the Pursuit of Heroism,* 13; Waldhorn, *A Reader's Guide,* 37; Donaldson, *By Force of Will,* 225; Mellow, *Hemingway,* 122; DeFalco, *Hero in Hemingway's Short Stories,* 138.

4. Lynn, *Hemingway,* 258–60. Carlos Baker was the first to observe that Harold Krebs's name is a compound of the first names of Harold Loeb, soon to be "immortalized" as Robert Cohn in *The Sun Also Rises,* and Krebs Friend (*Ernest Hemingway,* 585n). The information about Friend being a victim of shell shock is also in Reynolds, *Hemingway: The Paris Years,* 189; Paul Smith, *A Reader's Guide,* 70; and Mellow, *Hemingway,* 263. To be fair, Lynn also mentions this fact (*Hemingway,* 236), but he does not emphasize it as he does the age difference between Friend and his wife (236, 258), and he does not bring it up, despite its manifest relevance, when examining "Soldier's Home."

5. Reynolds, *Hemingway: The Paris Years,* 191; J. Gerald Kennedy and Kirk Curnutt, "Out of the Picture"; Kobler, "'Soldier's Home' Revisited," 378. For a thoroughly convincing refutation of Kobler, see Steven Trout, "'Where Do We Go from Here?'" 15–16. To Trout's rebuttal I would add that one of the reasons why Hemingway made the protagonist of "Soldier's Home" Harold Krebs from Oklahoma rather than Nick Adams was that he wanted to write a story about the homecoming of a veteran who, unlike Nick, had fought in many of the most horrific battles of the war. Had the story been about Nick Adams, Kobler's interpretation, although still irremediably flawed by poor evidence, might possibly carry some weight.

6. Frank O'Connor, *The Lonely Voice,* 166.

7. For my reading of "Hills Like White Elephants," see *Art Matters,* 198–203.

8. On the origins of the term "soldiers' home," see Trout, "'Where Do We Go from Here?'" 6–7; and Severo and Milford, *The Wages of War,* 133.

9. All citations of "Soldier's Home" are from *The Short Stories of Ernest Hemingway,* 145–53.

10. Trout, "'Where Do We Go from Here?'" 14–15. I am deeply indebted to Professor Trout's *tour de force* article, which came out in *The Hemingway Review* after an earlier version of this chapter first appeared in that journal. The historical context he provides on the Second Division further substantiates my interpretation of "Soldier's Home," and has enabled me, in this new version, to grasp Hemingway's narrative strategies and the entire text more fully.

11. In examining Hemingway's strategies for making this exposition more credible, I do not mean to posit a careless reader, only to suggest that these narrative strategies enable a reader to suspend his or her disbelief more easily. As for actual, rather than posited readers, it is striking how effectively Hemingway managed to get readers to accept some of these "facts" at face value. See, for instance, Petrarca, "Irony of Situation," 665; and Roberts, "In Defense of Krebs," 516.

12. Trout, "'Where Do We Go from Here?'" 14.

13. According to Trout, nearly 600,000 American soldiers were sent home immediately after the Armistice and "most of the remaining 3,400,000 received their discharges by the summer of 1919" ("'Where Do We Go from Here?'" 8).

14. Ellis W. Hawley, *The Great War and the Search for a Modern Order,* 21. I should add that enlisting in the Marines was more unusual. Steven Trout observes that in rural areas of Oklahoma "typically four or five men per county" joined the Marines. Most Oklahomans served in the 36th Division or the 90th Division, both of which saw casualties but neither of which came close to the casualty rate of Krebs's Second Division ("'Where Do We Go from Here?'" 17–18).

15. For a fuller explanation of *free indirect speech,* see *Art Matters,* 87–88. What is fascinating about Hemingway's prose in "Soldier's Home" is precisely his use of free indirect speech throughout, especially in the story's final paragraph, which completely merges the narrator with his focalizer.

16. These mock heroic phrases recall the brief prologue to F. Scott Fitzgerald's otherwise realist/naturalist 1920 story, "May Day," in which the main body of the text serves to puncture the prologue's representation of American culture's idealized self-fashioning of

the nation's role in the Great War. The prologue begins: "There had been a war fought and won and the great city of the conquering people was crossed with triumphal arches and vivid with thrown flowers of white, red, and rose" (97).

17. Trout, "'Where Do We Go from Here?'" 14–15.

18. This list specifically consists of the major battles in which my beloved friend, Sydney "Big Syd" Weinstein, who passed in January 2011, fought as a land mine specialist for the famed 36th Division of the 5th Army in the Second World War. I make the analogy to honor the enduring memory of Big Syd and the heroes of his generation, and because readers unacquainted with the battles of the First World War might not realize how emotionally a reader in 1924 would have responded to names like Belleau Wood and Soissons.

19. I am indebted to Susan F. Beegel, editor of *The Hemingway Review,* for pointing out this second way of interpreting Mrs. Krebs's removal of her glasses as a dramatic gesture, which, especially if Mrs. Krebs is wearing reading glasses, is more apt than my first, "myopic," reading of her action.

20. Peter L. Hays observes that Hemingway's "hardening bacon fat" may have been influenced by similar images in Ford Madox Ford's *Some Do Not* and James Joyce's "A Painful Case" and *Portrait of the Artist as a Young Man,* where they are used to express disgust regarding conventional sexual morality ("Soldier's Home," 21–22). Assessing Hays's observation, Paul Smith suggests that "the image of hardening grease seems to have taken on in those years an almost iconic association with a stultifying, normal, and homey morality" (*A Reader's Guide,* 70).

21. I am grateful to my friend Wendy Flory for pointing out the comic element, which I had hitherto not noticed, in this otherwise serious passage.

22. On *immediate speech,* see *Art Matters,* 88 and 110.

23. Eliot, "The Hollow Men," section V, lines 5–9, *Complete Poems and Plays 1909–1950,* 58.

24. On what I term the *float-off* as a strategy for concluding a story, see *Art Matters,* 149–53.

25. Raymond Williams, *The English Novel from Dickens to Lawrence,* 192.

26. My understanding of the American 1920s derives from numerous sources. Particularly valuable are Paula S. Fass, *The Damned and the Beautiful;* Frederick Lewis Allen, *Only Yesterday;* Geoffrey Perrett, *America in the Twenties;* William E. Leuchtenburg, *The Perils of Prosperity;* Ellis W. Hawley, *The Great War and the Search for a Modern Order;* David E. Kyvig, *Daily Life in the United States, 1920–1940;* David J. Goldberg, *Discontented America,* and, for literary history, Frederick J. Hoffman, *The Twenties,* Ann Douglas, *Terrible Honesty,* and Marc Dolan, *Modern Lives.* The best accounts of the American homefront during the war are David M. Kennedy, *Over Here,* and Ronald Schaffer, *America in the Great War.*

27. For a fuller explanation of what I mean by a *symbolic historical representation* and its relation to a *dialogical textualization,* see my "'America Can Break Your Heart,'" 483–84. Because I am coining two terms here, I should add that a symbolic historical representation need not necessarily emerge from a dialogical textualization as it does in *Huck Finn;* in other words, the time of the fabula and of the narrating present can be one and the same. For example, in *Moby-Dick,* Herman Melville critiques the vicious nativist response to Irish immigrants in the 1840s and 1850s (in a novel published in 1851) by contrasting

the responses of Ishmael with those of other characters toward Queequeg, a South Seas islander. This is a symbolic historical representation—with Queequeg representing the Irish "other"—and there is no gap between the fabula and the time of narration. See my "Making Mats," 40–42. The opposite of a symbolical historical representation would be a *reflection,* in which the text depicts a cultural phenomenon in a straightforward fashion, as in, for example, Stephen Crane's *Maggie,* Theodore Dreiser's *Sister Carrie,* or John Steinbeck's *The Grapes of Wrath.*

28. James R. Mellow shrewdly observes that in Hemingway's fiction a river generally "serves as a cleansing baptism, an absolution for past sins, a healing experience," as is the case with the Big Two-Hearted, the Irati (in *The Sun Also Rises*) and the Tagliamento (in *A Farewell to Arms*). But in "Soldier's Home" the "absence of the Rhine is, perhaps, a signal that there is no redemptive symbol in Krebs's circumstances—or in the story" (*Hemingway,* 124–25).

29. Dolan, "The (Hi)story of Their Lives," 50.

30. I am indebted to Marc Dolan for pointing out to me how oddly mixed the attire of the young women is.

31. Fass, *The Damned and the Beautiful,* 93, 280.

32. See Lamb, Exchange of Letters.

33. These anxieties were particularly acute during the 1920s and are part of the social experience of the period. In reality, of course, the family was not collapsing but rather undergoing fundamental changes as, according to Paula S. Fass, "emotional ties of warmth and amicability replaced [former ties of] respect and authority" and the family became less hierarchical and more democratic (*The Damned and the Beautiful,* 93).

34. Eliot, "The Love Song of J. Alfred Prufrock," stanza 3, *Complete Poems and Plays 1909–1950,* 4.

CHAPTER THREE

1. Hemingway wrote "The Killers" in Madrid on 15 May 1926. In August, he and Hadley returned by train to Paris from the Cap d'Antibes and Hemingway moved into a friend's apartment. There he corrected proofs of *The Sun Also Rises,* and during the first week of September wrote "A Canary for One," which was based on the train trip he had taken a few weeks earlier. Immediately after finishing the story, he started "In Another Country," another tale in which a man loses his wife, but one that was not autobiographical and that had clear thematic points. It also took him nearly two months to complete. See Lynn, *Hemingway,* 342–60; and Carlos Baker, *Hemingway,* 169–77.

2. Hilary K. Justice carefully scrutinizes the manuscripts of the story to read it as a textualization of Ernest's break-up with Hadley and the state of his impending marriage to Pauline Pfeiffer, as well as the first story he wrote in which his roles as private man, working writer, and celebrity author all came into conflict. In this persuasive biographical reading, the three wrecked train cars near the story's end become fictionalized equivalents of the three lives (Hadley's, Pauline's, and his) that he feared he might have ruined; the American lady comes to represent Pauline's mother, who at the time was a threat to end Pauline's relationship with him; and the "foreign" Swiss with whom the lady's daughter fell in love

stands for Hemingway's own sense of being viewed by the Pfeiffers "as a writerly 'other'" ("Courting Exposure," 73). Although I will purposefully be approaching the story here in a non-biographical manner, I should point out that Justice's article, Julian Smith's thematic examination, "'A Canary for One': Hemingway in the Wasteland," and Scott Donaldson's genetic study, "Preparing for the End," are the only examples of criticism that have been equal to the many excellences of this extraordinary story.

3. All citations of "A Canary for One" are from *The Short Stories of Ernest Hemingway,* 337–42.

4. See, for instance, Cunliffe, Dolch, and Hagopian, "A Canary for One."

5. Fitzgerald, "One Hundred False Starts," 132.

6. Flannery O'Connor, "Writing Short Stories," 96.

7. Ernest Hemingway, *A Moveable Feast,* 75.

8. Ernest Hemingway to Dr. C. E. Hemingway, 20 March 1925, *Ernest Hemingway: Selected Letters,* 153.

9. Flannery O'Connor, "The Nature and Aim of Fiction," 78.

10. Ernest Hemingway, interview by George Plimpton, 229.

11. Flannery O'Connor, "Writing Short Stories," 98, 99.

12. The only part of this reconstruction of the seating arrangement that needs some explanation is the matter of which way the narrator is facing, which is based on strong, if circumstantial, evidence. The narrator uses the words "looking back" to describe how he viewed Marseilles as the train is leaving it. Later, when they pass the three wrecked cars, he can see all three cars as his train passes them, but the American lady, when alerted to the wreck, can only see the last car. It is highly probable, therefore, that he is facing forward, and certainly likely that his wife is seated alongside him and not next to the American lady.

13. On Hemingway's innovative use of external focalization in first-person narratives, which he first employed in "chapter 3" of *in our time* ("Chapter II" of *In Our Time*) and that he pushes to its limits here in "A Canary for One," see *Art Matters,* 99–103. My analysis on those pages also illuminates the differences between Hemingway's externally focalized, first-person narration and what we see in a conventional first-person narration by contrasting the depictions of Twain's Huck Finn and the narrator in Hemingway's "After the Storm" to the sight of a sunken ship each wishes to loot.

14. See *Art Matters* (57–58) on what Ian Watt terms *delayed decoding* (*Conrad in the Nineteenth Century,* 175), a Stephen Crane technique that also enormously influenced Joseph Conrad. Also see *Art Matters* (61–62) for how Hemingway employs this same method of presenting sensory perceptions "as they appear in the experiencing consciousness, simulating how the mind records them before it starts processing them. The composition of such passages [as in the above one from Avignon station] seems informal and spontaneous, although of course Hemingway is deliberately crafting them" (*Art Matters,* 61). For a re-definition and full exploration of Hemingway's *impressionism,* as well as of *expressionism,* see *Art Matters,* chapter 3.

15. Scott Donaldson was the first to observe that the statement about the soldiers being too tall to stare, like the later line about how nothing had eaten any breakfast, are foreshadowings which "indicate that something is troubling" the narrator ("Preparing for the End," 206).

16. Carter, "'Nothing Had Eaten Any Breakfast,'" 10.

17. Cunliffe et al., "A Canary for One," 97.

18. Booth, *The Rhetoric of Fiction,* 274.

19. Unpublished manuscript excerpted in Phillips, *Ernest Hemingway on Writing,* 5–6.

20. Ernest Hemingway, *A Moveable Feast,* 75.

21. See *Art Matters,* chapter 3, especially 51–53.

22. Julian Smith, "'A Canary for One': Hemingway in the Wasteland," 356.

23. This is akin to how, in a naturalist story like Stephen Crane's "The Blue Hotel," a favorite of Hemingway's, the main characters, except for Scully and his son Johnny, are continually referred to as the Swede or the Dutchman, the Gambler, the Easterner, and the Cowboy, even though the names of the last two are mentioned at some point in the story.

24. Donaldson, "Preparing for the End," 208.

25. If I may be allowed a biographical intrusion, Ernest never stopped loving Hadley, even after their divorce and his subsequent marriage to Pauline Pfeiffer. But one also strongly senses, just in reading the story, that the narrator still loves his wife, an observation that has been made by many of my students over the years, none of whom were aware of the history of Ernest and Hadley's marriage and its aftermath.

26. Donaldson, "Preparing for the End," 209.

27. For a complete analysis of how dialogue in fiction functions, and exactly how Hemingway transformed the illustrative dialogue of previous fiction into the constructive dialogue that was his single greatest and most influential contribution to fictional craft, see *Art Matters,* chapter 8.

28. Ford, *Joseph Conrad,* 200–201.

29. Grebstein, *Hemingway's Craft,* 96.

30. Martin and Ober, "Hemingway and James," 470–71.

31. Ernest Hemingway, *The Sun Also Rises,* 251.

32. Bowen, "Notes on Writing a Novel," 255.

33. Julian Smith, "'A Canary for One': Hemingway in the Wasteland," 361.

34. For a definition and fuller understanding of what I mean by the term *disjunctive bump,* as well as Hemingway's strategies for negotiating it, see *Art Matters,* 144–53.

35. O'Faolain, *The Short Story,* 158.

36. Ernest Hemingway to Horace Liveright, 31 March 1925, *Ernest Hemingway: Selected Letters,* 154.

37. Flannery O'Connor, "The Teaching of Literature," 128.

CHAPTER FOUR

1. I am not counting among these my own 1996 article, which is a much earlier version of this chapter. Hays, "Hemingway and the Fisher King" (1966); Julian Smith, "Hemingway and the Thing Left Out" (1971); Monteiro, "Hemingway's Christmas Carol" (1972); and Moss, "Hemingway and the Thing Left In" (1990). The explication is by Gary Harrington, "Hemingway's 'God Rest You Merry, Gentlemen'" (1993). There are occasional brief mentions of the story in Hemingway scholarship, and Paul Smith devotes a short chapter to it in *A Reader's Guide* (246–51) in which he reconstructs the circumstances of its creation, re-

counts its publication history, and offers a shrewd critique of Hays, Julian Smith, and Monteiro.

2. Kruse, "Allusions to *The Merchant of Venice* and the New Testament," 72; Camastra, "Hemingway's Modern Hymn,'" 51, 64; Levitzke, "'In Those Days the Distances Were Very Different,'" 21, 22, 19, 23.

3. To be fair, these critics do address the question of the diminished first-person narrator, but they still fail to see the many functions such a narrator serves.

4. Most critics identify the narrator as a reporter, presumably because Hemingway was a young reporter in Kansas City in 1917–18. But there is no textual evidence to support such an assumption. In addition, as Horst Kruse points out, "Hemingway tried to avoid confusion of the narrator with the Hemingway or Nick Adams persona of his autobiographical fiction by deliberately deleting a reference to [the narrator's] occupation as a reporter from the final version of his manuscript" ("Allusions to *The Merchant of Venice* and the New Testament," 64). Hemingway also deleted from the story's final draft a remark made by Doc Fischer that might suggest the narrator is a reporter (see Kruse, 71). The conflation of the author with his narrators and focalizers remains an occupational hazard in Hemingway studies.

5. All citations of "God Rest You Merry, Gentlemen" are from *The Short Stories of Ernest Hemingway,* 392–96.

6. On the *present absence,* see *Art Matters,* 142–43.

7. Hawthorne, *The Scarlet Letter,* 35–36.

8. Rick Moss points out that "Dans Argent" is not idiomatic French, and speculates that the words the young narrator recalls seeing on the car hood "probably read 'Sans Argent,' a common expression meaning 'without Money'" ("Hemingway and the Thing Left In," 170). But this makes no sense as something that would be lettered on the hood of an expensive racing car, and Hemingway deliberately makes the car "silver." Idiomatic or not, "Dans Argent" is the most logical lettering and the only lettering the text supports.

9. In an excellent article on *The Sun Also Rises,* Katherine Calloway argues for the likelihood of Hemingway's familiarity with the Roman poet Horace and makes a strong argument for a deliberate Horace intertext throughout that novel, but she limits herself to merely mentioning the use of the name in this story ("'*Pulvis et Umbra Sumus,*'" 126). The expression, "What news along the rialto?" is from act 1, scene 3, of Shakespeare's *The Merchant of Venice.* Gary Harrington makes an interesting case for how the Shakespeare intertext contributes to Hemingway's treatment of religious intolerance in the story. He also notes that on the arch over the entrance to the Kansas City General Hospital, where young Hemingway stopped along his beat as a reporter, is inscribed Portia's speech on the "quality of mercy" from act 4, scene 1, of the play, which may explain why the phrase about the rialto suggests itself so readily to both Fischer and Hemingway ("Hemingway's 'God Rest You Merry, Gentlemen,'" 52).

10. The story was first published in 1933 as a limited, first-edition pamphlet. In that version, Wilcox tells the boy, "Oh go and jack off." When the story was reissued by Scribner's later that year, as part of the collection *Winner Take Nothing,* a dash replaced the words "jack off" against Hemingway's wishes, and this has been the case in all subsequent reprintings. See Paul Smith, *A Reader's Guide,* 247.

11. Ernest Hemingway to Robert Morgan Brown, 14 July 1954, quoted in Gajdusek, "Harder on Himself than Most," 365.

12. Gajdusek, "Harder on Himself than Most," 366.

13. On what I term the *Conradian split*, see *Art Matters*, 104–6.

14. On the difference between James's and Hemingway's opinions about choosing a focalizer in fiction, which derive respectively from the former's work in the novel and the latter's in the short story, see *Art Matters*, 106–8.

CHAPTER FIVE

Epigraph: "La peinture, va, Henri, c'est bougrement difficile. . . . On croit toujours la tenir, on n'y est jamais. . . . Il y a un métier par objet. On ne sais jamais son métier. . . . Je peindrais cent ans, mille ans sans m'arrêter, qu'il me semble que je ne saurais rien. . . . Moi, je me dévore, je me tue, à couvrir cinquante centimètres de toile. . . . N'importe. . . . C'est la vie. . . . Je veux mourir en poignant. . . ." (Paul Cézanne, quoted in Joachim Gasquet, *Cézanne*).

1. The best and fullest biographical account of the writing of this story is in Michael Reynolds, *Hemingway: The Paris Years*, 201–48. As far as I can tell, Paul Smith was the first to observe that Stein's famous comment was a response to the original ending of this story ("Hemingway's Early Manuscripts," 284–85); also see Mellow, *Hemingway*, 276–77; Stein, *The Autobiography of Alice B. Toklas*, 207; Ernest Hemingway to Ernest Walsh and Ethel Moorhead, c. 12 January 1925, *Ernest Hemingway: Selected Letters*, 144; Ernest Hemingway to F. Scott Fitzgerald, c. 24 December 1925, *Ernest Hemingway: Selected Letters*, 180. For three valuable analyses of the various manuscripts of the story, see Oldsey, "Hemingway's Beginnings and Endings," 218–24; Paul Smith, "Hemingway's Early Manuscripts," 280–86; and Paul Smith, "1924: Hemingway's Luggage," 45–52.

2. Malcolm Cowley, "Introduction," 48.

3. Philip Young, *Hemingway: A Reconsideration*, 6, 165–71, 47.

4. Edmund Wilson, "Hemingway: The Gauge of Morale."

5. Lynn, *Hemingway*, 10, 102–8; also see Lynn, "Hemingway's Private War." After railing against Young's thesis for several years, Hemingway suddenly agreed with the gist of it in letters to Malcolm Cowley (Lynn, *Hemingway*, 106–7) and to a *New York Times* reporter who was writing an introduction to a Hemingway reader (Ernest Hemingway to Charles Poore, 23 January 1953, *Ernest Hemingway: Selected Letters*, 798). Not surprisingly, Lynn views these letters as "warm-ups for the gloss he offered the public at large in *A Moveable Feast*" (*Hemingway*, 107).

6. Two excellent recent examples that fall broadly into the war-wound camp but that are focused on other matters are Philip Melling's study of the history of northern Michigan Indians that lies hidden beneath the surface of the story ("There Were Many Indians") and Sarah Mary O'Brien's application of Leo Marx's ideas on pastoralism to the text ("'I, Also, Am in Michigan'").

7. Lamb, "Fishing for Stories," 163.

8. Barthes, "The Death of the Author," 52–53.

9. All quotations of the final version of "Big Two-Hearted River" are from *The Short Stories of Ernest Hemingway*, 209–18 and 221–32, and all quotations of the original ending

that was deleted are from Ernest Hemingway, *The Nick Adams Stories*, 233–41. Because this is a longer story than the others we have been exploring, and since I will be moving back and forth between the two texts, to prevent confusion I will embed page numbers in the text as "BTHR" for the final version of the story and "OW" (for "On Writing," the title given to it by editor Philip Young in *The Nick Adams Stories*) for the original ending. Where no reference appears, the page of the quotation is the same as the next embedded reference.

10. Summerhayes, "Fish Story," 12.

11. Fredrik Chr. Brøgger identifies and traces the narrator's and Nick's very different voices and perspectives regarding nature throughout the text. He shows that "Nick's viewpoint is unabashedly anthropocentric; he is first and foremost concerned with what nature means to *him*." But the "narrator's relationship to nature is marked by a refusal to impose meaning on it[.]" Gradually, Nick's perspective demonstrates "development and progression" towards the possibility of becoming more like that of the narrator's. The story, Brøgger insightfully asserts, "is a tale not only of a man who needs to feel in control of his environment; it is at the same time the story of a man who tries to challenge that need" ("Whose Nature?" 24, 27, 26).

12. Ernest Hemingway to Philip Young, 6 March 1952, *Ernest Hemingway: Selected Letters*, 760. Despite his disgust at being psychoanalyzed in Young's book, Hemingway kindly and generously decided to give him permission to quote from his works. Michael Reynolds observes: "When Ernest received a copy of Young's paper presented at a professional meeting, it confirmed his worst fears. Young and others were practicing psychoanalysis without a license. . . . Despite his serious misgivings . . . Hemingway eventually gave in to Young's plea [for permission to quote from Hemingway's fiction] that his tenure and his family's well-being depended on the book. When Ernest learned that Young was a wounded veteran from World War II, he reluctantly told Charles Scribner, Jr., to give him permission to quote. Whatever Bledsoe [Young's editor] had to pay Scribner's for the permissions, Ernest instructed his publisher to give his half back to Young" (*Hemingway: The Final Years*, 254).

13. Ernest Hemingway to Robert McAlmon, c. 15 November 1924, *Ernest Hemingway: Selected Letters*, 133.

14. Borges, *Borges On Writing*, 59.

15. Ernest Hemingway to Robert McAlmon, c. 15 November 1924, *Ernest Hemingway: Selected Letters*, 133.

16. On the break-up between Hemingway and Bill Smith, see Reynolds, *Hemingway: The Paris Years*, 198, 251.

17. Although Helen was not the usual fictional name for the real-life Hadley and Hemingway himself claimed in 1925 that he had only used Hadley in one story, "Out of Season," nevertheless Bernard Oldsey notes that in one of the manuscripts of "Big Two-Hearted River" Hemingway had accidentally written "Hadley" instead of "Helen" ("Hemingway's Beginnings and Endings," 219). Given this slip, and how autobiographical the deleted ending is, I think we may safely assume that Helen is based on Hadley.

18. Kate was Bill Smith's sister, who later married John Dos Passos. The other characters are also unfictionalized real-life friends of Hemingway.

19. Maera (Manuel García López) would be dead of tuberculosis at age twenty-eight by the end of 1924. Perhaps, while watching Maera fight in Spain that July, Hemingway had learned that the matador was ill.

20. For a description of the *cabelleros en plaza,* see the glossary in Hemingway's *Death in the Afternoon.*

21. Ernest Hemingway, *Green Hills of Africa,* 109.

22. J. Gerald Kennedy, *Imagining Paris,* 92–95. This volume, I should add, is the most insightful criticism I've ever read on the American expatriates in Paris during the interwar years, as well as the finest book we have on the literary poetics of exile; it is also a brilliant study of the role of place on writing and in the construction of self-identity.

23. Ernest Hemingway to Howell Jenkins, c. 15 September 1919, *Ernest Hemingway: Selected Letters,* 28–29; Oldsey, "Hemingway's Beginnings and Endings," 219; Ernest Hemingway to Dr. C. E. Hemingway, 20 March 1925, *Ernest Hemingway: Selected Letters,* 153; Reynolds, *Hemingway: The Paris Years,* 202; Sheridan Baker, "Hemingway's Two-Hearted River," 157; Svoboda, "Landscapes Real and Imagined," 34, 41.

24. In this reading of the deleted ending I am purposely conflating Hemingway and Nick, a strategy I think entirely appropriate to a text that is probably not much more fictional than, say, *A Moveable Feast.* For a different approach, see Debra A. Moddelmog's intriguing article, "The Unifying Consciousness of a Divided Conscience," in which she employs the deleted ending to posit Nick as the implied author of *In Our Time.*

25. Speaking of a later part of the deleted ending, Paul Smith comments, "The obviously autobiographical character of this section is emphasized by the unnecessary appositive 'He, Nick'; it is as if he had to remind himself that he was writing a work of fiction" ("Hemingway's Early Manuscripts," 282). The "He, Nick" construction that Smith refers to comes in the part of the story where Hemingway is talking about writing like Cézanne painted ("OW" 239), but it also occurs in an earlier passage about Nick/Hemingway's friendship with Maera—"He, Nick, was a friend of Maera" ("OW" 237).

26. I simply cannot resist an anecdote dimly recalled from a quarter of a century ago. I can attest to its truth if not its absolute accuracy. A vegetarian who is disgusted by fishing, appalled by hunting, and horrified by bullfighting (the irony of my being a Hemingway scholar does not escape me), I grew up in the unnatural landscape of concrete, asphalt, red bricks, and gasoline fumes in the Bronx. Living in a similar environment in Cambridge, Massachusetts, and in the midst of writing on "Big Two-Hearted River," I found myself exasperated in attempting to keep track of which damned trout was which in the story's two versions. (I had even tried naming them as a mnemonic device—Little Joe, Hoss, Larry and Magic, Crockett and Tubbs— but that just gave me the giggles and made matters worse.) Growing increasingly sick of fish and desperately in need of a break, I turned on *The Tonight Show,* only to find Johnny Carson interviewing the actress Mariel Hemingway, who bears an uncanny resemblance to her famous grandfather. They were discussing—oh, the humor of the gods—trout fishing! When Johnny asked Mariel if she fished, she laughed and said something like, "I'm a Hemingway. Of course I fish." He then inquired if she used real bait or lures, and she sternly replied, "Hemingways never use lures." After the interview, I gave up and went to bed for some much needed sleep. And all night long I dreamed of trout.

27. Ernest Hemingway, *Green Hills of Africa,* 27.

28. Ernest Hemingway to Harvey Breit, 27 June 1952, *Ernest Hemingway: Selected Letters,* 770.

29. Hemingway may have heard from Gertrude Stein about Cézanne's personality and recognized its affinities with his own. Gertrude and her brother Leo knew Cézanne's friend, the legendary art collector Ambroise Vollard, and purchased Cézanne paintings from him (see Mellow, *Charmed Circle,* 5, 14). In 1926, Hemingway would borrow Vollard's book on Cézanne from Sylvia Beach (see Reynolds, ed., *Hemingway's Reading,* 197). Vollard's own temperament, by the way, had much in common with Cézanne's and Hemingway's.

30. Paul Cézanne to Paul Cézanne, Jr., 13 October 1906, *Paul Cézanne: Letters,* 327–28; Paul Cézanne to Émile Bernard, 23 October 1905, *Paul Cézanne: Letters,* 312; Ernest Hemingway, *Death in the Afternoon,* 2. Cézanne offers similar advice in several other letters. My understanding of Cézanne's aesthetics comes from a number of studies, especially Roger Fry, *Cézanne;* Kurt Badt, *The Art of Cézanne;* Richard Shiff, *Cézanne and the End of Impressionism;* and Pavel Machotka, *Cézanne: Landscape into Art.* The definitive study of the influence of artists on Hemingway is Emily Stipes Watts, *Ernest Hemingway and the Arts.* Other illuminating explorations of Cézanne's influence on Hemingway are by Ron Berman, "Recurrence in Hemingway and Cézanne"; Sheldon Norman Grebstein, *Hemingway's Craft,* 161–66; Kenneth G. Johnston, "Hemingway and Cézanne"; and Theodore L. Gaillard Jr., "Hemingway's Debt to Cézanne." Comparing the landscape descriptions of Seney in "Big Two-Hearted River" with earlier ones of Hortons Bay in "Up in Michigan," Johnston shows how Hemingway moved beyond "photographic realism" to a Cézanne-like aesthetic. Among the qualities that the two share, he singles out "[t]he oblique rendering of more than meets the eye; the repetition of line, color, and motif; the fusion of simplicity and complexity; the union of abstraction and reality; [and] the elimination of non-essential details" ("Hemingway and Cézanne," 30).

31. Ernest Hemingway, *Death in the Afternoon,* 191.

32. Grebstein, *Hemingway's Craft,* 164–65.

33. See Paul Cézanne to Émile Bernard, 15 April 1904 and 25 July 1904, *Paul Cézanne: Letters,* 296, 299.

34. Loran, *Cézanne's Composition,* 8.

35. Gaillard, "Hemingway's Debt to Cézanne," 67.

36. Quoted in Ross, "How Do You Like It Now, Gentlemen?" 36.

37. Ernest Hemingway to Gertrude Stein and Alice B. Toklas, 15 August 1924, *Ernest Hemingway: Selected Letters,* 122.

38. Ron Berman points out Cézanne-like *routes tournantes* in "Indian Camp," "The Three-Day Blow," "The Battler," "Big Two-Hearted River," "In Another Country," and "An Alpine Idyll." To these stories, we can add "Che Ti Dice la Patria?" "Ten Indians," "A Way You'll Never Be," "Wine of Wyoming," "Fathers and Sons," and "The Snows of Kilimanjaro" (they are also, of course, found throughout the novels). Berman also explains that many of the phrases Hemingway uses in his landscape depictions deliberately allude to parts of the lengthy titles of Cézanne's late landscape paintings, a sort of homage to the French master. See "Recurrence in Hemingway and Cézanne," 23–24.

39. Berman, "Recurrence in Hemingway and Cézanne," 25–26, 27, 32.

40. Berman, "Recurrence in Hemingway and Cézanne," 29.

41. Paul Cézanne to Émile Bernard, [1905], *Paul Cézanne: Letters,* 310–11; Paul Cézanne to Charles Camoin, 13 September 1903, *Paul Cézanne: Letters,* 291–92; Paul Cézanne to Charles Camoin, 9 December 1904, *Paul Cézanne: Letters,* 303–4.

42. Ernest Hemingway, *A Moveable Feast,* 13.

43. While acknowledging Hemingway's deep appreciation of Cézanne, Paul Smith makes this interesting and, I think, perceptive point: "That Hemingway chose a painter as Nick's master was as much a strategy to disclaim any other writer's influence as it was to admit that of any artist's" ("Hemingway's Early Manuscripts," 283). Of course, one of the artists whose enormous influence he was particularly ambivalent about admitting was Joyce, especially while writing a long story to conclude *In Our Time* that would serve the same purpose for his collection that "The Dead" had served for Joyce's *Dubliners.* Hence the silly Cézanne/Joyce binary of this fragment, which is so completely at odds with the enormous respect Hemingway always expressed for Joyce both publicly and privately.

44. Although he died a few months short of his sixty-eighth birthday, Cézanne would lament a month before his death: "Will I ever achieve the goal I have sought so fervently and pursued so long?" (Paul Cézanne to Émile Bernard, 21 September 1906, *Paul Cézanne: Letters,* 324).

45. Ernest Hemingway to Edward J. O'Brien, c. 20 November 1923, *Ernest Hemingway: Selected Letters,* 104.

46. Hemingway here images the act of writing much the same way as does James's dying writer Dencome in "The Middle Years": "We work in the dark—we do what we can—we give what we have. Our doubt is our passion and our passion is our task. The rest is the madness of art" ("The Middle Years," 354).

47. Mellow, *Hemingway,* 276.

48. Here I see the captured trout as metaphors for successful stories and the uncaptured trout as metaphors for stories too difficult, at this stage in his career, for him to complete successfully. Earlier, I viewed the trout as metaphors for the material of stories, the fabula that the act of fishing/writing turns into stories if it can catch them. In either case, the metafictional metaphor, as I have said, is inescapable.

49. Love, *Practical Ecocriticism,* 118.

50. Ernest Hemingway to L. H. Brague Jr., 22 February 1959, *Ernest Hemingway: Selected Letters,* 893.

51. Ernest Hemingway, *A Moveable Feast,* 76–77.

Works Cited

Allen, Frederick Lewis. *Only Yesterday: An Informal History of the 1920s.* 1931. New York: Harper Perennial Modern Classics, 2000.

Allen, Walter. *The Short Story in English.* Oxford: Clarendon/Oxford UP, 1981.

Badt, Kurt. *The Art of Cézanne.* Trans. Sheila Ann Oglivie. Berkeley: U of California P, 1965.

Baker, Carlos. *Ernest Hemingway: A Life Story.* New York: Scribner's, 1969.

Baker, Sheridan. *Ernest Hemingway: An Introduction and Interpretation.* New York: Holt, Rinehart, 1967.

———. "Hemingway's Two-Hearted River." 1959. In Jackson J. Benson, ed., *The Short Stories of Ernest Hemingway: Critical Essays.* Durham, NC: Duke UP, 1975. 150–59.

Barthes, Roland. "The Death of the Author." 1968. *The Rustle of Language.* Trans. Richard Howard. New York: Hill and Wang, 1986. 49–55.

———. "Introduction to the Structural Analysis of Narratives." 1966. *The Semiotic Challenge.* Trans. Richard Howard. New York: Hill and Wang, 1988. 95–135.

———. "The Reality Effect." 1968. *The Rustle of Language.* Trans. Richard Howard. New York: Hill and Wang, 1986. 141–48.

———. *S/Z.* Trans. Richard Miller. New York: Hill and Wang, 1974.

———. "Textual Analysis of a Tale by Edgar Allan Poe." 1973. *The Semiotic Challenge.* Trans. Richard Howard. New York: Hill and Wang, 1988. 261–93.

Beach, Sylvia. *Shakespeare and Company.* 1959. Lincoln: U of Nebraska P, 1980.

Beegel, Susan F. *Hemingway's Craft of Omission: Four Manuscript Examples.* Ann Arbor, MI: UMI Research Press, 1988.

Bennett, Eric. "Ernest Hemingway and the Discipline of Creative Writing, or, Shark Liver Oil." *Modern Fiction Studies* 56.3 (2010): 544–67.

Berkhofer, Robert F., Jr. *The White Man's Indian: Images of the American Indian from Columbus to the Present.* New York: Vintage, 1979.

Berman, Ron. "Recurrence in Hemingway and Cézanne." *The Hemingway Review* 23.2 (2004): 21–36.

Booth, Wayne C. *The Rhetoric of Fiction.* 1961. 2nd ed. Chicago: U of Chicago P, 1983.

Borges, Jorges Luis. *Borges on Writing.* Eds. Norman Thomas di Giovanni, Daniel Halpern, and Frank McShane. New York: Dutton, 1973.

Bowen, Elizabeth. "Notes on Writing a Novel." 1945. *Collected Impressions.* New York: Alfred A. Knopf, 1950. 249–63.

Brøgger, Fredrik Chr. "Whose Nature?: Differing Narrative Perspectives on Hemingway's 'Big Two-Hearted River.'" In Robert F. Fleming, ed. *Hemingway and the Natural World.* Moscow: U of Idaho P, 1999. 19–29.

Calloway, Katherine. "'*Pulvis et Umbra Sumus*': Horace in Hemingway's *The Sun Also Rises.*" *The Hemingway Review* 25.1 (2005): 120–31.

Camastra, Nicole J. "Hemingway's Modern Hymn: Music and the Church as Background Sources for 'God Rest You Merry, Gentlemen.'" *The Hemingway Review* 28.1 (2008): 51–67.

Carter, Steven. "'Nothing Had Eaten Any Breakfast': Hemingway's 'A Canary for One.'" *Prospero* 4 (1997): 5–15.

Carver, Raymond. Interview by Mona Simpson and Lewis Buzbee. 1983. In George Plimpton, ed., *Writers at Work: The* Paris Review *Interviews.* Seventh series. New York: Penguin, 1988. 299–327.

Cézanne, Paul. *Paul Cézanne: Letters.* Trans. Seymour Hacker. Ed. John Rewald. New York: Hacker, 1984.

Chatman, Seymour. *Story and Discourse: Narrative Structure in Fiction and Film.* Ithaca, NY: Cornell UP, 1978.

Chekhov, Anton. *Anton Chekhov's Short Stories.* Ed. Ralph E. Matlaw. Norton Critical Edition. New York: W. W. Norton, 1979.

———. *Letters of Anton Chekhov.* Trans. Michael Henry Heim and Simon Karlinsky. New York: Harper & Row, 1973.

———. *Letters on the Short Story, the Drama, and Other Literary Topics by Anton Chekhov.* Ed. Louis S. Friedland. New York: Minton, Balch and Company, 1924.

Comley, Nancy R., and Robert Scholes. *Hemingway's Genders: Rereading the Hemingway Text.* New Haven, CT: Yale UP, 1994.

Cowley, Malcolm. "Hemingway's Wound—And Its Consequences for American Literature." *The Georgia Review* 38.2 (1984): 223–39.

———. "Introduction" to *The Portable Hemingway.* 1944. Rpt. as "Nightmare and Ritual in Hemingway" in Robert P. Weeks, ed., *Hemingway: A Collection of Critical Essays.* Englewood Cliffs, NJ: Prentice-Hall, 1962. 40–51.

Crane, Stephen. "The Blue Hotel." 1898. *Stephen Crane: Prose and Poetry.* Ed. J. C. Levenson. New York: Library of America, 1984. 799–828.

Cunliffe, W. Gordon, Martin Dolch, and John V. Hagopian. "A Canary for One." In John V. Hagopian and Martin Dolch, eds., *Insight I: Analysis of American Literature.* Frankfurt: Hirschgraben, 1962. 96–99.

DeFalco, Joseph. *The Hero in Hemingway's Short Stories.* Pittsburgh: U of Pittsburgh P, 1963.

Dolan, Marc. "The (Hi)story of Their Lives: Mythic Autobiography and the 'Lost Generation.'" *Journal of American Studies* 27 (1993): 35–56.

———. *Modern Lives: A Cultural Re-Reading of the "Lost Generation."* West Lafayette, IN: Purdue UP, 1996.

Donaldson, Scott. *By Force of Will: The Life and Art of Ernest Hemingway.* New York: Viking, 1977.

———. "Preparing for the End: Hemingway's Revisions of 'A Canary for One.'" *Studies in American Fiction* 6 (1978): 203–11.

Douglas, Ann. *Terrible Honesty: Mongrel Manhattan in the 1920s.* New York: Farrar, Straus, and Giroux, 1995.

Eliot, T. S. *The Complete Poems and Plays 1909–1950.* New York: Harcourt Brace, 1962.

Fass, Paula S. *The Damned and the Beautiful: American Youth in the 1920s.* New York: Oxford UP, 1977.

Faulkner, William. *Absalom, Absalom!* 1936. New York: Vintage International, 1990.

Fenton, Charles A. *The Apprenticeship of Ernest Hemingway: The Early Years.* New York: Viking, 1954.

Fitzgerald, F. Scott. "May Day." 1920. *The Short Stories of F. Scott Fitzgerald: A New Collection.* Ed. Matthew J. Bruccoli. New York: Scribner's, 1989. 97–141.

———. "One Hundred False Starts." 1933. *Afternoon of an Author: A Selection of Uncollected Stories and Essays.* Ed. Arthur Mizener. New York: Scribner's, 1957. 127–36.

Flaubert, Gustave. *The Letters of Gustave Flaubert, 1830–1857.* Ed. and trans. Francis Steegmuller. Cambridge, MA: Belknap/Harvard UP, 1980.

Flora, Joseph M. *Hemingway's Nick Adams.* Baton Rouge: Louisiana State UP, 1982.

Ford, Ford Madox. *Joseph Conrad: A Personal Remembrance.* Boston: Little, Brown, 1924.

Fry, Roger. *Cézanne: A Study of His Development.* New York: Macmillan, 1927.

Frye, Northrop. *Anatomy of Criticism: Four Essays.* 1957. New York: Atheneum, 1967.

Gajdusek, Robert E. "Harder on Himself than Most: A Study of Hemingway's Self-Evaluation and Self-Projection in His Work." 1993. *Hemingway in His Own Country.* Notre Dame, IN: Notre Dame UP, 2002. 357–67.

Gaillard, Theodore L., Jr. "Hemingway's Debt to Cézanne: New Perspectives." *Twentieth Century Literature* 45.1 (1999): 65–78.

Gardner, John. *The Art of Fiction: Notes on Craft for Young Writers.* New York: Alfred A. Knopf, 1984.

Gasquet, Joachim. *Cézanne.* Paris: Les Éditions Bernheim-Jeune, 1921.

Genette, Gérard. *Narrative Discourse: An Essay in Method.* Trans. Jane E. Lewin. Ithaca, NY: Cornell UP, 1980.

Goldberg, David J. *Discontented America: The United States in the 1920s.* Baltimore: Johns Hopkins UP, 1999.

Grebstein, Sheldon Norman. *Hemingway's Craft.* Carbondale: Southern Illinois UP, 1973.

Gurko, Leo. *Ernest Hemingway and the Pursuit of Heroism.* New York: Crowell, 1968.

Harrington, Gary. "Hemingway's 'God Rest You Merry, Gentlemen.'" *The Explicator* 52.1 (1993): 51–53.

Hasbany, Richard. "The Shock of Vision: An Imagist Reading of *In Our Time.*" In Wagner-Martin, ed., *Ernest Hemingway: Five Decades of Criticism.* 224–40.

Hawley, Ellis W. *The Great War and the Search for a Modern Order: A History of the American People and Their Institutions, 1917–1933.* New York: St. Martin's, 1979.

Hawthorne, Nathaniel. *The Scarlet Letter.* 1850. New York: Penguin Classics, 1986.

Hays, Peter L. "Hemingway and the Fisher King." *The University Review* 32.3 (1966): 225–28.

———. "'Soldier's Home' and Ford Madox Ford." *Hemingway Notes* 1 (1971): 21–22.

Helstern, Linda Lizut. "Indians, Woodcraft, and the Construction of White Masculinity: The Boyhood of Nick Adams." *The Hemingway Review* 20.1 (2000): 61–78.

Hemingway, Ernest. *By-Line: Ernest Hemingway: Selected Articles and Dispatches of Four Decades.* Ed. William White. New York: Scribner's, 1967.

———. *Death in the Afternoon.* New York: Scribner's, 1932.

———. *Ernest Hemingway: Selected Letters, 1917–1961.* Ed. Carlos Baker. New York: Scribner's, 1981.

———. *A Farewell to Arms.* 1929. New York: Scribner's, 1969.

———. *Green Hills of Africa.* 1935. New York: Scribner's, 1963.

———. Interview by George Plimpton. 1958. In George Plimpton, ed., *Writers at Work: The* Paris Review *Interviews.* Second series. New York: Penguin, 1963. 217–39.

———. *A Moveable Feast.* New York: Scribner's, 1964.

———. *The Nick Adams Stories.* Ed. Philip Young. New York: Scribner's, 1972.

———. *The Short Stories of Ernest Hemingway.* New York: Scribner's, 1954.

———. *The Sun Also Rises.* 1926. New York: Scribner's, 1954.

Hemingway, Mary Welsh. *How It Was.* New York: Alfred A. Knopf, 1976.

Hoffman, Frederick J. *The Twenties: American Writing in the Postwar Decade.* 1955. Rev. ed. New York: Free Press, 1965.

Holder, Alan. "The Other Hemingway." 1963. In Wagner-Martin, ed., *Ernest Hemingway: Five Decades of Criticism*. 103–109.

Hotchner, A. E. *Papa Hemingway: A Personal Memoir*. New York: Random House, 1966.

James, Henry. "The Middle Years." 1893. *Henry James: Complete Stories 1892–1898*. Eds. David Bromwich and John Hollander. New York: Library of America, 1996. 335–55.

Johnston, Kenneth G. "Hemingway and Cézanne: Doing the Country." *American Literature* 56.1 (1984): 28–37.

———. *The Tip of the Iceberg: Hemingway and the Short Story*. Greenwood, FL: Penkevill Publishing, 1987.

Joost, Nicholas. *Ernest Hemingway and the Little Magazines: The Paris Years*. Barre, MA: Barre Publishers, 1968.

Justice, Hilary K. "Courting Exposure: The Composition of Hemingway's 'A Canary for One.'" *Resources for American Literary Study* 27.1 (2001): 65–77.

Kennedy, David M. *Over Here: The First World War and American Society*. Oxford: Oxford UP, 1980.

Kennedy, J. Gerald. *Imagining Paris: Exile, Writing, and American Identity*. New Haven, CT: Yale UP, 1993.

———, and Kirk Curnutt. "Out of the Picture: Mrs. Krebs, Mother Stein, and 'Soldier's Home.'" *The Hemingway Review* 12.1 (1992): 1–11.

Kobler, J. F. "'Soldier's Home' Revisited: A Hemingway *Mea Culpa*." *Studies in Short Fiction* 30 (1993): 377–85.

Kruse, Horst H. "Allusions to *The Merchant of Venice* and the New Testament in 'God Rest You Merry, Gentlemen': Hemingway's Anti-Semitism Reconsidered." *The Hemingway Review* 25.2 (2006): 61–75.

Kyvig, David E. *Daily Life in the United States, 1920–1940: How Americans Lived through the Roaring Twenties and the Great Depression*. Chicago: Ivan R. Dee, 2004.

Lamb, Robert Paul. "'America Can Break Your Heart': On the Significance of Mark Twain." In Robert Paul Lamb and G. R. Thompson, eds. *A Companion to American Fiction, 1865–1914*. Oxford, UK: Blackwell Publishing, 2005. 468–98.

———. *Art Matters: Hemingway, Craft, and the Creation of the Modern Short Story*. Baton Rouge: Louisiana State UP, 2010.

———. Exchange of Letters with John Leonard. *The Hemingway Review* 15.2 (1996): 131–37.

———. "Eternity's Artifice: Time and Transcendence in the Works of Ernest Hemingway." *The Hemingway Review* 4.2 (1985): 42–52.

———. "Fishing for Stories: What 'Big Two-Hearted River' Is Really About." *Modern Fiction Studies* 37.2 (1991): 161–82.

———. "Hemingway's Critique of Anti-Semitism: Semiotic Confusion in 'God Rest You Merry, Gentlemen.'" *Studies in Short Fiction* 33 (1996): 25–34.

———. "The Love Song of Harold Krebs: Form, Argument, and Meaning in Hemingway's 'Soldier's Home.'" *The Hemingway Review* 14.2 (1995): 18–36.

———. "Making Mats or, The Literary Critics (A)board the *Pequod:* Melvillian Thoughts on Reading and Interpretation." *The Centennial Review* 41.1 (1997): 17–61.

Larguier, Léo. *Le Dimanche avec Paul Cézanne (Souvenirs).* Paris: L'Édition, 1925.

Leuchtenburg, William E. *The Perils of Prosperity, 1914–1932.* 1958. Second ed. Chicago: U of Chicago P, 1993.

Levitzke, Shannon Whitlock. "'In Those Days the Distances Were Very Different': Alienation in Ernest Hemingway's 'God Rest You Merry, Gentlemen.'" *The Hemingway Review* 30.1 (2010): 18–30.

Loran, Erle. *Cézanne's Composition: Analysis of His Form with Diagrams and Photographs of His Motifs.* Berkeley: U of California P, 1947.

Love, Glen A. *Practical Ecocriticism: Literature, Biology, and the Environment.* Charlottesville: U of Virginia P, 2003.

Lynn, Kenneth S. *Hemingway.* New York: Simon and Schuster, 1987.

———. "Hemingway's Private War." *Commentary* 72.1 (July 1981): 24–33.

Machotka, Pavel. *Cézanne: Landscape into Art.* New Haven, CT: Yale UP, 1996.

Martin, W. R., and Warren U. Ober. "Hemingway and James: 'A Canary for One' and 'Daisy Miller.'" *Studies in Short Fiction* 22.4 (1985): 469–71.

Melling, Philip. "'There Were Many Indians in the Story': Hidden History in Hemingway's 'Big Two-Hearted River.'" *The Hemingway Review* 28.2 (2009): 45–65.

Mellow, James R. *Charmed Circle: Gertrude Stein & Company.* Boston: Houghton Mifflin, 1974.

———. *Hemingway: A Life Without Consequences.* Boston: Houghton Mifflin, 1992.

Melville, Herman. *The Confidence-Man: His Masquerade.* 1857. *Herman Melville: Pierre; Israel Potter; The Piazza Tales; The Confidence-Man; Uncollected Prose; Billy Budd, Sailor.* Ed. Harrison Hayford. New York: Library of America, 1984. 835–1112.

Moddelmog, Debra A. "The Unifying Consciousness of a Divided Conscience: Nick Adams as Author of *In Our Time. American Literature* 60.4 (1988): 591–610.

Monteiro, George. "Hemingway's Christmas Carol." *Fitzgerald/Hemingway Annual* (1972): 207–13.

Moss, Rick. "Hemingway and the Thing Left In 'God Rest You Merry, Gentlemen.'" *The Hemingway Review* 9.2 (1990): 169–73.

Nabokov, Vladimir. *Lectures on Literature.* Ed. Fredson Bowers. New York: Harcourt Brace Jovanovich, 1980.

O'Brien, Sarah Mary. "'I, Also, Am in Michigan': Pastoralism of Mind in Hemingway's 'Big Two-Hearted River.'" *The Hemingway Review* 28.2 (2009): 66–86.

O'Connor, Flannery. *Mystery and Manners: Occasional Prose.* Eds. Sally Fitzgerald and Robert Fitzgerald. New York: Farrar, Straus & Giroux, 1969.

———. "On Her Own Work." 1963. *Mystery and Manners.* 107–18.

———. "The Nature and Aim of Fiction." *Mystery and Manners.* 63–86.

———. "The Teaching of Literature." 1963. *Mystery and Manners.* 121–34.

———. "Writing Short Stories." *Mystery and Manners.* 87–106.

O'Connor, Frank. Interview by Anthony Whittier. 1958. In Malcolm Cowley, ed., *Writers at Work: The* Paris Review *Interviews.* First series. New York: Penguin, 1977. 161–82.

———. *The Lonely Voice: A Study of the Short Story.* 1963. New York: Harper and Row, 1985.

O'Faolain, Sean. *The Short Story.* 1951. Old Greenwich, CT: Devin-Adair, 1974.

———. *The Vanishing Hero: Studies in Novelists of the Twenties.* London: Eyre & Spottiswoode, 1956.

Oldsey, Bernard. "Hemingway's Beginnings and Endings." *College Literature* 7.3 (1980): 213–38.

Perrett, Geoffrey. *America in the Twenties: A History.* New York: Simon and Schuster, 1982.

Petrarca, Anthony J. "Irony of Situation in Ernest Hemingway's 'Soldier's Home.'" *English Journal* 58 (1969): 664–67.

Phillips, Larry W., ed. *Ernest Hemingway on Writing.* New York: Scribner's, 1984.

Rayfield, Donald. *Anton Chekhov: A Life.* New York: Henry Holt, 1998.

Reynolds, Michael. *Hemingway: The Final Years.* New York and London: W. W. Norton, 1999.

———. *Hemingway: The Paris Years.* Oxford: Basil Blackwell, 1989.

———. *Hemingway's First War: The Making of* A Farewell to Arms. Princeton, NJ: Princeton UP, 1976.

———, ed. *Hemingway's Reading, 1910–1940: An Inventory.* Princeton, NJ: Princeton UP, 1981.

Roberts, John J. "In Defense of Krebs." *Studies in Short Fiction* 13 (1976): 515–18.

Ross, Lillian. "How Do You Like It Now, Gentlemen?" 1950. In Robert P. Weeks, ed., *Hemingway: A Collection of Critical Essays.* Englewood Cliffs, NJ: Prentice-Hall, 1962. 17–39.

Ryan, Ken. "The Contentious Emendation of Hemingway's 'A Clean, Well-Lighted Place.'" *The Hemingway Review* 18.1 (1998): 78–91.

Sanford, Marcelline Hemingway. *At the Hemingways: A Family Portrait.* Boston: Little, Brown, 1962.

Schaffer, Ronald. *America in the Great War: The Rise of the War Welfare State.* New York: Oxford UP, 1991.

Severo, Richard, and Lewis Milford. *The Wages of War: When America's Soldiers Came Home—From Valley Forge to Vietnam.* New York: Simon and Schuster, 1989.

Shakespeare, William. *The Comical History of the Merchant of Venice, or Otherwise Called the Jew of Venice.* 1600. *The Norton Shakespeare Based on the Oxford Edition.* Eds. Stephen Greenblatt et al. New York and London: W. W. Norton, 1997. 1090–1145.

Shiff, Richard. *Cézanne and the End of Impressionism.* Chicago: U of Chicago P, 1984.

Smith, Julian. "'A Canary for One': Hemingway in the Wasteland." *Studies in Short Fiction* 5.4 (1968): 355–61.

———. "Hemingway and the Thing Left Out." *Journal of Modern Literature* 1.2 (1970–71): 169–82.

Smith, Paul. "Hemingway's Early Manuscripts: The Theory and Practice of Omission." *Journal of Modern Literature* 10.2 (1983): 268–88.

———. "1924: Hemingway's Luggage and the Miraculous Year." In Scott Donaldson, ed. *The Cambridge Companion to Ernest Hemingway.* Cambridge: Cambridge UP, 1996. 36–54.

———. *A Reader's Guide to the Short Stories of Ernest Hemingway.* Boston: G. K. Hall, 1989.

Stein, Gertrude. *The Autobiography of Alice B. Toklas.* 1933. *Selected Writings of Gertrude Stein.* Ed. Carl Van Vechten. New York: Vintage, 1972. 1–237.

Stevens, Wallace. *Letters of Wallace Stevens.* Ed. Holly Stevens. New York: Alfred A. Knopf, 1966.

Strychacz, Thomas. *Hemingway's Theaters of Masculinity.* Baton Rouge: Louisiana State UP, 2003.

Summerhayes, Don. "Fish Story: Ways of Telling in 'Big Two-Hearted River.'" *The Hemingway Review* 15.1 (1995): 10–26.

Svoboda, Frederic J. "Landscapes Real and Imagined: 'Big Two-Hearted River.'" *The Hemingway Review* 16.1 (1996): 33–42.

Tillich, Paul. *The Courage to Be.* 1952. New Haven, CT: Yale UP, 1971.

———. *Systematic Theology.* Vol. 1. Chicago: U of Chicago P, 1951.

Trout, Steven. "'Where Do We Go from Here?': Ernest Hemingway's 'Soldier's Home' and American Veterans of World War I." *The Hemingway Review* 20.1 (2000): 5–21.

Vollard, Ambroise. *Paul Cézanne: His Life and Art.* Trans. Harold Livingston Van Doren. New York: N. L. Brown, 1923.

Wagner-Martin, Linda, ed. *Ernest Hemingway: Five Decades of Criticism.* East Lansing: Michigan State UP, 1974.

Waldhorn, Arthur. *A Reader's Guide to Ernest Hemingway.* New York: Farrar, Straus & Giroux, 1972.

Warren, Robert Penn. "Ernest Hemingway." 1951. In Wagner-Martin, ed., *Ernest Hemingway: Five Decades of Criticism.* 75–102.

Watt, Ian. *Conrad in the Nineteenth Century.* Berkeley: U of California P, 1979.

Watts, Emily Stipes. *Ernest Hemingway and the Arts.* Urbana: U of Illinois P, 1971.

Welty, Eudora. "Looking at Short Stories." 1949. *The Eye of the Story: Selected Essays and Reviews.* New York: Vintage, 1979. 85–106.

———. "Writing and Analyzing a Story." 1955. *The Eye of the Story: Selected Essays and Reviews.* New York: Vintage, 1979. 107–15.

Wharton, Edith. *The Writing of Fiction.* 1925. New York: Octagon Books, 1966.

Williams, Raymond. *The English Novel from Dickens to Lawrence.* 1970. London: Hogarth, 1984.

Williams, Wirt. *The Tragic Art of Ernest Hemingway.* Baton Rouge: Louisiana State UP, 1981.

Wilson, Edmund. "Hemingway: Gauge of Morale." *The Wound and the Bow.* 1947. *The Triple Thinkers & The Wound and the Bow.* Boston: Northeastern UP, 1984. 174–97.

Young, Philip. "Big World Out There: The Nick Adams Stories." 1972. In Jackson J. Benson, ed. *The Short Stories of Ernest Hemingway: Critical Essays.* Durham, NC: Duke UP, 1975. 29–45.

———. *Ernest Hemingway: A Reconsideration.* 1952. Rev. ed. University Park: Pennsylvania State UP, 1966.

Index

Advance mention, 81–83; *defined:* by Barthes, 81, by Genette, 82
Advance notice, 82; *defined* by Genette, 82, 202n84
Algabeño, José García, 175
Allen, Frederick Lewis, 204n26
Allen, Walter, 201n74
American Expeditionary Force (A.E.F.), 96, 203n13; Marine Brigade of the Second Division, 94, 96, 203n14
Anderson, Sherwood, 3, 153
Antisemitism and Jewish stereotypes, 156, 157, 159–65, 166
Armistice of 1918, 96, 107, 203n13

Babel, Isaac, xi
Badt, Kurt, 212n30
Baker, Carlos, 11, 197n5, 197n6, 198n7, 198n15, 201n74, 202n4, 205n1
Baker, Sheridan, 90, 179
Bakhtin, Mikhail M., xiii, 106
Banks, Russell, xi
Barthes, Roland: cultural code, 38–39, 199n47; death of the author, xiii–xiv, 170; foreshadowing, 81; hermeneutic code, 33, 36–37, 133; proairetic code, 33–34; reality effect, 200n57. *See also* Cultural code; Hermeneutic code; Proairetic code
Beach, Sylvia, 212n29
Beattie, Ann, xi
Beauvoir, Simone de, xi
Beegel, Susan F., 201n70, 204n19
Belleau Wood, Battle of, 99, 204n18
Bellow, Saul, xi
Bennett, Eric, 197n3
Berenson, Bernard, 112, 201n59
Berkhofer, Robert, Jr., 199n49
Berman, Ron, 186, 212n30, 212n38
Bird, Bill, 173
Birth of a Nation, The, 200n52
Black Sox Scandal of 1919, 107
Böll, Heinrich, xi
Borges, Jorge Luis, 172
Bowen, Elizabeth: on dialogue, 22, 146
Breit, Harvey, 153, 202n76, 212n28
Brøgger, Fredrik Chr., 171, 210n11
Broom (magazine), 164
Burroughs, William, xi
Butler, Robert Olen, xi
Byron, George Gordon (Lord Byron), 144

Caesarean sections in the U.S., 58
Calloway, Katherine, 208n9
Camastra, Nicole J., 154–55
Camus, Albert, xi
Carson, Johnny, 211n26
Carter, Steven, 129
Carver, Raymond, xi; on relationship between life and fiction, 8
Cather, Willa, xv, 111
Cela, Camilo José, xi
Cézanne, Paul, 123, 211n25; artistic techniques analyzed, 183–87, 212n30; central or culminating point, 184–85; H on, 183, 185, 213n43; influence on H, xi, 183, 186–88, 190, 212n30, 212n38; on his own painting, 167, 209n (epigraph), 213n44; *routes tournantes,* 86, 212n38; temperamental similarities to H, 183, 212n29
Chandler, Raymond, xi
Chatman, Seymour, 33
Chekhov, Alexander P., 16, 198n27, 199n45
Chekhov, Anton, xi, 14, 118; "Chekhov's gun," 51, 200n55; on depicting consciousness, 16; on effacing the author, 14, 16; on indirection, 38; on limiting details, 16, 33; on omission, 12, 14; on treatment of theme, 13

Cheyenne Autumn (film), 200n52
Closerie des Lilas (Parisian café), 7, 9
Comley, Nancy R., 201n74
Conrad, Joseph, 142, 206n14
Conradian split: *defined,* 156, 209n13
Cowley, Malcolm, 168, 169, 201n74, 209n5
Crane, Stephen, xi; "The Blue Hotel," 207n23; impressionism of, 126, 206n14; influence on H, 62, 126, 206n14; *Maggie,* 204–5n27; "The Open Boat," 117–18; *The Red Badge of Courage,* 106
Cultural code: *defined,* 38–39, 199n47, 200n52; in "God Rest You Merry, Gentlemen," 163; in "Indian Camp," 38–42, 53–54, 58, 61, 77; in "Soldier's Home," 92, 108
cummings, e. e., 188
Curnutt, Kirk, 91

Daily Star (Toronto newspaper), 5–6
Davis, Rebecca Harding, 129
Debs, Eugene V., 107
DeFalco, Joseph, 90, 201n74
Delayed decoding: *defined,* 62–63, 126, 206n14
Dialogical text: *defined,* 106, 204n27; *Adventures of Huckleberry Finn,* 106–7; *The Red Badge of Courage,* 106; *The Scarlet Letter,* 106; "Soldier's Home," 105–11, 205n33
Dialogue: H's technique of, 142, 198n30, 207n27. *See under individual H stories*
Díaz, Junot, xi
Dickinson, Emily, 68
Didion, Joan, xi
Disjunctive bump: *defined,* 148, 207n34
Dolan, Marc, 108, 204n26, 205n30
Donaldson, Scott, 90, 112–13, 137, 201n74, 205–6n2, 206n15
Dos Passos, John, xi, 111, 168, 210n18
Douglas, Ann, 204n26
Dreiser, Theodore, 111, 205n27; influence on H, 62; *Sister Carrie,* 204–5n27

Echo scenes: *defined* by Reynolds, 81; in "Indian Camp," 30, 83
Ellipses, 35; functions of, 68. *See under individual H stories*
Ellison, Ralph, xi
Eliot, T. S., xi, 176, 201n68; "The Hollow Men," 104, 111; "The Love Song of J. Alfred Prufrock," 111
External focalization, 63, 97, 100, 102, 187; *defined,* 29, 53, 125, 201n68; H's innovative use in first-person narration, 125, 206n13; and stream-of-consciousness, 128

Fabula time, 34–35, 63, 131, 199n37. *See also* Narrative time
Fass, Paula S., 109, 204n26, 205n33
Faulkner, William, xi, 199n47; *Absalom, Absalom!,* xv, 79, 202n77
Fitzgerald, F. Scott, xi, 1, 111, 182; "May Day," 203–4n16; on writers, 117
Flappers, 108–9
Flaubert, Gustav, 182; on effacing the author, 16
Float-off ending, 75, 104–5, 149; *defined,* 201n69, 204n24
Flora, Joseph M., 39, 71, 197n2, 201n74
Flory, Wendy Stallard, 204n21
Focalization, xi, 80, 165, 209n14; *defined,* 29, 199n32, 201n68, 206n13. *See under individual H stories. See also* External focalization
Ford, Ford Madox, 6, 7, 10–11, 142, 204n20
Ford, John, 200n52
Free indirect discourse, 97, 98, 99, 100, 102, 103, 104–5, 109–10, 179; *defined,* 97, 203n15
Friend, Krebs, 91, 202n4
Fry, Roger, 186, 212n30
Frye, Northrop: on function of criticism, xvii

Gaillard, Theodore L., Jr., 184, 212n30
Gajdusek, Robert E., 165
García Márquez, Gabriel, xi
Gardner, John: the "fictional dream," 19; use of auxiliaries in fiction, 15
Genette, Gérard, 199n37; *defines* advance mention, 82–83; *defines* advance notice, 82, 202n84
Gilchrist, Ellen, xi
Glasgow, Ellen, 111

Gogol, Nikolai, 95
Goldberg, David J., 204n26
Gordimer, Nadine, xi
Gorky, Maxim, 16, 199n33
Grebstein, Sheldon Norman, 142, 184, 212n30
Greco-Turkish War, 107
Greene, Graham, xi
Griffith, D. W., 200n52
Gurko, Leo, 90, 201n74
Gurliand, Ilia, 200n55

Harrington, Gary, 207n1, 208n9
Hasbany, Richard, 90
Hawley, Ellis W., 204n26
Hawthorne, Nathaniel, 95; *The Scarlet Letter,* 106, 156
Hays, Peter L., 153–54, 204n20, 207–8n1
Helstern, Linda Lizut, 10, 58, 201n74
Hemingway, Dr. Clarence (H's father and model for Dr. Adams in "Indian Camp"), 7, 9–10, 50, 72, 84–85, 91
Hemingway, Ernest
—anxiety and suicide, 10, 12–13, 64, 85
—and Cézanne. *See under* Cézanne, Paul
—childhood-wound thesis, 184; and "Big Two-Hearted River" 169–70, 174, 177–78, 191; *defined,* 169; and "Soldier's Home," 90–92, 93, 100–102, 105. *See also* H: war-wound thesis
—and creative writing curricula, xiv, 197n3
—critiques antisemitism and Jewish stereotypes, 156, 157, 159–65, 166
—impressionism in, xv, 30–31, 42, 53, 62–63, 74–75, 83, 119, 121–22, 125, 126, 129, 132–33, 183–84, 187, 201n68, 206n14.
—influence on other authors, xi
—on literary critics and criticism, 89, 120, 151, 153, 155, 171, 210n12
—and masculinity, 10, 11; Strychacz on, 59–60, 200n51, 201n60. *See also* Masculinity
—mistreatment of H at *Daily Star,* 5–6,
—novels and books:
By-Line: Ernest Hemingway: Selected Articles and Dispatches of Four Decades, 84
Death in the Afternoon, 14, 26, 62, 76, 81, 176, 182, 184, 211n20, 212n30
Farewell to Arms, A, 6–7, 81, 90, 205n28
Green Hills of Africa, 176, 182
in our time (1924), 3, 5, 7, 72, 168, 173, 175, 197n5, 198n22, 206n13
In Our Time (1925), 3, 83, 111, 167, 168, 174, 190, 206n13, 211n24, 213n43
Moveable Feast, A, 3, 119, 132, 185, 187, 192, 209n5, 211n24
Nick Adams Stories, The, 8, 11, 83, 171, 197n3, 209–10n9
Sun Also Rises, The, 111, 146, 153–54, 164, 173, 202n4, 205n28, 205n1, 208n9
Three Stories & Ten Poems, 5, 7
Winner Take Nothing, 208n10
—pre-Christmas 1923 visit home, 7, 9
—on rejections of his early stories, 8
—repetition compulsion, 90, 168–69
—short stories:
"After the Storm," 206n13
"Alpine Idyll, An," 212n38
"Battler, The," 212n38
"Big Two-Hearted River," xvii, 8, 16, 89–90, 111, 167–92, 197n1, 205n28, 209n1, 209n5, 209n6, 210n11, 210n17, 211n24, 211n25, 211n26, 212n30, 212n38, 213n48; biographical background of, 168, 178–79, 209n1; Brøgger's interpretation of, 171, 210n11; bullfighting as metaphor for writing in, 176; Cézanne's influence on H in, 183–88; common ground of Young's and Lynn's interpretations, 169–70, 171; complex objective correlative (impressionism) analyzed, 185–87; fishing as metaphor for writing in, 174–75, 181–82, 182–83, 185–87, 188–92, 213n48; H on Cézanne in, 183, 185, 187, 188, 213n43; homoerotic bonding in, 174; impressionism in, 183–84, 185–87; J. Gerald Kennedy's interpretation of, 177–78; Lynn's childhood-wound interpretation of, 169, 174, 177, 191, 209n5; memory and writing, 174–75, 175–76, 177, 178, 179; as metafiction, 167, 175, 176, 177, 178, 179, 188–89, 190–92, 213n48; plot summarized, 170–71; questions raised by text, 170–71; rabbit as metaphor for writer in, 189; *route*

Hemingway, Earnest (*continued*)
tournante in, 185–87; Seney, Michigan in, 170, 178–79, 181; the swamp, 170, 171, 172, 172–73, 188, 191–92; Young's war-wound interpretation of, 168–69, 171, 174, 177, 191, 210n12. *See also* H: short stories: "On Writing"
"Canary for One, A," xvi, 47, 112–50, 205n1, 205–6n2, 206n12, 206n13, 206n14, 206n15, 207n25; American lady's function in, 121, 123–24, 126–27, 128, 133, 134–35 (her function summarized), and *passim;* biographical contexts of, 112, 205n1; biographical interpretations dominate criticism of, 112, 205–6n2, 207n25; canary as symbol, 129, 137, 144; dialogue analyzed, 134–37, 141–46; ellipses in, 123, 125, 127; external focalization with first-person narration in, 125, 128, 206n13; focalization in, 116, 126, 131–33, and *passim;* hermeneutic code in, 126, 133; hypothetical questions posed, 114–15; impressionism in, 119, 121–22, 125, 126–27, 128, 129, 131–33, 139–40, 204n14; indirection in, 128, 133, 142; initial list of observations about, 115–17; intertextuality with Henry James's "Daisy Miller," 144; irrelevance of theme in, 117–18; omission in, 127, 128, 132; plot summarized, 112–14; purpose of the disguised first-person narrator, 131–33; purpose of the lack of exposition in, 115, 119; purpose of the story, 118–19, 149; purpose of the summarized clothing passage in, 138–39; recapitulation with variation in, 127, 145; repetition in, 117, 124–25, 127, 141–42, 144–45; seating arrangement in compartment reconstructed and analyzed, 121–22, 142, 206n12; surprise ending defended, 114, 148–49; train as symbol of marriage in, 119–20; train wreck as multilayered symbol in, 146–47; train's function as a technical device in, 120–21, 123, 124, 125, 127, 128, 129–30, 130–31, 147; significance of Vevey's *Trois Couronnes* hotel in, 144; unities in, 121, 124–25, 130–31
"Cat in the Rain," 135, 164, 174, 197n1
"Che Ti Dice la Patria," 212n38
"Clean, Well-Lighted Place, A," 13, 47–48, 200n54
"Cross-Country Snow," 174, 197n1
"Day's Wait, A," 83
"Doctor and the Doctor's Wife, The," 90–91, 174, 197n1
"End of Something, The," 173, 174, 197n1
"Fathers and Sons," xvi, 84–85, 164, 212n38
"God Rest You Merry, Gentlemen," xvi–xvii, 153–66, 207n1, 208n4, 208n8, 208n9, 208n10; antisemitism and Jewish stereotypes critiqued in, 156, 157, 159–65, 166; biblical passages influencing the boy's self-mutilation, 158; boy's amputated penis as symbol of Doc Fischer, 160; censored, 208n10; Christmas carol allusion in, 164; critical interpretations of, 153–55, 208n9; dialogue analyzed, 161–64; Doc Fischer's "otherness," 159–60, 161–64; French racing car in, 156, 208n8; functions of the first-person narrator in, 165–66; as metacriticism, 153, 155, 166; mutilated boy as text in, 157–59; narrator not necessarily a reporter in, 155, 208n4; narrator's name ("Horace") in, 157, 208n9; omission of abortions in, 159–60; present absence in, 156; semiotic confusion in, 155 (*defined*), 155–66 *passim;* Shakespearean intertext in, 157, 208n9; story as H's self-accusatory apology to Harold Loeb, 164–65
"Hills Like White Elephants," 92, 135, 159, 203n7
"In Another Country," 112, 166, 205n1, 212n38
"Indian Camp," xvi, 3–85, 112, 119, 127, 133, 134, 172, 179, 180, 197n1, 200n51, 201n74, 212n38; advance mentions (foreshadowing) in, 50–51, 73, 81–82, 82–83; advance notices in, 82; authorial intrusions in/focalization errors,

40, 43, 58, 59, 65; biographical background of, 3, 5–8; biographical contexts within the story, 8–10, 50, 65, 72; Caesarean paragraph analyzed, 52–55; complex unity of, 80–83; cultural codes in, 38–42, 53–54, 58, 61, 77; dialogue analyzed, 31–32, 45–52, 54, 55–56, 57, 59, 60–62, 65, 67, 69–73; echo scene in, 30, 81, 83; ellipses in, 34–36, 52, 54, 67–68; external focalization in, 29, 53, 63; final version analyzed, 26–83; finessing challenges in focalization, 35, 40, 42–45, 57, 63, 65–66; float-off ending, 75; hermeneutic code in, 37–38, 40, 43, 44, 46, 49, 50, 57, 60, 66–67, 77, 81; illustrative stamp of, 83; Indian father's suicide discovery paragraph analyzed, 62–66; indirection in, 38, 66–67, 76, 77; objective correlatives in, 55–56, 73–75; omission in, 34, 47, 52–53, 55, 61, 67–68, 73–74, 76; ontological shock in, 9, 12–14, 19–21, 27, 67, 76–77, 80–81; part four (the denouement), 67–79, 201n74; part one (from the opening through the arrival at the camp), 27–39; part three (from the aftermath of the operation through the discovery of the suicide), 56–67; part two (from entering the shanty through the operation), 39–56; plot summarized, 3–4; recapitulation with variation in, 73, 74–75; repetition in, 46, 56, 66, 70, 74–75; retrospective notices in, 82; sequence displacement in, 66; third-person fixed internal focalization in, 26–27, 28–29, 35, 40, 41, 42–45, 50, 52–55, 56–57, 63, 65–66, 77, 80; ultimate mystery in, 77–79, 201–2n74; use of light imagery in, 30, 38, 69, 80–81. *See also* Indians and Indian cultures; H: short stories: "Three Shots"

"Killers, The," 50, 112, 200n57, 205n1

"Mr. and Mrs. Elliot," 92, 174, 197n1

"My Old Man," 3, 179

"Now I Lay Me," 89–90, 128

"On Writing": analyzed, 171, 172–82, 183, 187–90; conflation of Nick and H in, 173, 179–80, 210n17, 210n18, 211n24, 211n25, 212n30; discarded as end of "Big Two-Hearted River," 168, 172

"Out of Season," 3, 5, 135, 174, 210n17

"Revolutionist, The," 198n22

"Short Happy Life of Francis Macomber, The," 135, 198n22

"Snows of Kilimanjaro, The," 190–91, 212n38

"Soldier's Home," xvi, 89–111, 112, 119, 134, 155, 187, 197n1, 202n4, 203n5, 203n10, 203n11, 203n15, 205n28; battles Krebs fought in, 99; bifurcation of summary and scene in, 91–93; breakfast scene analyzed, 100–102, 110, 204n19, 204n20, 204n21; childhood-wound interpretation of, 90–91, 92, 100–102, 203n4; cultural significance of, 105–11, 205n33; as dialogical text, 105–11, 205n33; derivation of the name "Harold Krebs," 91, 202n4; exposition analyzed, 94–100, 107–8, 203n11; float-off ending in, 104–5; free indirect discourse in, 97, 98–99, 100, 102, 103, 104, 105, 109–10, 203n15; hometown girls analyzed, 100, 103–4, 108–9; illustrative stamp of, 105; main link between summary and scene, 103, 104; Marine Brigade, 95–96, 203n14; 1919 date of the fabula, 96–99, 107, 109–10, 203n13; objective correlative (hardening bacon fat) in, 101, 102, 204n20; omission in, 103; other interpretations of, 91; repetition in, 103; story title's deliberate ambiguity, 93–94; symbolic historical representation of early to mid-1920s, 105–11, 205n33; war-wound/alienated veteran interpretations of, 89–90, 91–92, 94–96, 203n4, 203n5

"Ten Indians," 212n38

"Three Shots": savagely critiqued, 11–12, 13–14, 14–26, 26–27, 28–29, 72, 172; awful dialogue in, 22–23; good dialogue in, 23–25; reason why deleted from "Indian Camp," 10–11, 13–14

"Three-Day Blow, The," 173, 174, 197n1, 212n38

Hemingway, Earnest *(continued)*
"Up in Michigan," 3, 7, 11, 212n30
"Way You'll Never Be, A," 128, 212n38
"Wine of Wyoming, The," 212n38
—techniques. *See under* the following individual entries and *under* individual stories by H: Advance mentions, Advance notices, Delayed decoding, Dialogical text, Dialogue, Disjunctive bump, Echo scenes, Ellipses, External focalization, Fabula time, Float-off ending, Focalization, Free indirect discourse, Identification tags in dialogue, Illustrative stamp, Implication Omission, Impressionism, Indirection, Narrative time, Objective correlative, Omission, Recapitulation with variation, Repetition, Retrospective notice, *Route tournante,* Sequence displacement, Symbolic historical representation, Symbols, Verb tenses
—war-wound thesis, 209n5; and "Big Two-Hearted River," 168–70, 174, 177–78, 191, 209n6; *defined,* 168–69; and "Soldier's Home," 89–90, 91, 93–94, 97, 100, 102, 105, 202n4. *See also* H: childhood-wound thesis
—wounded at Fossalta di Piave, 90, 168–69, 191
—on writing and his art, 167–192, *passim;* "the actual things . . . that produced the emotion," 184; "all stories . . . end in death," 81; "any part you make will represent the whole," 26; "art endures forever," 176; "do it from inside yourself," 183; "feel something more than they under[stand]," 132, 185; "more fun than anything," 180; "the more you read, the more there will be," 3; the mystery in all great writing, 79, 182; "no other thing mattered," 192; on omission, 53; "one page of masterpiece to ninety one pages of shit," 1; "a perpetual challenge . . . and it makes me happy," 167; "poetry written into prose," book epigraph (vii); "prose is architecture," 184; "a prose that has never been written," 182; "real beyond any reality," 132; "the roughest trade of all," 112; "sequence of motion and fact which made the emotion," 62; similes as "defective ammunition," 59; "the stories are written so tight," 1, 81–82; technique is "most visible in its imperfection," 14; "there is always change and always movement," 5; "three cushion shots," 75; "to actually make it alive," 119; on tricks, 181–82; "truer than anything true," 151; value of "an unhappy childhood," 84
Hemingway, George (H's uncle), 7, 10, 23, 42
Hemingway, Grace Hall (H's mother), 7, 12, 72, 90–91, 92
Hemingway, Hadley Richardson (H's 1st wife), 5–7, 9, 112, 120, 130, 149, 173–74, 180, 205n1, 205n2, 207n25, 210n17
Hemingway, John Hadley Nicanor "Bumby" (H's 1st child), 5, 7, 9
Hemingway, Mariel (H's granddaughter), 211n26
Hemingway, Mary Welsh (H's 4th wife), book epigraph (vii), 197n4
Hemingway, Pauline Pfeiffer (H's 2nd wife), 112, 205–6n2, 207n25
Henry, O. (William Sydney Porter), 114
Hermeneutic code, 33, 92, 97; *defined,* 36–37; in "A Canary for One," 126, 133; in "Indian Camp," 37–38, 40, 43, 44, 46, 49, 50, 57, 60, 66–67, 77, 81. *See also* Proairetic code.
Hindmarsh, Harry, 5–6
Hoffman, Frederick J., 90, 91–92, 204n26
Holder, Alan, 201n74
Horace (Quintus Horatius Flaccus), 157, 208n9

Identification tags in dialogue, 32, 47, 49, 50, 56, 143; general analysis of functions, 47–48
Illustrative stamp, xi, 83, 105; *defined,* 83, 202n86
Immigration Restriction Acts, 108, 164–65
Implication omission, 68; *defined,* 34, 199n36
Impressionism, xi–xii, xv; *defined,* 62–63, 125, 126–27, 128, 129, 132–33, 184, 201n68, 206n14. *See also* H: impressionism in

Indian camp (type of camping), 10, 170
Indians and Indian cultures, 10, 39, 40–42, 43–44, 54, 58, 62, 64, 209n6; white cultural code stereotypes of, 39, 40–42, 54, 58, 61, 69, 75, 77, 199n49, 200n52
Indirection, 38, 66–67, 76, 77, 128, 133, 184; in dialogue, 69–73, 142

James, Henry, xi, xvii, 98, 119, 165–66, 209n14; "Daisy Miller," 144; "The Middle Years," 190, 213n46
Jazz Age, 110–11
Johnston, Kenneth G., 201n74, 212n30
Joost, Nicholas, 201n74
Joyce, James, xi, xiv, 11, 176, 179, 182, 188, 204n20, 213n43; on H, book epigraph (vii)
Justice, Hillary K., 112, 205–6n2

Kafka, Franz, 148
Kennedy, David M., 204n26
Kennedy, J. Gerald, 91, 177–78, 211n22
Kerouac, Jack, xi
Kobler, J. F., 91, 203n5
Kruse, Horst H., 154, 208n4
Ku Klux Klan, 108
Kyvig, David E., 204n26

Lamb, Robert Paul, 200n52, 201n74, 211n26; *Art Matters,* xi–xvii, 92, 132, 198n30, 199n32, 199n36, 201n61, 201n63, 201n66, 201n68, 201n69, 202n86, 203n7, 203n15, 204n22, 204n24, 206n13, 206n14, 207n21, 207n27, 207n34, 208n6, 209n13, 209n14
Laxness, Halldór, xi
Le Clézio, Jean-Marie Gustav, xi
League of Nations, 107
Leonard, Elmore, xi
Leuchtenburg, William E., 204n26
Levitzke, Shannon Whitlock, 154
Lewis, Sinclair, 111
Liveright, Horace, 1, 202n82, 207n36
Lloyd George, David, 5
Loeb, Harold, 164–65, 202n4
London, Jack: influence on H, 62
Loran, Earl, 184
Lost Generation, 90, 108
Love, Glen A., 191
Lynn, Kenneth S., 11, 90–91, 92, 169–70, 171, 198n9, 198n10, 202n4, 205n1, 209n5

Machotka, Pavel, 212n30
Maera (Manuel García López), 175, 176, 211n19
Mailer, Norman, xi
Malamud, Bernard, xi
Marine Brigade (Second Division). *See under* American Expeditionary Force
Martin, W. R., 144
Marx, Leo, 209n6
Masculinity, 10, 11, 41, 54, 59–60, 61, 77; Strychacz on, 59–60, 200n51, 201n60
Maupassant, Guy de, xi, 14, 114
McAlmon, Robert, 168, 179, 210n13, 210n15
McCarthy, Cormac, xi
Melling, Philip, 209n6
Mellow, James R., 90, 190–91, 202n3, 202n4, 205n28, 209n1, 212n29
Melville, Herman: "Bartleby, the Scrivener," 117; on fiction and religion, 79; *Moby-Dick,* 204–5n27
Milford, Lewis, 203n8
Moddelmog, Debra A., 211n24
Modernist fiction, 121; relationship between form and cultural critique, xiv–xv
Monteiro, George, 154–55, 207–8n1
Moreseschi, Alessandro, 154
Moss, Rick, 154, 208n8
Munonye, John, xi

Nabokov, Vladimir, 77
Narrative time, 131; *defined,* 34–35, 199n37. *See also* Fabula time
Native Americans. *See under* Indians and Indian culture
Norris, Frank, 129

Ober, Warren U., 144
Objective correlative, 56, 73–75, 101, 102, 125, 187, 201n68, 204n20
O'Brien, Edna, xi
O'Brien, Edward J., 6, 213n45
O'Brien, Sarah Mary, 209n6

O'Connor, Flannery, xi; on fiction's rules, 44; on modern fiction, 119; on psychological criticism, 89; on reader's need to understand craft, xvii, 87, 149–50; on symbols in a story, 120; on theme, 118; on "ultimate mystery" in the short story, 77–78, 79
O'Connor, Frank, xv, 92–93; analogy between fiction and playwriting, 16, 33
Oe, Kenzaburo, xi
O'Faolain, Sean: xi, 14, 27, 201–2n74; on camera angle, 199n38; on how a story speaks for all of a life, 149; on use of details, 20
Ojibwas and Ojibwa culture. *See under* Indians and Indian culture
Oldsey, Bernard, 209n1, 210n17
Omission, xi, xvi, 11, 34, 47, 52, 53, 55, 61, 68, 73–74, 76, 84, 97, 103, 127, 128, 132, 159–60, 171–72, 178, 184–85, 201n70; in Cézanne, 184–85; H on, 53, 132. *See also* Ellipses
Ontological shock: *defined,* 9, 12; in "Indian Camp," 12–14, 19–21, 27, 67, 76–77, 80–81, 198n19

Palmer Raids, 107
Pentecost, John ("The Ghee"), 173, 174, 178
Perrett, Geoffrey, 204n26
Petrarca, Anthony J., 203n11
Pissarro, Camille, 183
Plimpton, George, 89, 151, 197n4
Poe, Edgar Allan, xi, 57, 80, 121
Poore, Charles, 209n5
Pound, Ezra, xi, 6, 7–8, 173
Present absence, 156; *defined,* 156, 208n6
Proairetic code: 68, 77; *defined,* 33–34, 37. *See also* Hermeneutic code
Proust, Marcel, 190

Recapitulation with variation, 73–75, 127, 145; *defined* 74, 201n66
Red Scare of 1919, 107
Repetition, xi, 46, 56, 66, 70, 74–75, 103, 117, 124–25, 127, 162–64, 168, 173, 181, 212n30; in dialogue of "A Canary for One," 141–42, 144–45
Retrospective notice, 82; *defined,* 82, 202n84
Reynolds, Michael, 81, 91, 197n5, 197n6, 198n9, 198n10, 202n4, 209n1, 210n12, 210n16, 211n23, 212n29
Roberts, John J., 203n11
Route tournante, 185–87, 212n38
Ryan, Ken, 200n54

Salinger, J. D., xi
Sanford, Marcelline Hemingway (H's sister), 7, 198n13
Sarraute, Nathalie, xi
Sartre, Jean-Paul, xi
Schaffer, Ronald, 204n26
Scholes, Robert, 201n74
Scribner, Charles, Jr., 210n12
Scribner's Magazine, 112
Semiotic confusion, 155–66; *defined,* 155
Seney (Michigan), 10, 170, 178–79, 181, 212n30
Sequence displacement, 66; *defined,* 66, 201n63
Seton, Ernest Thompson, 10
Severo, Richard, 203n8
Shakespeare, William, 154, 157, 208n9
Shiff, Richard, 212n30
Smith, Bill, 172–74, 210n16, 210n18
Smith, Julian, 112–13, 133, 147, 153–54, 206, 207–8n1
Smith, Kate, 174, 210n18
Smith, Paul, 197n1, 202n4, 204n20, 207–8n1, 208n10, 209n1, 211n25, 213n43
Social experience (versus social reality), 95–97, 109, 110–11, 205n33; *defined,* 105
Soissons, Battle of, 99, 204n18
Soldiers' homes, 94, 203n8
Stein, Gertrude, 3, 6, 183, 185, 209n1, 212n29; influence on H, xi, 168, 188, 201n61
Stein, Leo, 212n29
Steinbeck, John, xi, 204–5n27
Stevens, Wallace, xv
Strychacz, Thomas, 39, 59–60, 200n51, 201n60
Sullivan, Harry Stack, 101
Summerhayes, Don, 171

Svoboda, Frederic J., 179
Symbolic historical representation (versus reflection), 105–11, 205n33; *defined,* 106–7, 204–5n27
Symbols and symbolism, 30, 39, 41, 50, 51, 54, 59, 74, 82–83, 107, 109, 113, 119–20, 129, 135, 137, 140, 143, 144, 146, 160, 173, 175, 186, 187, 191, 200n51, 205n28; Flannery O'Connor on, 120; H on, 120

Theme, 4–5, 9, 12–14, 26, 74, 91, 96, 99, 113, 115; Chekhov on, 13; Flannery O'Connor on, 118, 155–56, 168, 205n1, 205–6n2; H's great theme, 10; purposes and limitations of, 112, 117–18
36th Division of the Fifth Army (World War Two), 204n18
This Quarter (magazine), 168
Tillich, Paul, 12, 198n19
Toklas, Alice B., 6, 185
transatlantic review (magazine), 6, 7, 10–11
Trout, Steven, 96, 203n5, 203n8, 203n10, 203n13, 203n14
Twain, Mark (Samuel Langhorne Clemens), 176; *Adventures of Huckleberry Finn,* 68, 106–7, 206n13
Tzara, Tristan, 11

Updike, John, xi

Vargas Llosa, Mario, xi
Verb tenses, 21, 44–45, 63, 92, 144–45, 148–49, 156; misuse of, 14–17, 18–19; problem of past progressive openings in stories, 14–15; reader shifts past tenses, 199–200n50
Veteran's Bureau Scandal of 1923, 107
Vittorini, Elio, xi
Vollard, Ambroise, 212n29
Volstead Act, 107

Walcott, Derek, xi
Waldhorn, Arthur, 72, 90
Walker, Al, 178
Warren, Robert Penn, 90
Watt, Ian, 126, 206n14
Watts, Emily Stipes, 212n30
Waugh, Evelyn, xi
Weinstein, Sydney "Big Syd," 204n18
Welty, Eudora, xi, 14, 38, 201–2n74; on relationship between life and fiction, 8; on reticence in fiction, 36, 133
Wharton, Edith: on story openings, 14–15
Williams, Raymond, 105, 106
Williams, Terry Tempest, xi
Williams, Wirt, 201n74
Wilson, Edmund, 151, 169, 201n74
Wilson, Woodrow, 107, 200n52
Wister, Owen, 75

Yezierska, Anzia, 111
Young, Philip, 11, 72, 89–90, 91, 168–70, 197n3, 201n74, 209–10n9; H's dealings with, 171, 209n5, 210n12

Zola, Émile: influence on H, 62